Robert M. Kaplan is Clinical Associate Professor in Psychiatry at the Graduate School of Medicine at the University of Wollongong. A writer, historian and speaker, he has written and spoken on medical, psychiatric, criminal and historic topics. His book *Medical Murder: Disturbing Tales of Doctors Who Kill* was published by Allen & Unwin in 2009. To recover from the effort of writing this book, he has thrown himself into a fiction project, working title *Seven Suicides*. His ever-diminishing circle of friends constantly implores him to defer his plan to be a comedian and return instead to his rabbinical roots.

THE
EXCEPTIONAL
BRAIN

AND HOW IT CHANGED THE WORLD

ROBERT M. KAPLAN

ALLEN&UNWIN

First published in 2011

Copyright © Robert M. Kaplan 2011

Allen & Unwin
Sydney, Melbourne, Auckland, London

83 Alexander Street
Crows Nest NSW 2065
Australia
Phone: (61 2) 8425 0100
Fax: (61 2) 9906 2218
Email: info@allenandunwin.com
Web: www.allenandunwin.com

Cataloguing-in-Publication details are available
from the National Library of Australia
www.trove.nla.gov.au

ISBN 978 1 74237 444 4

Set in 11.5/15 pt Sabon by Midland Typesetters, Australia
Text design by Nada Backovic Designs

10 9 8 7 6 5

Printed and bound in Australia by The SOS Print + Media Group.

MIX
Paper from
responsible sources
FSC FSC® C011217
www.fsc.org

The paper in this book is FSC® certified.
FSC® promotes environmentally responsible,
socially beneficial and economically viable
management of the world's forests.

CONTENTS

CONTENTS

This book is dedicated to my grandfather, Sam Kaplan, originally from Shadova, who fled Lithuania to escape Tsarist persecution, settled in South Africa and established a family that thrived and flourished in all its human manifestations.

INTRODUCTION

One morning my grandfather, Sam Kaplan, then in his early fifties, was found lying on the ground. Roused, he could not speak, appearing confused and not recognising people around him. Admitted to hospital, he was seen by a neurosurgeon. The tests gave no indication of what was wrong, and the decision was made to take a brain biopsy through a small opening in the skull. The biopsy, the surgeon told my father, showed that Sam had Alzheimer's disease, the condition described the previous century by Alois Alzheimer and regarded as a predecessor to senile dementia.

'We have no choice,' the neurosurgeon said, 'but to do a lobotomy'.

The family, in the days when the doctor, particularly a specialist, was regarded as the highest authority, if not a god, agreed.

And so it was done. The surgery would have been a freehand procedure with two holes bored on opposite sides of the frontal skull and what was known as a leucotomy knife inserted in each orifice. It was at this point that the skill and expertise of the neurosurgeon would come to the fore to ensure that the white matter fibres connecting the frontal section of the brain were severed without affecting other structures. On the day, these considerations were absent from the operating theatre and, as the results indicated, the effect was akin to shoving a screwdriver into the brain cavity and waggling it around.

Sam Kaplan never spoke again and never rejoined the world after his collapse. He had been a restless and gregarious man who loved company and conversation. He could talk with family, friends or just about anyone he would find and bring home until the early hours of the morning—if not later, had his wife Bertha not intervened and ushered the visitors out.

Now Sam developed an alarming set of behaviours requiring him to be in a nursing home for the rest of his days. He would try to eat anything and everything if left unrestrained, making no discrimination between food and objects such as bedsheets, blankets and curtains. He lost the capacity to recognise objects and, at least part of his behaviour — known as hyperorality — was to substitute for this by fondling the item in his hand or putting it in his mouth. His mood was placid, unchanging; he was quite indifferent to anything that occurred around him. A rational, intelligent, affectionate and informed man all his life, he had no awareness of even his own identity. The world around him meant nothing. He no longer recognised his family.

In an attempt to break through the wall of silence that surrounded him, his grandson, barely four years old, was brought to him. In the past, Sam had loved to see him. It made no difference. Mute, incomprehending, he showed no response. His family was by now resigned to a situation that they could only attribute to God or fate (depending on how far they had moved from Talmudic piety along the path of rational agnosticism). The little boy, who by now you will have realised is the author, was ushered out to play on the flowing lawns of the nursing home, this being one of the first memories of his life.

I knew little else of the story aside from occasional vignettes given me by my father, a man who was more interested in such matters as the directing skills of Ken Russell or the flight path of the coleus butterfly. While the situation puzzled me, Alzheimer's disease, hyperorality and leucotomy were hardly the stuff of my early life. I was more interested in the spring hatching of trout in the Lourens River, wondering whether I would ever manage to read *Ulysses* (I did, eventually) and finding an occupation which, for a range of reasons, after a prolonged gestation at 34 years I found myself a psychiatrist. During this time these issues faded into the background, but they had an odd habit of emerging every now and then to trouble, even taunt me.

As I learned about the brain and its behaviour, Sam's story began to make sense. He had been rendered mute by a stroke. The brain biopsy was unlikely to have shown that he had Alzheimer's disease, but rather that there was an increase in Alzheimer bodies, which we now know to be neurofibrillary tangles—clumps of amyloid protein—for which there could have been any number of causes as there are always some present in the brain, increasing with age.

But regardless of the events that led to Sam's collapse and loss of speech, it was not disease, but his doctor, that led to the dreadful disarray that afflicted him for the rest of his life. For, in performing a free-hand leucotomy for reasons that even in the limited knowledge of those days would have been incomprehensible, the doctor and his loose swipes effectively disconnected Sam's temporal lobes from the rest of the brain, resulting in the state called Klüver-Bucy syndrome.

The events after the time that I began to have a faint understanding of what had happened to Sam Kaplan shall be deferred (that is, until I finish the long-delayed autobiography) to bring us to the more immediate circumstances that led to this book. My psychiatric training was weighted towards neuropsychiatry (psychiatric aspects of organic brain disease) and liaison psychiatry (psychiatric aspects of physical disorders). This was a combination with which I was perfectly comfortable and has remained the mainstay of my clinical practice.

However, in the last decade I resumed my long-deferred project to understand human evolution and prehistory, particularly in southern Africa. Things fell into place. In order to understand just how we became truly human and developed those features that make us both more adapted and capable than our nearest primate cousins, as well as retaining uniqueness in personality, it became clear that two features in our development are crucially important. These are the capacity of the brain to develop altered states, allowing fantasy, spirituality and creativity; and laterality, the critical change in the orientation of the brain that allows this capacity. This book reflects my interest in these features of the human brain.

The account that follows makes no pretence to be systematic, comprehensive or definitive. I have unashamedly followed a historical account. In some cases, I have given an abbreviated account of the brain issues; in others, I have gone into some detail. This is my choice and I hope the reader approves. I have followed a rough chronological order, although this begins to unwind by the time of the nineteenth century. Where possible, I have interspersed the relevant chapter with the account of the neuroscientist or neurosurgeon involved, but this is scarcely consistent.

What I have *not* done is attempt to write a book with academic pretensions. I have gone to some lengths to avoid medical and scientific jargon; where unavoidable, I have provided explanations. I have provided only a few lists that are necessary for explanation. I have tried to keep the use of neuroanatomical terms down to an absolute minimum; consequently, the enthusiastic amateur will not find this much of a guide to home neurosurgery. A reading list contains the books and articles that I think are most reader-friendly.

I hope the stories of these individuals are of interest and the descriptions of their brains manage to be coherent and useful without becoming cloying or overwhelming. In the end, every author writes for an ideal reader who, oddly, bears a remarkable resemblance to themselves. I hope you enjoy the book. I have.

DAIDALOS

*I stand in the bright sunlight with closed
eyes and face the sun. Then I move my
outstretched, somewhat separated, fingers
up and down in front of the eyes, so that
they are alternately illuminated and shaded.
In addition to the uniform yellow-red that
one expects with closed eyes, there appear
beautiful regular figures that are initially
difficult to define but slowly become
clearer. When we continue to move the
fingers, the figure becomes more complex
and fills the whole visual field.*

JAN PURKINJE

It is 78,000 years ago. On the southern coast of Africa, a group of humans are in a cave alongside a series of rock ledges and reefs on the coastline. The sea (later to be known as the Indian Ocean) is bright blue. The rocks are covered with shellfish; as a wave withdraws, serried rows of shells, cysts, bladders and tubes spurt and squish and suck. Small fish swim in the gullies, octopi and crayfish scuttle under ledges or hide beneath swaying kelp. Seabirds hover and squawk, plunging whenever they see some item of food. Further out to sea there is the occasional spout of spume as a whale, looking for a suitable place to calve, comes to the surface.

The cave, which we now call Blombos, is spacious, tapering towards the back. The floor is covered with a carpet of shells, crunching underfoot, slowly pounded into a layer to record the presence of a generation, thousands of layers multiplying as the millennia pass. The inhabitants stand around or sprawl. They wear little aside from animal-skin loin cloths, the children scuttle around naked. One of the younger women, showing the first glow of pregnancy, is more ornately decorated. In her hair are several bone needles. Around her neck hangs a necklace made of twine from a local bush strung with rows of shells of the limpet crab, found in the lagoon. The shells, rubbing softly against her skin, have acquired a glowing patina that brings out the natural colours in the shells.

In the centre of the group, squatting on his heels, surrounded by a scattered pile of red ochre chips, is a man with a stone in his hand. The squatting man, whom we shall call Daidalos in honour of Daedalus, the skilled and cunning artificer of Greek mythology, is trying to explain to his audience what had happened to him the night before. Driven by an urge he could not understand, Daidalos left the cave and squatted on a rock outside that gave him a clear view of the skies. This was something he did frequently, fascinated by both the sparkling stars that appeared to resemble animal shapes and the trajectory of the moon across the inverted bowl of the sky. These inspections left him with a sense of contentment and he would always sleep well afterwards. But this night was different. The sky was unusually clear, the moon was full and, as he sat down and took up his position, a blazing comet shot across the sky before disappearing in a shower of sparks.

For several hours, Daidalos stared directly at the incandescent moon, occasionally shifting his position to adjust to its arc, blinking only when he could not keep his eyelids apart. Before long, he began to experience changes. His instinctive awareness of where he was and what was around him began to waver and flicker. He seemed to be plummeting or soaring; he could not say which; he felt he no longer owned his body. Then, to his shock, he realised that he was looking down at his body squatting on the rock. In his ears, there was a humming noise. The sense of whirling and tumbling increased, whatever concept he had of the present was lost and he felt he was being absorbed into the sky. The bright moon seemed to have receded and the patterns of the constellations drew closer, flickering, winking and sparkling. The stars coalesced to form regular patterns that he had never seen in the natural world. The patterns, which we call geometric, had precise and regular forms with rectangles, series of blocks like bricks in a wall, nested curves and circles, and a single diamond shape that expanded to a shimmering pattern, forming a cross-hatched grid. At its apogee, several glowing spots shot across the grid like lines of unleashed energy.

Daidalos had little recall of what happened after that. Several hours later, before dawn, he found himself awake. He picked himself up off the rock and returned to the cave.

Now he wanted to tell his companions of his experience. But Daidalos lacked the verbal capacity. At that stage, humans still used a protolanguage, limited to doing not much more than naming items, accompanied by hand gestures, facial expression, grunts and other noises. None of this repertoire would assist him to describe an experience that was beyond anything he, or they, had encountered.

The group, of whom he was the natural leader, stared at him quizzically. At a loss, Daidalos looked around him. Among the pile of ochre chips, left from a recent exercise to prepare red body paint and mastic—used as a glue to attach small stone points to spear tips—were several larger lozenge-shaped ochre pieces. He picked up a little slab, indicating to the group with his free hand that he wanted to explain what he had seen the previous night. Suddenly, without quite realising what he was doing, with a pointed cutting stone tool in his right hand, the ochre slab in his left, he began to drag the point across the flat ochre surface, going back and forth. He stopped and looked at what he had created. Nodding his head, he inspected the little slab. On the surface, in a series of lacerations, was inscribed the geometric crosshatching pattern he had seen the previous night. He realised there was still something missing. In two firm swipes, he pulled the cutting tip across the pattern, etching in the energy lines that had exploded across his vision the night before.

Pleased, he held out the inscribed tablet to his audience who crowded around. What he had done was to create what may well have been one of the first graphic examples of symbolism, the critical feature of modern behaviour that separated the new humans from every species that had come before it. Tossed into the rubble, it was to lie undisturbed for another 78,000 years until a team of archaeologists brought it to the attention of the world.

Daidalos' Brain

The people in Blombos Cave were modern humans—*Homo sapiens*—who had the same anatomy as we do. They arose from what is known as the speciation event 195,000 years ago. From that point, with minor variations, humans have not changed anatomically. Early humans had the same brains we have and the capacity to demonstrate what we call modern behaviour. While they appear to have first arisen in the region of modern Ethiopia, they moved to the south of Africa. But they were never destined to stay in one place and the human adventure commenced 50,000 years ago; they began moving out through the narrow neck connecting Africa with the Levant, or across the Red Sea by the Arabian Peninsula, going on to colonise every environment on the planet.

Fast forward to the present. Excavations at Blombos Cave reveal a mass of artefacts going back as far as 130,000 years. The findings include incised bone tools, exquisitely facetted opal-shaped stone tools, many in shining silcrete which had to be obtained from a long distance away, and ochre shards used for decoration.

Two small inscribed ochre slabs caused a sensation. The careful dating (78,000 years) of the level in which the ochre slabs were found was incontestable and led to headlines around the world. Even the shapes were unusual, suggesting a deliberate intention to create some kind of panel, rather than being the off-cuts from grinding ochre for other uses. The geometric patterning was undoubtedly human. There was no evident way in which the inscriptions on the ochre could have occurred through natural processes, accident or any other means; they resulted from deliberate human intention and could only have been applied by people with well-developed eye–hand coordination in a hand adapted to precision-grip activities, such as manufacturing stone tools. Once the implications of the ochre inscriptions were absorbed, the Blombos investigators unveiled another revelation: a mollusc shell necklace, using limpet snail shells similar to those found in a nearby lagoon, the shells revealing a deliberate piercing to pass a string or hide cord through and showing signs of wear.

The unavoidable conclusion is that the artefacts indicate that the Blombos people were able to demonstrate what we call modern behaviour. The artefacts are the material indication of our capacity for symbolic behaviour, the basis of language.

The dating of the finds was a body blow to the prevailing view that the first modern human behaviour had occurred around 40,000 years ago in Europe during the transition from the middle to the upper Palaeolithic, suddenly appearing at the same time as the Neanderthals were replaced by modern humans. This resulted in subsistence farming and settlement, stone tools, organised hunting, reliance on blade technology and long-distance procurement of raw materials. The Eurocentric view of modern humans had been under assault for some time and, like all deeply held beliefs, was reluctantly, to say the least, surrendered by the establishment. It had become evident that modern behaviour had arisen far earlier at a number of scattered sites around Africa. Rather than being a 'revolution', this process occurred over long periods in different groups around the continent, who made small changes that slowly accumulated. The progress was not linear. Some groups did not survive; in which case, their innovations and developments were not passed on.

The most significant breach in the wall of denial arose in the last two decades with the findings at the Klasies River Caves, further east of Blombos along the same Indian Ocean coast. KR, as it became known, yielded a series of stone tools and related artefacts over a period of 60,000 years, showing the unmistakable presence of what is known as Middle Stone Age (MSA) tools going back as far as 115,000 years. MSA tools were a further development in stone tool technology. Their makers cut blades and cutters off a stone core, but more importantly, the tools' variation in size, shape and utility indicated the ability of the tool maker to think three-dimensionally, to plan ahead to flake the core, to show others how to repeat the process and, in all likelihood, to choose different ways of making tools.

The argument over what constitutes human modernity has raged for some time, but there is widespread agreement that at the heart of this concept is the capacity for symbolic behaviour — which can be summed up in one word: language. Language can express itself with the use of speech, the design of advanced stone tools requiring forethought and planning, and artistic or spiritual behaviour.

Pre-Blombos, the argument was slowly but surely shifting to acceptance of an African evolution, as opposed to a European 'revolution' around 40,000 years ago. To ram home the point, archaeologists have since found inscribed ochre at another site, Pinnacle Point, up the road from Blombos, dated to an incredible 164,000 years ago.

But the Blombos findings came first, and confounded everyone. In addition to the crosshatched ochres, there were over 8,000 used pieces of ochre plus the perforated shell beads used for personal ornaments. Stone tools are one thing; after all, there is evidence of the first use of stone tools by hominins in Ethiopia going back 2.6 million years, and the development of such technology, albeit in fits and starts, would have been intuitive. But the inscribed geometric symbols, as well as the use of shells for ornamentation, laid to rest the old paradigm. Post-Blombos, there was only one logical conclusion: fully modern people had evolved in southern Africa by 78,000 BCE and were demonstrating symbolic behaviour with ornaments and abstract designs.

We know that the Blombos humans had the anatomical capacity for language (brains with a speech centre and changes in the upper airway to permit vocalisation), but we have no other way of knowing how they spoke, only that they had the capacity for abstract thinking, the mental manifestation that results in symbolic activity.

So can we explain how the geometric grid patterns could have arisen? We cannot say for sure if they were produced in an altered state of consciousness, although this is a reasonable supposition. The images do not exist in nature. The only place from which they could arise was somewhere within the brain of the inscriber.

A possible explanation for the inscriptions comes from visual neurophysiology, long a matter of speculation but escalating into a science in the last century. Sensory deprivation can produce visual forms such as rows of dots, geometric patterns and mosaics. Flashes of light at certain frequencies produce hallucinations of intricate patterns and vivid colours. But the most detailed way to study geometric illusions and hallucinations is through the effects of hallucinogens.

As we have seen, Klüver described the geometric patterns that he hallucinated, dividing these into categories known as form constants. These included: tessellopsia (grid patterns construed by subjects as brickwork, lattices, netting, crazy paving, cobwebs and chequerboards); dendropsia (irregular branching forms described as maps, trees or branches); and polyopsia (reduplication of images, both geometric and iconic).

Visual hallucinations can occur in those with impaired vision, altered states of consciousness and pathological states (such as strokes, infections and macular degeneration). A migraine can also produce a hallucination, or scotoma, known as a 'fortification illusion': a luminous, jagged arc starts near the centre of the field of vision and expands until it passes beyond the periphery. Migraines can induce visions of latticed, faceted and tessellated motifs, as well as images reminiscent of mosaics, honeycombs, Turkish carpets or moiré patterns.

Geometric visual illusions are also experienced in hypnagogic states (perceptual changes occurring at the point of waking or falling asleep), hypoglycaemic coma or by looking at disks with rotating black, white or coloured sectors. Among the descriptions of hallucinations occuring at the sleep–wakefulness boundary are luminous wheels and whirling suns.

Our current knowledge of the origin of visual hallucinations comes from psychiatrist Dominic ffytch, who used the latest technology to show that the geometric patterns, occurring in a range of normal or pathological circumstances, arise from the structure of groups of cells in areas V1 and V2 of the occipital (visual) cortex. According to ffytch, reflecting these anatomical structures, visual hallucinations are located in the world around us, not in the mind's eye. They are not under our control, in the sense that we cannot bring them on or change them as they occur. They look real and vivid, although the things one sees may be bizarre and impossible.

In short, geometric visual phenomena are wired into the human brain, originating in the visual cortex. The anatomical structure of the cells determines the shapes, which are perceived as arising externally. The geometric grids etched on the Blombos ochres were in all likelihood form constants produced in trance states. We don't know how these states were produced, but we do

know that one of the earliest modern humans, all that time ago in
Blombos Cave alongside a sparkling African ocean, was inspired
to scratch out what he saw on the soft stone surface, leaving an
enduring and poignant reminder of our brain's first steps to take
control of the world around it.

HEINRICH KLÜVER

*... the question we wish to answer is:
What is it that determines the directions
and turns of behaviour? More specifically,
what are the factors which impart certain
directions to the animal's behaviour in
situations in which reactions to sensory
stimuli are performed? What are, briefly
speaking, the determinants of sensory
responses? We are not interested in the fact
that there is such a thing as 'behaviour';
we are interested in the factors responsible
for certain kinds of behaviour.*

Heinrich Klüver, one of the foremost psychologists of his time, had a significant influence on neuroscience. He is most famous for his experiments with the hallucinogenic drug peyote and surgery on monkeys, producing what became known as temporal lobe syndrome or Klüver-Bucy syndrome. His work highlighted for the first time the critical role of the brain's temporal lobes.

Klüver was born in Schleswig-Holstein, Germany, in 1897. After reluctantly serving as a private in the German Army, he studied psychology at the University of Berlin and the University of Hamburg. Disillusioned by the chaos and extremism of post-World War I Germany, in 1923 he travelled to the United States, where he stayed for the rest of his life.

After interludes at the University of Minnesota and Columbia University, Klüver moved to the University of Chicago where he worked up to the year before his death. There he was by far the brightest light in an unusually strong field of neuroscientists, including such luminaries as Karl Lashley, Percival Bailey, Stephen Polyak, Charles Herrick and Roy Grinker. Famously reticent, Klüver avoided all administrative and teaching duties and would only allow certain approved visitors beyond the locked door into the inner sanctum of his laboratory.

Klüver's early interest was in eidetic imagery (that is, the capacity for strong mental images), which most people know as a photographic visual memory. The problem was to create this in the laboratory for research purposes. Klüver stumbled upon a reference in the literature to a plant that, upon ingestion, was capable of generating eidetic phenomena in people who did not normally experience them. Mescal buttons or peyote (the dried tops of the cactus *Lophophora williamsii*) induced visions thought to resemble visual eidetic imagery.

This was many years before anyone had considered using hallucinogenic drugs for scientific research. However, there were some precedents. At the end of the nineteenth century, neurologist Weir Mitchell described the mescaline visions he experienced: '. . . a rush of countless points of white light swept across (my) field of view, as if the unseen millions of the milky way were to flow a sparkling river before the eye'.

And, sexologist Havelock Ellis:

> I would see thick, glorious fields of jewels, solitary or clustered, sometimes with a dull rich glow. Then they would spring up into flower-like shapes beneath my gaze, and then seem to turn into gorgeous butterfly forms or endless folds of glistening, iridescent, fibrous wings of wonderful insects . . .

Klüver laid hands on the plant, and on 18 October 1925, with the aid of a laboratory assistant at the University of Minnesota, consumed it 'with the object of producing experimentally phenomena that are, or are comparable to, eidetic images'.

In his mescalinised state, Klüver experienced recurring visual forms, comparing them with a painting by Miro. The boundaries between the subjective and objective world, he said, tended to disappear. The results were so spectacular that Klüver declared that the importance of 'the divine plant', as he later called it, for psychological research could not be questioned. Psychoactive compounds were an important tool in the study of visual abilities such as colour and space phenomena, dreams, illusions and hallucinations. In addition, mescaline could assist in understanding the thinking of schizophrenics. This led to his 1928 book, *The 'Divine' Plant and its Psychological Effects*.

Klüver then injected mescaline into monkeys, finding that it produced peculiar chewing and licking movements, as well as convulsions—symptoms arising from the temporal lobes, the lobes on each side of the cerebral hemisphere that play a central role in regulating thoughts and feelings. To confirm his observations, he wanted to remove the monkeys' temporal lobes to see if these symptoms ceased.

Lacking the surgical skills, Klüver joined forces with neurosurgeon Paul Bucy. On 7 December 1936, Bucy removed the left temporal lobe from 'Aurora', an aggressive female rhesus monkey who was so vicious that laboratory workers could not deal with her.

The next morning, Bucy got a call from Klüver, who exclaimed, 'What did you do to my monkey?' Aurora had become so tame she allowed people to approach and handle her without any response. Her tolerance, or rather indifference, improved even more when Bucy removed the other temporal lobe.

They repeated the surgery on a number of monkeys, finding a specific pattern of behaviour which Klüver and Bucy called the 'temporal lobe syndrome'; in honour of their work, we have since then called it Klüver-Bucy syndrome.

The five main symptoms of the KBS are:

1   Psychic blindness—the inability to recognise and detect the meaning of objects by sight in the absence of visual problems.

2   Hypermetamorphosis—a condition characterised by an immediate motor response upon the presentation of a visual object, regardless of its nature.

3   Oral tendencies, such as examining objects by licking, biting and chewing them; as well as changes in dietary habits including the ingestion of large quantities of meat which was almost never observed in normal monkeys.

4   Tameness, placidity and indifference; the absence of social behaviours.

5   Hypersexuality, manifesting with an increase in genital manipulation, heterosexual and homosexual behaviours. The monkeys appeared to lose all restraint in this regard.

Klüver described these experiments as 'the most striking behaviour changes ever produced by a brain operation in animals'. The unexpected findings directed his research to the study of the functions of the temporal lobe in primates and people.

Bucy later said:

> *The discovery of the syndrome of bilateral destruction of the temporal lobes came by chance and without prior planning—but not by accident. This discovery was the result of the action of a well-prepared, active, alert mind, which perceived the unexpected and recognized its importance.*

Klüver went on to make other important contributions to neuro-anatomy. However, his temporal lobe studies had the greatest effect. In fields such as neurology, neurosurgery, psychiatry and psychology, Klüver-Bucy syndrome was a springboard for under-standing dementia, epilepsy and other brain disorders. In humans, Klüver-Bucy syndrome will only occur when there is considerable destruction of the brain tissue, such as in certain dementias or (as in Sam Kaplan's case), accidental or misplaced therapeutic intervention.

Klüver-Bucy syndrome exposes the functioning of an area of the brain that has a critical role in the features that make us intensely human, arguably definably human: emotions, spirituality, creativity, empathy, attachment and language. Whereas previously the frontal lobes were regarded as critical for defining intellect, it was realised that the temporal lobes and their underlying struc-tures, which we call the limbic system, are just as important. The limbic system is a complex set of nerve junctions integrat-ing bodily activities, such as appetite, pain and breathing, with the emotions which, like a London tube train, ricochet around a circuit before being filtered through to the frontal areas to be incorporated in our thoughts. Together, these regions are called the temporo-limbic zone.

Klüver-Bucy syndrome arises from the removal (or inactiva-tion) of the temporo-limbic zones. This helps us to understand the reverse situation: how these areas of the brain function, particularly when they do so excessively; in other words, the mirror image of Klüver-Bucy syndrome.

These features can only occur as a result of the unique feature of the human brain: the rotation from the anterior/poste-rior axis to the left (well, almost always to the left, rather than the right)—what the *Top Gear* people refer to as torque. Asym-metry is unique because the brain is symmetrical in other species. The evolutionary event that produced this shift was the definitive event—known as the speciation event—separating us from all who had come before, leading to the development of symbolism, which in simpler terms we can call the capacity for language and creativity.

The speciation event occurred between 195,000 and 205,000 years ago in Africa, in the heat-blasted rolling badlands of Ethiopia. From that point, anatomical evolution essentially stopped. With the brain now equipped with symbolic language, we have remained in the same shape, give or take a few minor modifications, ever since. From this point, this brain changed the world around it. And what a world the brain created.

NQABAYI

A long, long time ago, we, the Bushmen, roamed these mountains, masters of the unpredictable ways of nature. We were nomads then, moving with the great herds of game and the changing of seasons. When the animals migrated we followed, leaving no houses or roads to mark our presence here. All we left behind was our story painted in the rock, in the shelters, the story of sacred animals and our journeys to the spirit world. These mountains once gave us shelter and the herds of antelope gave sustenance, and meaning to our lives. Especially the eland, for it is the animal of the greatest spiritual power. For us, it is the animal of well being and healing, of beauty and peace and plenty. The eland could take us on journeys to the world beyond and connect us to God.

UNNAMED MEMBER OF THE SAN PEOPLE

In 1992, in a remote and isolated part of the Drakensberg mountains in the eastern Cape Province of South Africa, archaeologists Geoff Blundell and Sven Ouzman were searching for rock paintings. Towards the end of a long and fruitless day, a breaking storm forced them to dash to a distant rock enclave. As they gazed around, they realised they had stumbled onto a treasure trove. Hidden behind a fallen boulder was a six-metre-high (20-foot) rockface with 231 painted images. These paintings were found to illustrate hitherto unknown aspects of the history and culture of an extinct people and have been described as the Rosetta Stone of Southern African rock art. Inevitably, the site became known as the Storm Shelter.

The Storm Shelter panel is a unique and beguiling palimpsest. Human and totemic animals, both enlarged and diminished, are interspersed with the characteristic figure of rock art, therianthropes—combined human and animal features in a single figure. These are exquisitely detailed, with some bizarre features, for example, a beautifully outlined antelope head with a protruding tongue and an uplifted right arm. The antelope figure morphs into a human with cloven hoofs. Several human figures are in a squatting position, typical of this style. Many heads are exceptionally large with exaggerated facial features, showing details of nose, eyes, lips, ears and mouths. Superimposed on other images are translucent white human figures with ferocious teeth, grotesque claws, shrunken bodies and enlarged penises. On one side of the panel, a narrow red line fringed with red dots winds its way not just around the images, but in and out of the rockface, a thread or rope between the material world on one side of the rockface and the spirit world within. The overall effect is deeply aesthetic, poignant, disturbing and utterly compelling.

The paintings at Storm Shelter are the work of San hunter-gatherers. Who were the people who left these exquisite works, remaining hidden, unseen and unknown, brought to our attention only by the chance event of finding shelter from a storm?

The Drakensberg has between 35,000 and 40,000 works of San art at 500 different caves and cliff overhang sites and is the largest collection of such work in the world. At Ndedema Gorge, for example, 3900 paintings have been recorded at seventeen sites. Sebaayeni Cave contains 1146 individual paintings.

Since the beginning of human time, the San (Europeans called the people Bushmen; San, meaning 'outsider' is the preferred term) roamed southern Africa, from the Zambezi to the Cape of Good Hope, from the Atlantic to the Indian Ocean. Their superb adaption to this lifestyle left them unprepared to deal with the incursion of settler groups, first the southward-moving Bantu people, then the Europeans. The southerly groups, such as the /Xam of the Cape and the Maluti San of Lesotho, became extinct towards the end of the nineteenth century; of those, only the !Kung, who live in the Kalahari Desert of Namibia and Botswana, survived. Today there are about 85,000 San left in the Kalahari Desert, Botswana, Namibia, Angola, South Africa, Zimbabwe and Zambia.

The people known as the /Xam sought their last refuge in the south Drakensberg, known for good reason as Nomansland. After 25,000 years, harried by all around them, they knew they faced extinction. The last sighting in the Drakensberg mountains was in the early 1880s. They lived in caves and overhangs in the cliffs, leaving their legacy on the sandstone walls. Accounts from that period suggest that the last group was led by a man called Nqabayi, known for his painting skill.

With history rather than destiny in mind, was the man who painted these pictures appealing to the spirit gods, or aware that the end was nigh, leaving a last plea to history? What we know with greater certainty is how such pictures are produced. In recognising Nqabayi's work, we can take the liberty of reconstructing the events surrounding it. Although San groups travelled over a wide area, they maintained contact with other groups at regular intervals and came together for ritual exchange of gifts, dances and to swap partners to improve the gene pool. These gatherings occurred on a regular basis, in much the same way as later farming communities would celebrate harvests and seasonal events.

San society was truly egalitarian, a reflection of the fragility of their existence and their small numbers—the first (and last) such society in history. There was no concept of leaders or designated roles such as shamans, spirit diviners, artists or healers; this was done by anyone who had the capacity to do so. All we know from the ethnographic records is that healers were male and rock art was done by men, although women were depicted in painting. Dance had the goal of inducing various levels of altered states of consciousness. The San believe that those who go into a trance can cure the sick, communicate with dead or absent relatives, ask the gods to produce rain, find animals to hunt and enhance group cohesion. There are still groups in the Kalahari Desert that practise trance rituals, although the tradition of painting is forever lost.

The dances, often starting during the day with the sun blazing down, go on for hours until illuminated only by the flickering flames of camp fires and the twinkling of the stars. As it has throughout history, a full moon would have a spiritual significance under these circumstances. The women clap and sing as the men dance around the fire. The dancers move round in a circle, stomping their feet, clapping their hands and singing. The sound effects are facilitated by dried seed pods dangling from the wrists and ankles. The women and children sit in the centre as a claque, adding a backup to the auditory production from the moving line. While women mostly stayed within the centre, children could run around the dancing figures or join in, but not stay long enough to go into trances—the maternal role was to stay with the children to ensure their safety in a procedure that could produce intense effects.

Trance states are produced by autohypnosis, overbreathing, dehydration, pain and continuous rhythmic activity coupled with intense sensory overload. Hallucinogens, known as *dagga* (cannabis) and *buchu*—are rarely used by the San. The onset of a trance is signalled by dramatic changes, regarded as the moment when 'potency'—inner spiritual power in the stomach—begins to 'boil'. The first sign of the onset of a trance is the interruption of the gait and balance. Muscular weakness, especially in the legs, leads to the knees turning in, feet rotating out from their usual forward axis. The dancer will stagger and falter, struggling to stay upright. Contraction of the axial muscles of the back and neck causes intense pain, pulling the head back over the neck. The spasms also constrict the abdominal muscles, causing agonising cramp, leading to a hunched-over posture. Skin changes, known as piloerection, an exaggerated form of what we experience as goose bumps, affect the hair roots. Perspiration will pour off the dancer till his body is covered by a film of moisture. The combined physical and psychological effects can be too intense for many, who fall to the ground trembling violently as if having a seizure. Members of the audience rush over to protect them from falling into the fires, taking them to the side.

Once in a trance, all sense of time or place vanishes, the dancer is no longer in the material world but travelling in the San cosmos, either in the sky above or the ground below. He is believed to change into a totemic animal, tapping its power to cure the sick, make rain or control prey animals. Now in the healer role, they are finally ready to receive messages from the spirits and to attend to the unwell who they embrace, bathing with their perspiration, rubbing on the magic substances that promote recovery. Healers frequently have nosebleeds, rubbing the blood on their patients to keep evil and sickness at bay.

The dances go on through the night. It takes some time to recover from a trance. When it is over, the healer will go into a deep sleep, often lasting all day. The daily life of the hunter-gatherers will resume, but the trance state leaves a lingering pattern of images, sounds, senses and emotions of their excursion to the San cosmos. It was important to record these eidetic images, both as a testimony to the miracle-working role of the spirits and to create what can only be described as a spiritual altar or tabernacle—rock art—to be used on other sacred occasions.

The San artists did not have any concept of representational art as we know it, rather an overweening urge to depict the spiritual, which may be the most enduring and characteristic human trait.

San religion is based on the ritual interaction between the material and spirit worlds. The San belief system arose many thousands of years ago. Intrinsic to this was the production of rock paintings and engravings. The oldest known San images, known as Apollo 11 (from the Apollo 11 flight which occurred at the same time as the paintings were discovered), have similar elements to the recent San depictions. Pieces of the rock are dated to 27,000 years ago (some have even argued that they go back as far as 57,000 years).

The San cosmos has three levels. The spirit world is above and below the real world, connected to the material world by places such as waterholes and caves. San art is a re-creation of the shamanic visions of the spirit world. This gives the paintings an inherent power, represented by the use of blood as a binder to stick the pigments (ochre, clay or charcoal) to the rockface.

Why rock painting, as opposed to rock engraving, was chosen is not clear. The surviving material indicates that rock painting was carried out in a broad zone extending down the coastal area of Namibia, around the Cape and as far up as present-day Mozambique. Rock engraving was done more in the inland areas. There is no evidence why the one medium was chosen above the other, although geography must have been important, desert areas being less likely to have suitable caves, rockfaces and cliff overhangs, and more likely to have plenty of scattered rocks.

The rockface, ledge or cave used for painting was not a random selection based on the availability of a convenient, perhaps shaded, smooth rock surface. The site, a hillock, ridge or mountain, was chosen deliberately for its position in relation to the trajectory of the sun or the stars, mostly facing east or north. Such sites often have archaeological evidence of regular habitation, with artefacts such as stone tools, animal bones, ornamental beads and the detritus of the painter, like ochre shards. The artist might use the entire rockface for the painting, but often restricted it to the area around a depression or crack on the surface. The rockface was regarded as a membrane with the imperfections representing portals to the underlying spirit world. The best evidence for this is seen at many sites where there is repeated overpainting, regardless of the availability of other uncluttered or unused surfaces.

San rock art imagery would include symbols of supernatural potency; images of trance, healing, dances and shamans in a trance; zoomorphically transformed shamans as therianthropes; monsters and malevolent spirits; groups of images that could be made by one or more painters; and superimpositions to show the interception of the spirit realm with the material world.

San rock art portrays metaphors, symbols and hallucinations derived from the trance experience. At many sites, energy lines weave in and out of the rock, connecting people and places to the spirit world. Clapping women, nosebleeding, flywhisks and bows are commonly portrayed. There are caricatures of the totemic animals they hunted and revered, notably the eland, the largest antelope. One of the spirits who frequently features in the paintings is /Kaggen, the trickster mantis who can influence events, transform himself and perform magic tricks. Paintings also include scenes and practices in the material world. Among more recent paintings are historical images depicting interactions with first the Bantu people and then the Europeans, with scenes of ox-wagons and mounted men with rifles—a terrible, poignant omen of their fate.

San shamans are said to 'die' when they enter the trance state, and artists depict an analogy between 'dying' shamans and dying eland: both tremble, sweat profusely, lower their head, stagger, bleed from the nose and finally collapse unconscious. In addition, a dying eland's hair stands on end, just as a shaman experiences piloerection during a trance. Like the dying eland, entranced shamans often bleed from their nose, experience excruciating physical pain and their arms stretch behind them in emulation of splayed limbs of the eland as the transport into the spirit world takes place.

Therianthropic figures are often surreal, with irregular heads suggesting an altered state of being. Human figures in San art could be markedly elongated, distorted or even microscopic. They can be seen in the bending-forward posture, typical of the state described by shamans as potency boils in their stomachs, their muscles contract and they bend forward, often requiring the aid of one or two 'dancing sticks'. Paintings show spirits leaving the top of the head, representing sickness being expelled through a 'hole' in the back of a shaman's neck. The 'lion's hair' (piloerection) that grew on the back of a man in a trance was often present. San use the word 'nose' to mean a shaman's ability to go into trance and enter the spirit world. Hand-to-nose postures is seen in the paintings and is connected with the potency of nasal blood.

The ritual and symbolic significance of the dying eland, the moment when the spirit of the beast passed to the heavens, had intense iconic significance. It was the incarnation of the great experience of the San hunter who would shoot an antelope with a poisoned arrow, track it for days and nights while the toxin seeped in, the weakened animal's path becoming more erratic until the last steps of its death frenzy. The beast would stumble, stagger forward, the front knees buckling, the hooves turning in, the head first drawn back and then slowly falling down on the chest. The moment of exsanguination, both tragic and ecstatic for the hunter, was characterised by the gush of bright red blood from the nostrils. Like the dying eland, dancers would emulate that moribund haemorrhage as they went into a trance, if necessary induced by using reeds or sticks to get their noses to bleed.

Nqabayi's Brain

*These states, whether dreams, trances, or
day-time confrontation with the spirits,
are regarded as reliable channels for the
transfer of new meaning from the other
world into this one ... Though dreams may
happen at any time, the central religious
experiences of Jul'hoan life are consciously
and, as a matter of course, approached
through the avenue of trance ... Contact
with the beyond is regularly made, and
all who come to the dance experience an
uplifting energy which they feel to be a
necessary part of their lives.*

MEGAN BIESELE

San rock art is more, much more, than the depiction of the events
experienced during dances. Among hunter-gatherer societies—
the first groups of humans on earth—the capacity to explore
altered states of consciousness allowed the development of spiritual beliefs, creativity and a human sensibility. Those individuals
with the capacity to develop altered states of consciousness to
engage in spiritual activities are known as shamans—the term is
now used in a generic sense.

Shamans, the world's oldest professionals, were versatile
specialists. They were humanity's first physicians, magicians,
artists, storytellers, timekeepers and weather forecasters. Acting
on behalf of their communities, shamans purported to contact
spirits, heal the sick, control animals, change the weather or
foretell the future. Shamans were the first ritual specialists in
hunter-gatherer society, and persisted in settled societies where
they became integrated with other religions.

Shamans operated by deliberately altering their conscious state to contact spiritual entities in 'upper worlds', 'lower worlds' and 'middle earth' (that is, material reality). Trance states, as we have noted above, can be induced by a variety of means including hyperventilation, audio driving (such as drumming or clapping), sensory deprivation, pathological conditions, migraine, pain, fasting, meditation, prolonged rhythmic dancing, flashing lights and hallucinogen-induced trance.

The man credited with interpreting the images in rock art is David Lewis-Williams, Professor Emeritus of Cognitive Archaeology at the University of the Witwatersrand in Johannesburg. He did this by studying the ethnographic records done at the end of the nineteenth century, laboratory studies of hallucinogens and common themes in hunter-gatherer art. From this he came up with the revolutionary explanation that is now widely accepted. The images in the paintings arise during trance and represent an extension of the spirit world to which the shaman would travel. This insight not only changed our understanding of San rock art, but all rock art.

In order to understand trance states, a review of human consciousness is necessary. Contrary to the popular view, there are no clearly defined barriers between being fully alert and aware and being deeply unconscious. The daily sleep–wake cycle leads from alert states to daydreaming to dreaming to the deepest level of sleep.

Altered states of consciousness—a more scientific way of categorising trance—arise in a variety of ways, including from pathological states. These intensified states are similar in many ways to dreams, but are more vivid, prolonged and intense. This was shown in laboratory studies with hallucinogens such as LSD. Test subjects pass through three stages to the deepest level of trance, experiencing a range of hallucinations and perceptual changes. The hallucinations followed a consistent pattern as the subjects went deeper into trance, affected by cultural variations.

Unfortunately, all research in this field ended due to concerns about drug abuse. After four decades, this hiatus is coming to an end. Any doubts about the validity of the laboratory studies have been removed by the groundbreaking work by Griffiths, the first scientific study in more than four decades to examine the effects of the hallucinogenic drug psilocybin. Middle-aged emotionally stable college graduates were given either psilocybin or methylphenidate (better known as Ritalin) in two separate sessions. Twenty-two of thirty-six subjects who received psilocybin had a 'complete' mystical experience, compared to four of thirty-six on methylphenidate. Furthermore, followed up two months later, sixty-seven per cent of subjects rated the psilocybin experience as either the single most meaningful experience or among the five most meaningful experiences of their lives.

The process of trance follows a neurophysiological path that is constant in all humans, although some features may vary with circumstances, for example, not all the stages are present and cultural factors can also influence the content of images. The behaviour of the human nervous system in an altered state of consciousness creates the illusion of dissociation from one's body, often by flight, passing through a vortex or tunnel, or being submerged under water.

Stage 1. Entoptic hallucinations arise in the structure of the nervous system and can be reproduced by physical pressure on the eyeball (also known as phosphenes) and migraines. Subjects 'see' the luminous, flickering, geometric forms known as entoptics, phosphenes or form constants). Entoptic visions include lines, nested curves, circles, clouds of bright dots, undulating or zigzag lines and grids and the moon-shaped illusions found in migraines.

Stage 2. Subjects try to make sense of the geometric images. For example, they may interpret a collection of small circles as a flight of bees. Subjects then pass through a vortex or tunnel, often with a bright light at the end. This sensation resembles accounts of near-death experiences during which the nervous system begins to alter its functioning and to shut down.

Stage 3. Hallucinations occur independently of the structure of the nervous system, derived from culturally mediated memories. They comprise full-blown hallucinations of monsters, people, animals, buildings and so forth. Hallucinations are often projected onto surfaces such as ceilings or walls. Subjects now take part in their hallucinations.

Hallucinations are compelling and involuntary experiences of perception in the absence of appropriate sensations, such as vision or hearing. Experiences interpreted as perceptions of the world, including our own bodies, can arise from normal stimuli or internally, as hallucinations, through spontaneously or induced physiological activity. When experienced as external events of illusory movement, hallucinations can be experienced in right or left area of vision.

Hallucinations may be auditory, visual, touch, smell or taste. They range from simple unstructured sensations to complex meaningful objects and scenes. Geometric visual hallucinations occur after taking hallucinogens, viewing bright flickering lights, on waking or falling asleep, in 'near-death' experiences, sensory deprivation states or migraine. It has long been recognised that hallucinations occur in situations such as fasting, 'solitary musing' and lack of sleep. With sensory deprivation, individuals experience phenomena such as flashes of light, spots, simple geometric patterns and complex integrated events. Hallucinations can be induced by hypoxia in mountaineers at high altitude, near-drowning, test pilots exposed to high G-forces, cosmonauts, and from near-death experiences involving out-of-body experiences, hallucinations, tunnel or vortex travel and a sense of contact with other beings.

In summary, all hallucinatory images are derived from the underlying architecture of the nervous system from where they arise, although they can be induced by a variety of means, and are affected by cultural issues.

Shamans are believed to be able to contact the spirits or powers by leaving their bodies. During an out-of-body experience, the subject seems to be awake and able to view his body and the world from a location outside the physical body.

Depersonalisation, another component of trance states, is frequently associated with déjà vu, dizziness and mystical experiences. Depersonalisation arises from the brain, arterial disease of the brain, post-encephalitic states, brain damage, anxiety disorders and temporal lobe epilepsy. Autoscopy (literally, seeing oneself) is a closely related experience characterised by the experience of looking at one's body, usually from above. Related, if not rare, phenomena include internal autoscopy, where subjects can 'see' inside their own bodies with the organs on display like in a butcher's rack.

Out-of-body experiences and autoscopy are associated with sensations of floating, flying, elevation or rotation; visual body-part illusions such as shortening, transformation or movement of an extremity; and the experience of seeing one's body only partially. The phenomenon of micro- or macro-somatognosia, that is, altered perceptions of body image (also known as the 'Alice in Wonderland' syndrome), is caused by migraines, epilepsy, schizophrenia, drug reactions, brain tumours and encephalitis.

A disturbance of self-image that can occur in a trance state is lycanthropy, the belief that one has been changed into an animal. This can occur in psychoses, dissociative states, epilepsy and from hallucinogenic drugs. Patients believe they change to birds, bees and frogs, in addition to a range of totemic animals such as lions, tigers, wolves and horses. There is a single case report of an unfortunate individual who became convinced that he was a gerbil.

Can we compare the modern mind with that of the hunter-gatherer shaman, whether in the Upper Palaeolithic or the earliest San healers? Phenomena associated with altered states of consciousness, such as epilepsy, schizophrenia, mania, depersonalisation, autoscopy, hallucinations and lycanthropy, all arise in the brain, predominantly from the limbic system, the neuroanatomical basis of emotion, experience and expression. Each of us perceives, imagines and dreams the world around us in drastically different terms, yet all of this originates from the same material sphere: the brain. While culture influences the content of our thoughts, feelings and perceptions, we have the same brain as the cave painter of Chauvete Cave in France, the rock engraver of Wildebeeskuil in South Africa or the rock painter of Storm Shelter.

Southern African San rock art, despite the depredations of several hundred years of settler society and the virtual driving of the San into extinction, is the largest collection in the world, the enduring legacy of those artists and intensely spiritual people, using tools which by the time of the Greeks or the Pharaohs would have been regarded as primitive, creating visions and images of extraordinary beauty and feeling that would evoke the admiration of a Leonardo or Picasso. Their legacy is ours and we can look at the images, knowing that behind the rock membrane lie the haunted spirits of the first people on earth.

NORMAN GESCHWIND

*Few scientists create revolutions, and
the revolution in aphasia occurred in the
1860s with Broca and in the 1870s with
Wernicke. Most people who advanced their
field must disagree with their predecessors
to some extent and in some measure
destroy the past; they must also disagree
with their contemporaries and so increase
chaos. Usually a field is least usefully active
when it is apparently least chaotic.*

NORMAN GESCHWIND

Where lies the soul of man? The question has troubled sages, seers, shamans and philosophers since the beginning of time. The Hebrews thought the soul and the emotions lay in the midriff. According to the Greeks, one got the humours (feelings) below the diaphragm and the vapours (the mind) above it. As for the brain, it kept the ears apart; they had no word for it other than 'thing in the head'. These views put something of a damper on brain research for well beyond the next millennium.

However, following the Renaissance, the focus shifted. Shake-speare referred to the brain as that 'which some suppose the soul's frail dwelling-house'. Leonardo da Vinci, whose restless mind seemed to involve him in every aspect of science, was a pioneer, dissecting the brain and developing an ingenious method of inject-ing wax to demonstrate the outline of the ventricles where the vital substance of the soul was supposed to reside. Not until the Enlightenment was it considered incontestable that the soul arose in the brain, but this hardly solved the problem. In order to wrest the body from the faltering grasp of the church, dualism had to be invented. The man for the hour was that ubiquitous Frenchman René Descartes, who declared that the body (meaning the brain) and soul were separate, with the soul located in the pineal gland, which he thought to be the only truly unilateral and non-replicated part of the brain (and therefore not part of it).

It was a nice idea, but Descartes was wrong about the pineal, a tiny nodule located in the centre of the underside of the brain. But while the priests retained their hegemony of the soul, the body was the property of physicians and scientists. The brain now lay ready to be unveiled as the seat of all that was human. As far back as 1658, Thomas Hobbes had decided that thought was produced by the motion of bodies—no surprise considering his preoccupation with enlarged cetaceans as demonstrated by his famous book *Leviathan*. William Gilbert, in the sixteenth century, was largely responsible for giving us the word electricity from the Greek word *elektron* (meaning 'amber') and the development of the Leyden jars, an early method of storing static electricity, a kind of proto-battery. John Walsh believed that nervous activities occurred as a result of compressed electric fluid and got John Hunter, the famous surgeon and anatomist, to dissect a torpedo, an electric ray. David Hartley in his 'doctrine of mechanism' (1749) described the rhythmic movements of the brain as vibrations superimposed on them. Thoughts, he proposed, arose from vibratruncals, the finetuning of these entities.

It became established that the nervous system operated by that unique force of nature, electricity, and the function of the nerves in the body began to be teased out. The person credited with defining their role is Luigi Galvani from Bologna. In 1790 Galvani used the Leyden jar on the nerve of a frog's leg to get it to jump, showing that muscle contraction occurs with electrical stimulation of the nerve. He speculated that 'nervous electrical fluid' was the cause of the transmission of energy.

Galvani's findings led to an acrimonious dispute with Alessandro Volta, another example of the tolerant objectivity that scientists are supposed to bring to their work. Based at Lake Como, Volta believed that all living tissue generated small voltages, which changed with activity or injury. Therefore, while all physiological activities, including nervous transmission, were electrical, Volta claimed that the frog muscle had contracted by accident, not through induced electrical transmission. Volta did find that current flowed between two dissimilar metals, the basis of what we later came to know as the battery. History, however, vindicated Galvani, leaving Volta to content himself with being the inventor of the battery and having the volt named after him — there are worse consolations for a scientist.

By the eighteenth century, the concept of animal electricity was transposed into the theory of magnetism, a short step to the work of Franz Mesmer, which centred on influencing the nervous system through hypnotism. This led to the rise of Joseph Gall, who believed the skull moulded itself on the brain, hence a study of its outer contusions, in other words the bumps on the skull, was a guide to the underlying personality, a practice that became known as phrenology.

In the nineteenth century, the work of Hermann von Helmholtz, Charles Sherrington and others led to the wide acceptance that the brain, like the rest of the nervous system, functioned by electrical transmission. Oddly, the trend to locate all thoughts and emotions in the brain was resisted by William James, the father of US psychology, a confirmed hypochondriac who believed that abdominal activity was the precursor of deep feelings.

Neuroscience, as we now call the investigation of the nervous system, was moving in two directions. Firstly, there was neuropathology, dissecting brains and examining slides. This was helpful in illuminating neurological disorders, but had little to offer psychiatry. Then, with Theodor Meynert in the lead, there was neurophysiology, an attempt to bridge the mind–body gap by measuring electrical currents in nervous tissue. The young Freud, a Meynert protégé, spent many happy hours dissecting the gonads of the electric eel investigating such issues.

After 1870, there were some promising developments. Fritsch and Hitzig used the exposed brains of casualties of the Franco-Prussian War (1870) for experimentation, stimulating the brain tissue to produce movement on the opposite side of the body. Richard Caton was able to produce an electrical tracing from the brain of an animal. Brain stimulation then passed to the Russians. In 1913, the Russian neurophysiologist W.W. Prawdicz-Neminski did a brain wave tracing (called the electrocerebrogram) of the dog, but the focus remained on peripheral or individual nerves.

These results, although regarded as interesting, were not taken further. If putting a current through a frog's leg nerve got the muscle to contract, could one *read* the brain's electrical output to get the brain to reveal its secrets? The problem lay in the technology. Measurement of the electrical impulse in a single animal nerve in a laboratory is one thing; measuring the electrical discharge of the living human brain beneath the skull is entirely different, well beyond the capacity of the available technology at the time.

With the onset of the twentieth century, electrical measurement of physiological events culminated in Willem Einthoven's invention of the ECG (electrocardiogram) in 1903. The ECG provided a huge stimulus to cardiac and respiratory medicine. Those working with the brain were dismissive of the likelihood that the electrical output of such a richly complex organ could be measured, while their endeavours were largely focused on making traces of individual neurons.

But the brain remained largely impenetrable. It was not until neurologists began to correlate particular behaviours with specific areas of the brain (known as cerebral localisation) that this changed. The studies of Paul Broca and Carl Wernicke on stroke patients showed the left hemisphere structures that subserve language. A further spur to these studies was the famous case of Phineas Gage, who had a rod fired through his frontal lobes from an explosion when tamping a railway line charge, resulting in a complete personality change from a God-fearing model citizen to swearing unreliable wandering ne'er-do-well. This suggested that restraint and civility reside in the frontal lobes.

After 1915 the study of cerebral localisation virtually died out. That is, until a 1968 study by the man who was to be known as the father of behavioural neurology: Norman Geschwind. Geschwind showed that a structure known as the planum temporale was larger on the left side of the brain than on the right. The lateral shift of the brain results in a significant expansion around the left temporo-occipital region—the speech centre. Laterality determined the dominance of the hemisphere, affecting handedness, intellectual, verbal and special skills. This was also gender-specific: females are more strongly right-handed, acquire words more rapidly and have faster brain growth; men, by contrast, have greater adult brain size, more asymmetry and better spatial ability. The resurrected interest in cerebral laterality resulted in studies of the role of asymmetry in conditions such as dyslexia, handedness, schizophrenia and creativity. Geschwind's studies revealed a constellation of behaviours found in creative individuals and uncovered the role of a particular part of the brain, known as the limbic system, in human mood, behaviour and thinking. Our understanding of the brain has never been the same since.

Geschwind, the charismatic pioneer of the mind–brain frontier, was one of the most influential neurologists of the later twentieth century. Geschwind's modus operandi was elegantly simple: 'Every behaviour has an anatomy' (meaning neuroanatomy). His method was to observe specific behaviour, including deficits, in as much detail as possible; localise brain abnormalities, either in pictures of the living brain or at the autopsy table;

correlate behaviour and brain damage; and then draw conclusions. Geschwind thought that temporal lobe epilepsy provided the ideal model to correlate disorders of mind with pathological brain anatomy and physiology, going so far as to say that the personality changes in temporal epilepsy may be the most important condition in psychiatry.

Born on 8 January 1926 in New York City, Geschwind went to Harvard University in 1942 to study mathematics. After a stint in the Army, he studied social psychology and cultural anthropology. Intending to become a psychiatrist, he was deterred by the dominance of psychoanalysis, which he regarded as scientifically untenable, and changed to neurology. Graduating from Harvard Medical School in 1951, Geschwind worked in London before returning to Boston.

Geschwind read the classic nineteenth and early twentieth century neurology texts, exposing him to classic localisation theory. His research studied the neurological basis of language and higher cognitive functions. This included conditions like aphasia (language difficulties due to brain damage), epilepsy, dyslexia and abnormal cerebral symmetry. He coined the term behavioural neurology to describe the study of higher brain functions.

Geschwind's study of what was known as the epileptic personality has greatly informed my conception of the individuals in this book. This condition, known and described since biblical times, played a role in the stigmatising of the disorder. In 1951 French neurologist Henri Gastaut described some of its features. But Geschwind's paper on hypergraphia (excessive writing) brought to the fore what was to be known as Geschwind syndrome.

Geschwind syndrome crosses the boundaries between psychiatry and neurology, and leads to a revolution in our understanding of disorders such as manic-depressive illness and schizophrenia.

Geschwind syndrome occurs in patients with temporal lobe epilepsy resulting in complex partial seizures. It does not occur with generalised epilepsy, where the electrical discharge affects the entire surface of the brain. Mania, LSD, cocaine, manic-depressive illness and temporal lobe epilepsy can produce Geschwind syndrome. Furthermore, it can occur as a normal variant in individuals who do not have a brain disorder.

Geschwind syndrome only affects a small group of people with temporal lobe syndrome—probably less than ten per cent—but their behaviour is unmistakable. They can be among the most difficult individuals to encounter, particularly in the clinic or hospital. Studies have shown that throughout history, Geschwind syndrome is present among the seers, prophets, mystics, saints, artists, writers and creative souls in society. While the religiosity and hypergraphia can result in a unique capacity to inspire, it can also cause extreme moralisation, pedantry and possessiveness.

Geschwind was careful to distinguish the syndrome from changes that could occur at the time of the seizure (ictal) or just before or after (peri-ictal). Such changes included psychosis, confusion and automatism. Geschwind syndrome is a state that occurs between seizures as a result of constant excitation of the temporo-limbic neurones through a process known as kindling. The increased neuronal activity exacerbates the usual behaviour mediated by the temporo-limbic region.

Geschwind syndrome is a mirror image of Klüver-Bucy syndrome, a condition created by surgical removal of the temporal lobes, and its features are the reverse of the classical symptoms of Klüver-Bucy syndrome. As such, it represents an intensification of the characteristics that make us most human.

Geschwind wanted to avoid pathologising the syndrome, describing patients as having a behaviour pattern, rather than a personality disorder. Individuals with Geschwind syndrome have behaviours that are largely affective, creative and spiritual. The most prominent features are hypergraphia (an uncontrollable urge to write) and religiosity. Other features include viscosity of thinking, possessiveness, hypermoralising, chronic anger, absent or unusual sexuality, and inability to respond to social cues. The behaviour is often perceived by others as tendentious, rebarbative, confrontational or divisive.

Hypergraphia, the most notable feature of Geschwind syndrome, is defined as the intellectualised expression of elated mood. It occurs in a minority of cases, estimated at around eight per cent. Hypergraphia has plagued (or blessed, depending on one's perspective) some of our most prolific authors, as well as artists. Most people with Geschwind syndrome, however, are all-too-human, not great artists, writers, painters, religious figures. It is not hypergraphia that makes someone creative, but its effect on the manner and form of the creative activity. Such patients present with a pile of notebooks, each page filled with detailed descriptions of their obsessions, the writing often filling the margins and accompanied by drawing. To read these works is a near-impossible task in view of the repetitiveness and insignificance of the issues described in such detail.

A number of artists and religious figures display distinct Geschwind syndrome features, showing that in a suitably talented and motivated individual, hypergraphia and religiosity would act as a magnifier of the underlying impulse. The list of such people includes Paul of Tarsus, Immanuel Swedenborg, Fyodor Dostoevski, St Birgitta, Edward Lear, Joseph Smith, George Gershwin and St Catherine; others (the evidence is weaker) include Julius Caesar, the Prophet Muhammad and Isaac Newton. Hypergraphia can be expressed not only in writing, but in other graphic activities. A phenomenal example is the artist Pablo Picasso, who started drawing at the age of three, continuing until he died at 93, was unable to go through a day without working on his art, whether painting, drawing, sketching or sculpting. There is nothing to indicate that Picasso ever had a brain disorder such as epilepsy or manic-depression. As the chapter on Leonardo indicates, his phenomenal output, notably his voluminous diaries, indicate that he too had hypergraphia.

After hypergraphia, religiosity is the most prominent feature of Geschwind syndrome. There is a well-documented association of the onset of religiosity with epileptic seizures, particularly in temporal lobe epilepsy. The theology is extreme, demanding impossibly high standards of worship or conformity—that ranting man harassing the public with a sign predicting the end of the world could have Geschwind syndrome. It can also manifest with pseudo-philosophical speculation, for example, the poet Samuel Taylor Coleridge poured out torrents of the stuff.

The thinking of Geschwind syndrome patients is described as viscosity—'stickiness'—a peculiar, tedious and obsessive pattern in which they cannot conclude an idea and move on, making them extremely difficult to have a conversation with (and, of course, to read). Their viscosity and insensitivity extends to social interaction. They respond poorly to social cues, refusing to end conversations to such an extent that they may continue to talk even after a door is closed in their face. At the same time, they are almost pathologically intolerant, intensely critical of others but prone to take offence at minor slights. Older psychiatrists still speak of how the epilepsy wards in an asylum were like a bomb waiting to go off, constantly seething with conflicts and arguments.

Most Geschwind syndrome patients have a global hyposexuality: loss of interest in sex; a smaller group develop sexual perversions, in some cases among the most extreme kind, and often very sudden in onset. Patients can have changes in sexual orientation; they may alternate between homosexuality and heterosexuality as their seizure frequency changes. The case that is frequently quoted is the man with temporal lobe epilepsy who could become sexually aroused only at the sight of a safety pin, a response attributed to faulty brain wiring. For this reason, any patient who suddenly develops a sexual perversion should be tested to exclude brain pathology. As would be expected, men with Geschwind syndrome have difficult relationships with women, which is exacerbated by their abnormal sexuality.

When Geschwind syndrome arises, it presents abruptly, often causing consternation to those around the affected person. There is the account of an athletic instructor who suddenly became consumed with the idea of writing something important. Another patient started to keep a minute-by-minute log of his feelings and relationship to God. According to neurologist Pierre Gloor, Geschwind syndrome may not be apparent unless doctors search for it. 'It hits you in the eye in less than ten per cent of cases, but that doesn't mean it doesn't exist in a somewhat hidden form in some other patients. Sometimes you have to dig for it.'

David Bear and Paul Fedio designed a rating scale, known as the Bear-Fedio Inventory, to confirm the presence of Geschwind syndrome. After some modifications, the Bear-Fedio Inventory has shown that Geschwind syndrome occurs with temporal lobe epilepsy.

The area of the brain involved in Geschwind syndrome is called the temporo-limbic region. The temporal lobes are the areas on each side of the brain towards the back, bulging out slightly. Connected to the temporal lobes is a network with extensive connections going deep into the brain known as the limbic system (*limbus* means lobe in Latin). The limbic system and the temporal lobes function as the gatekeepers to consciousness, where the sensory world meets the emotions and regulates our reactions to drives such as aggression, fear, hunger and sexuality. In short, this is the primary area of the brain involved with those utterly human features of thought, mood and behaviour—key features of which we refer to as personality.

Too many and too rapid electrical connections in the temporo-limbic zone cause changes. Critical features of human behaviour—religiosity, creativity, ethics, inventiveness and individuality—are magnified to an extraordinary extent. The technical term for this is 'limbic hyperconnection'. In essence, Geschwind syndrome results from overcharging the temporo-limbic system.

Imagine if the part of your brain that processes feeling and drives your creative and spiritual urges is an electric motor that operates within a certain range; given a higher voltage than it is intended for, it over-runs but is not necessarily more efficient and may burn out. It is as if the normal resting voltage in these nerve cells between seizures is six volts; with a seizure, it spikes to twelve volts but then settles; in those with Geschwind syndrome the resting voltage is eight volts.

As a result of the overcharging, Geschwind syndrome causes what Geschwind called an excessive investment of the environment with limbic significance:

> *External stimuli begin to take on great importance; this leads in turn to increased concern with philosophical, religious, and cosmic matters. Since all events become charged with importance, the patients frequently resort to recording them in written form at great length and in highly charged language.*

Geschwind syndrome is another demonstration of how the brain makes us what we are: remarkably adaptive, communicative and capable, as well as remarkably individual in our characteristics. Truly human. And we have much to thank Norman Geschwind for. The explanations that follow in the succeeding chapters owe much to his fine Talmudic touch.

Norman Geschwind died in 1984, far too soon, leaving a rich legacy we are only starting to appreciate. Geschwind had originally intended to become a rabbi. His defection to medicine may have deprived his congregation of some marvellous sermons, but it was neurology's gain—as well as humanity's. Reading his work is an unadulterated pleasure, each line clear, elegant and meticulous. An inspirational teacher, his work was continued by his protégés, including Frank Benson, Antonio Damasio and Marsel Mesulam.

Not long before his death in 1984, Geschwind wrote:

Behavioural change in temporal lobe epilepsy deserves very special consideration, since it is probably the only cause of major change in behaviour for which we have a plausible mechanism of pathogenesis ... The importance of this syndrome results from its clinical fascination, its frequency, and from its unique capacity to present to us a clear-cut physiological paradigm for the occurrence of behavioural change after alterations in the brain.

THE PROPHET EZEKIEL

*These are the words of the Lord: See, I am
taking the children of Israel from among
the nations where they have gone, and will
get them together on every side, and take
them into their land: And I will make them
one nation in the land, on the mountains
of Israel; and one king will be king over
them all: and they will no longer be two
nations, and will no longer be parted into
two kingdoms*

Ezekiel 37:

The Old Testament (hereafter referred to as the Bible) is the history of Israelite peoples expressed through their prophets. Starting with Moses (Abraham was a proto-figure), prophets mediated between their people and an unflinching Yahweh who required them to keep to his rules in order to maintain their chosen status. Until the Babylonian exile, prophets delivered their messages orally; after the exile their words were recorded to ensure wide circulation, the prophesies turning more towards the divine, becoming intensely apocalyptic. The history of the prophets continues until shortly before the destruction of the Second Temple; after this, great Jewish history is no longer written and the period of diaspora commences.

The word 'prophet', derived from the Greek, means '*one who speaks forth, or one who speaks of the future*'. Prophets were unique figures who functioned as ethical and moral innovators, as well as revealers of the future. While the prophets were mostly male, there were women: Miriam, Deborah, Huldah, Nodiah and Isaiah's wife, many engaging in Jezebel-like activities. Their audience was not always quite as convinced of their ability, so they would be variously referred to as religious officials, political advisers, guardians of religious traditions, isolated mystics or simply ecstatics out of control.

Who were the people we know as prophets? Background, class and upbringing were irrelevant and they often came from the most humble of circumstances. Having the role of a prophet thrust on one, then or now, was not a fate an individual would seek. Prophets were not born, but chosen, whether they wished it or not. Jesus' comment about being a prophet without honour in one's own land was not made casually; it was a brutal recognition of the difficult, confrontational and frequently lonely terrain in which the prophet operated.

The prophet had a supranormal connection with God through ecstatic trances. The means for God to communicate was by taking control of the prophet's speech and actions; alternatively, the prophet's spirit (or soul) could leave the body and travel to the world of the spirits. This manifested itself in loss of consciousness, physical collapse, obsessive behaviours, garbled speech and visions or hallucinations. Jeremiah spoke of 'My anguish, my anguish, I writhe in pain', while Ezekiel wrote how the spirit lifted him up or entered into him and he would shake like a drunken man.

The prophet–people relationship was reciprocal, but inevitably awkward. Prophets were capable of bringing about changes in their societies by bringing messages from the divine realm. Some prophets demonstrated their oracles with symbolic acts. Isaiah, for example, walked naked through the streets of Jerusalem for three years. Jeremiah smashed a pot to demonstrate the destruction of Jerusalem. Ezekiel made an elaborate drawing of the Jerusalem siege to demonstrate what was happening.

Thought to possess extraordinary power, prophets had a special charisma. At the same time, their status depended on the society in which they functioned. They had to cope with the immensity of the intense relationship with an awesome god; there was no place for a tolerant or caring attitude to their flock. Prophets spent most of their time raging about the immorality and idolatry of a people who, mostly, displayed not the slightest inclination to change their ways while continuing to worship whatever god or idol was fashionable and partake in the always pleasurable activities that such worship permitted. Change only occurred when disaster was unavoidable or, even worse, afterwards. For prophets, this meant that they spent most of their time despairing at the feckless way in which their injunctions were ignored, despite the imminence of the disasters they predicted.

This did not make for a pleasant workplace. Prophets were even less tolerant towards their own kind and conflicts with the competition were common, an early form of turf war, as it were. Any prophet who spoke in the name of other gods was subjected to the death penalty. Ezekiel, for example, cursed the prophets still active in Jerusalem as apostates.

Regardless of the cultural group or society, whether designated as shamans, priests, diviners, sages or prophets, behaviour that would be designated as an illness or even criminal in other individuals was regarded as an essential feature of these people's professional function. Within a particular society, possession was expected to follow a standard pattern. Violent or uncontrolled behaviour was considered a sign of possession by evil spirits or mental illness. When this failed to occur, or the prophet deviated from the pattern, it was taken as a sign of the failure of their powers.

Which brings us to the march of history. It is a critical period for the Jewish nation. Over 600 years had elapsed since the Israelites had established themselves in Canaan, and almost 400 years had gone by since Solomon erected the Temple. On 16 March 597 BCE Jerusalem fell to Nebuchadnezzar II of

Babylon. He pillaged the Temple and took King Jehoiachin, his court and a group of prominent citizens back to Babylon. The Babylonians allowed the exiles to keep their religious and national identity and use their skills as artisans.

This led to an ambiguous situation. Before the exile, Jewish faith was based on worship of God at the Jerusalem Temple. As long as the Temple stood, the exiled Israelites believed that they would eventually return to Jerusalem. Until then, they needed to adapt to life in a foreign land. While keeping their religious and national identities, many Jewish people became part of Babylonian society.

Ezekiel (meaning 'God strengthens' or 'May God strengthen') is one of the Major Prophets, and the only prophet to have operated outside the Holy Land, that is, in Mesopotamia (present-day Iraq). He was a priest descended from the Priest Zadok, as was his father Buzi, a pedigree making him a member of the Judean elite. Combining duties as priest and prophet was unusual, if not unique. His work has come to us in the Book of Ezekiel. Providing extensive references, Ezekiel allows his prophesies to be placed in a historical context. The first date in the book is 593 BCE, five years after the first group of exiles were deported to Babylon. The latest dated oracle occurs in April of 571 BCE; consequently, the date of his ministry is accepted as being from 593 to 571 BCE.

Ezekiel's prophetic message commences with repentance and salvation; following the fall of Jerusalem, it becomes one of judgment and restoration associated with a utopian vision of the new Israel. Intrinsic to this is the doctrine of personal retribution. Written entirely in the first person, the Book of Ezekiel leaves the reader in no doubt that the author is the prophet receiving messages from God to chide, berate, intercede and provide solace to his suffering people. This, however, does not help to explain some of the most puzzling passages, which conflict strongly with basic Jewish theological principles, to say nothing of passages of unadorned sadism and misogyny that still have the capacity to shock.

Unique among the books of the Bible, the Book of Ezekiel continues to attract, fascinate and, it must be said, on occasions repel. The author's attitudes, values, intentions, ideas and emotions suffuse the text in an utterly compelling manner, allowing an opportunity to explore the mentality of a historical figure, who although interceding between his people and the monolithic God, was nevertheless human and subject to all the exigencies of material existence.

The narrative is characterised by lucid parables and the most extensive use of symbolism in the Bible. Widely regarded as the finest literary work in the Old Testament, the Book of Ezekiel is distinguished by well-defined passages of prose and poetry; the poetry is rhythmical, the text written in an elegant prose style. The style is characterised by rich imagery, detailed descriptions, repetitions of words and phrases and, at times, extreme coarseness, even obscenity. For reasons both theological and prurient, the rabbis advised men not to read it until they were aged forty, and women not at all. This explains why it is comparatively less well known than other books, despite its historical and theological importance.

Ezekiel provided a solution to the problem of living in a foreign land. He is held as the originator of that essential feature of diaspora life, the synagogue. Even more important, Ezekiel laid down what was to be the central ethical principle of Judaism, the shift from collective to individual guilt. In a radical leap, he declared that the individual alone bears responsibility for his deeds: 'A child shall not suffer for the iniquity of a parent, nor a parent for the iniquity of a child; the righteousness of the righteousness shall be his own.'

The innocent, in other words, cannot be held liable for the guilty; each one must atone for their own sins: 'The soul that sinneth, it shall die.' In the history of moral philosophy, this was a turning point, the equivalent in scientific terms of Galileo's viewing the moons of Jupiter through his telescope. It is the precept which illustrates the divine instruction to the Jewish people to be 'a light unto the Gentiles'.

Ezekiel was born during the time of the spiritual reform of King Josiah. He settled with a community at Tel-Abib (Tel Abubu, 'the hill of the storm god') on the banks of the Chebar near Nippur in Babylonia. The Book of Ezekiel gives little detail about Ezekiel's life and there is no other historical evidence. He is mentioned only twice by name: in an early reference and in Chapter 24. It seems he was influenced by his predecessor, the Prophet Jeremiah. Ezekiel was married, but it is unlikely he had children. He lost his wife in the ninth year of exile, although how this occurred is unknown. The circumstances and time of his death are also unknown. His tomb is reputed to be located at Al Kifl in the neighbourhood of Hilla in modern-day Iraq.

Ezekiel commences his work with words that echo down through history:

> Now it came to pass in the thirtieth year, in the fourth month, on the fifth day of the month, that I was in the midst of the captivity by the river of Chebar; and the heavens were opened, and I saw visions of God.
>
> On the fifth day of the month; this was the fifth year of the captivity of King Joakim.
>
> And the word of the Lord came to Ezekiel the priest, the son of Buzi, in the land of the Chaldeans, by the river of Chebar; and the hand of the Lord was upon me.
>
> And I looked, and, behold, a sweeping wind came from the north, and a great cloud on it, and there was brightness round about it, and gleaming fire, and in the midst of it as it were the appearance of amber in the midst of the fire, and brightness in it.

We are transported back two and a half millennia to the Fertile Crescent where civilisation began, the deliberate use of the first-person tense (the only time in the Book of Ezekiel) leaves us in no doubt that Ezekiel intends us to see the past through his eyes—a prophet and a rabbi, but a great historian too. What follows is one of the great prophetic visions, far richer in its visual and auditory elements than those relayed by the other prophets. God approaches Ezekiel as a divine warrior, riding in his battle chariot. The chariot vision has led to an entire school of eschatological study (a doctrine concerning the last things, or end of the world, such as death, the Last Judgment) and resurfaces in the hallucinations of John of Patmos, the New Testament author of the Book of Revelation.

God commissions Ezekiel to be a prophet and a watchman in Israel: 'Son of man, I am sending you to the Israelites'. The chariot is drawn by four creatures, each with four faces (of a man, a lion, an ox and an eagle) and four wings. The creatures could travel forwards and backwards, up and down, and moved in flashes of lightning. Beside each living creature was a beryl-coloured wheel, constructed as a wheel within a wheel, with tall and awesome rims that had eyes all around. The auditory accompaniment to this scene is intense: 'And there came a voice from above the dome of their heads'. The wings of the creatures make 'the sound of mighty waters like the thunder of the almighty, a sound of tumult like the sound of an army'.

Visions occur at regular intervals. Ezekiel is instructed to build a brick model of Jerusalem with a metal plate that represents the ongoing Babylonian siege. He then lies on his left side with the model resting on him for 390 days (representing the 390 days of Israel's punishment); then on the right side for forty days (representing the forty days of Judah's punishment).

One of the most evocative interactions occurs when Ezekiel is asked to eat the Holy Torah rolls which taste 'as sweet as honey'. There are more visits to the Temple, the return of the chariot, and a flight to Jerusalem to warn the inhabitants of the impending tragedy.

Ezekiel predicts destruction and exile, followed by God's forgiveness, using a magnificent (and very modern) metaphor: 'I will remove the heart of stone from their flesh, and give them a heart of flesh.' The exile Jewish community repeatedly visit Ezekiel for guidance, only to receive a less than benevolent response. Their moral failings will lead to the destruction of the Temple. Exile is their punishment for disobedience. Ezekiel is enraged not only because of their apostate behaviour, but for the injury inflicted on the majesty of God. He condemns King Zedekiah's policy of resistance against Babylon in the hope that they would be saved by the alliance with Egypt, clashing with the prevailing view that exile was temporary and such alliances would provide security.

The ferocity and vehemence of Ezekiel's sermons in the text is hard enough to read several millennia later. His prophesies make no provision for tolerance and frailty. The effect on those who had to listen to the ranting philippics must have been aversive, so it is no surprise the relationship was tense on both sides. He became the cynosure of the exiles, a figure of derision, if not fun, to the community, who only came to listen to him for entertainment. In return, an exasperated Ezekiel describes his 'impudent and stubborn' flock as a rebellious house.

On the other hand, if Ezekiel's behaviour seems extreme, no prophet had to go to such lengths to convince their audience because of their resistance to his message. Threats of vengeance to the enemies of Israel, notably the Edomites, Moabites, Philistines and Ammonites, follow (this is the chapter quoted by Samuel L. Jackson's character in the movie *Pulp Fiction*).

History now intervenes. Jerusalem falls and is sacked in 586 BCE, terminating the political and religious institutions of old. The exiles are devastated. Their hopes of continuing the link with the Temple have been negated. With Ezekiel's prophesies vindicated, his audience, at last, pays attention.

Ezekiel now offers hope: once the exile community returns to devout worship, they will eventually triumph and rebuild the new

Temple. For those who survived the sack of Jerusalem, he has not a shred of mercy; there is no compassion or chance of redemption for them; only the purified members of the exile community will be allowed to return to the rebuilt Temple in future: 'I sought for anyone among them who would repair the wall and stand in the breach before me on behalf of the land, so that I would not destroy it; but I found no one'.

The marvellous but still mystifying vision of the Valley of the Dry Bones follows. God leads Ezekiel to a valley filled with desiccated bones. At the prophet's words, the bones sew themselves back together, flesh and skin cover them and the corpses come alive, a mass reincarnation that symbolises the restoration of Israel. One explanation for the story is that Nebuchadnezzar abducted the male youths of Israel to Babylon where their beauty so entranced the Babylonian women he had them executed and their bodies mutilated; hence Ezekiel brought them back to life.

Ezekiel receives other messages, including commands to shave his head, eat bread made from human and animal dung, and dig a hole in the temple wall when escaping from Jerusalem during the siege. The head-shaving command has received much attention from theologians delving deeply into its spiritual and symbolic meaning. Yet the interpreters cannot avoid the fact that head shaving (let alone eating hair) is in dramatic contrast to the usual biblical instruction to remain unshaven in response to loss or grief.

On the same basis, the bizarre dictum to eat bread made from first human, then animal dung remains a deeply shocking statement, one that runs so contrary to Jewish views on cleanliness and purity that rabbinical interpreters over the next two millennia were unable to come up with any explanation. One explanation, moving out of the religious loop, is coprophilia—an obsession with emptying bowels and faecal matter that can have sexual overtones. This is admittedly a long bow to draw, considering the absence of any similar injunction in the text, but in view of the sadomasochistic descriptions elsewhere, there is a case to be made.

In the conclusion of the Book of Ezekiel, having established his moral authority, as well as been vindicated in his predictions, Ezekiel envisages a theocratic community established around the restored Temple in Jerusalem. The Temple will be gloriously restored and the people of God would be blessed as never before. The Messianic times will return with prosperity in the Kingdom of God. In the climax of his utopian vision, the twelve resurrected tribes were given land defined in the visions of the archaic land of Canaan.

Ezekiel's Brain

Ezekiel was a most unusual individual. There are indications that his prophetic role was neither desirable nor tolerable. He expresses the desire to be freed of the prophetic burden with 'and though they cry within my hearing with a loud voice, I will not listen to them'. That he was a priest, a prophet, a seer and a visionary is beyond doubt. Like the literary output of a later figure of not insignificant spirituality, Fyodor Dostoevski, his book is a monument to the symptoms that played such a role in shaping it. The frequency of his visions—he had ninety-three of them—was far greater than that of any other prophet, including Moses who not only led his people for a longer time, but arguably had a far more intense relationship with God. Considering the dramatic nature of his visions, his capacity to travel through time and space, and other extraordinary, if not baffling behaviour, Ezekiel has received a good deal of attention from pathographers, psychohistorians, psychiatrists and psychologists, not to say theologians and historians, who have come up with a range of explanations to explain his behaviour.

If we scan the known terrain of psychiatry and neurology, what conditions could be responsible? Schizophrenia, a severe psychotic disorder, is characterised in the acute phase by thought disorder, hallucinations and delusions, in addition to symptoms such as catatonia, depersonalisation and depression. It is worth noting that the first descriptions we have of schizophrenia come from the Assyrian Codex of approximately 2500 years ago—not greatly removed in time or place from Ezekiel's situation.

Command hallucinations, hearing conversations between two or more people about oneself, non-verbal auditory phenomena, and auditory and visual hallucinations are all features of schizophrenia. In the Book of Ezekiel, these include: 'He said to me; mortal eat this scroll that I give to you and fill your stomach with it. Then I ate it; and in my mouth it was as sweet as honey.' Then there are the shaving of Ezekiel's head and the command to dig a hole in a wall in his escape from the city of Jerusalem during the siege:

> The word of the Lord came to me ... Dig a hole through
> the wall in their sight and carry the baggage through
> it ... I did just as I was commanded brought out my
> baggage by day as baggage for exile and in the evening
> I dug through the hole with my own hands.

Ezekiel hears people gossiping about him: 'As for you mortal your people who talk about you by the walls and at the doors of the house say to one another each to a neighbour'; 'Come and hear what the word is that comes from the Lord.' He also hears the conversations God was having with others: 'To others he said within my hearing "pass through the city and kill, your eyes shall not spare".' His use of the phrase 'in my sight' is interpreted to mean that others must have observed him.

However, several issues mitigate against the diagnosis of schizophrenia. Firstly, paranoia is not exclusive to schizophrenia, but can occur in other psychiatric conditions. The prophetic state was one that promoted discord, tension and suspiciousness, if not open confrontation. Secondly, schizophrenia can occur with other disorders, temporal lobe epilepsy being a common example. Thirdly, it would be unusual for someone with a severe psychotic disorder to maintain an active role as a spiritual leader to his people for (at least) twenty-two years. Fourthly, hypergraphia (as opposed to repetitive but largely meaningless scrawling) is not a feature of schizophrenia. Fifthly, while Ezekiel was extremely obsessional, there is nothing to indicate the disorganised thinking found in schizophrenia. Finally, visual hallucinations can occur in a wide range of situations, both normal and pathological, but are not a regular feature of schizophrenia.

Other conditions to consider are manic-depressive psychosis and migraine. Ezekiel would have had any number of reasons to be depressed, not least being the spiritual leader of a community more interested in assimilating with the Persian lifestyle (known for its pursuit of hedonism), and coping with the death of his wife (regardless of the 'command' not to feel grief). In a psychotic depression, a patient may hear voices commanding them to kill their children to spare them further suffering. Before labelling the command to eat the scroll which turns from ashes into honey as psychotic, it is worth considering the intense symbolism, for example, as a show of devotion to experience the sweetness of the word of God, a metaphor found frequently throughout the Bible and therefore not regarded as an expression of a mental disorder. Migraine can produce graphic visual hallucinations, but would not lead to any other changes.

Having excluded these conditions, we are left with one disorder. Ezekiel is one of the earliest examples of temporal lobe epilepsy described (the first is in the Book of Numbers) and one of the more florid examples of Geschwind syndrome we are likely to see. The Book of Ezekiel describes typical features including hypergraphia and religiosity, pedantry and obsessiveness, extreme sexual fantasies associated with intense misogyny, insensitivity to the feelings of others and stickiness of thinking, manifesting in repetitiveness, anger and emotionally discordant behaviour.

Since it was first described, temporal lobe epilepsy has been associated with intense religious experiences, a dreamy mystical state and disturbances of identity, perception or orientation. Other features include fainting spells, mutism, out-of-body experiences, time and space travel, the well-known *déjà vu* and *jamais vu* experiences and other neuropsychiatric phenomena, notably sleep paralysis.

Ezekiel's experiences include many of these phenomena. He lies in a mute state on the ground for long periods. The altered sense of time is evident here — he claims to lie on one side for nearly 400 days. He travels at will between Tel-Abib and Jerusalem, penetrating the walls of the Temple. From the start of his account, he has visual hallucinations associated with intense auditory reactions, notably rushing or whirring sounds. The visions are elaborate, intense and highly structured; such phenomena are rarely seen in conditions such as schizophrenia or manic-depression, but have a remarkable resonance with trance experiences.

Hypergraphia is the diagnostic symptom of Geschwind syndrome. Ezekiel is the fourth longest book in the Old Testament — more than fifty per cent longer than Leviticus — and only three per cent shorter than Genesis, which covers a vastly greater timespan in history. Ezekiel's hypergraphia and stickiness are evident in many lines, for example:

> *Then came the word of the Lord unto me, saying 'Son of man, speak unto the elders of Israel, and say unto them, 'Thus saith the Lord God; Are ye come to inquire of me? As I live, saith the Lord God, I will not be enquired of by you.' ... And say unto them, Thus saith the Lord God ...*

This is a graphic example of Ezekiel's inability to let go of anything once he has seized on it, almost crippling his ability to conclude the paragraph. We probably don't have a better example of Geschwind syndrome hypergraphia until the eighteenth-century novels of Fyodor Dostoevski. Yet, almost despite himself, once he does break away from the viscous phrases, Ezekiel is able to write chapters of intensely lyrical prose or poetry—literature of the highest order.

Ezekiel's religiosity is by any standards extreme, even when compared to other prophets. His attitude to his peers, the other biblical prophets, is no different to the severe criticism he gave the people for their moral turpitude. In his remorseless and intolerant philippic, not even Noah, Daniel or Job could redeem themselves. If nothing else, anticipating Savonarola by two millennia, this attitude reveals the extraordinary degree of his remorseless moralising from which no one was exempt. This is a good demonstration of how Ezekiel's hypermoralising and insensitivity to social boundaries, to say nothing of his lack of empathy, come together.

In addition to the perceptual changes, altered orientation and disturbed identity, Ezekiel's personality reveals itself in the richly symbolic parables. When his wife dies, Ezekiel is commanded not to grieve for her, only to 'sigh, but not aloud'. This can only be described as an extraordinary reaction. It would be next to impossible to consciously refuse to allow oneself not to experience intense sadness under such circumstances. Not only is the instruction counter-intuitive (God constantly tells the prophets that the people should grieve and mourn their losses), but a manifestation of Ezekiel's 'sticky' personality, for example, his intolerance to social mores, as well as emotional rigidity.

Ezekiel's injunctions for moral behaviour and worship extend to the obsessive; he is compulsive about the minutiae of religious worship and cannot be distracted from this. His recurrent use of the terms 'Mortal' and 'Son of Man' is not only idiosyncratic for the time, but a reflection of his pedantic thinking, if not obsession, with eschatological matters.

Ezekiel constantly demonstrates another feature of Geschwind syndrome, namely viscosity. Whenever he has to describe a place or a situation, he descends into an obsessional preoccupation with details that has the effect of antagonising the reader, making it difficult to get to the conclusion. The best example of the stickiness is when he inspects the rebuilt Temple. A copper-coloured man carrying a ruler guides Ezekiel through the temple. They stop at every wall, window, door and altar to take measurements, which Ezekiel dutifully records in his book. He writes down elaborate descriptions of statues and carving. Ezekiel is preoccupied with the number twenty-five: the gate is twenty-five cubits wide; its length is fifty cubits; the distance from gate to gate is a hundred cubits; the inner court is a hundred cubits square; the total measurement of the temple area five hundred square cubits. Just when it seems as if he changes to other figures — the measurement of the steps of the ascent to the level of the sanctuary begins with the figure seven; the inner court is reached by eight steps; the level of the temple building is reached by a further ten steps — the measurement of the steps forming the ascent as a whole adds up to the figure twenty-five.

Towards the end of his mission, Ezekiel has an apocalyptic vision (the theologians like to call this his apotheosis) of the Twelve Tribes of Israel being resurrected, reunited and allocated their land in two rectangular rows. In the allocation of land, the system of measurement is still listed as twenty-five thousand cubits by twenty-five thousand. This arrangement pays no attention to geopolitical realities, let alone the fact that even the Israelites accepted that ten of the tribes had disappeared into history and the geography of the territory made the disposition untenable.

Ezekiel's attitude to women goes way beyond the extreme. Taking into account that Old Testament women were often described as feckless, seductive and immoral, his portrayal of them as harlots is only the start. In Chapter 16, he uses the story of a marriage that fails; God is the husband, Jerusalem is the wife.

As a literary analogy this is superb—the relationship falters, then fails and the wife becomes a whore, nothing less than an insatiable nymphomaniac: 'You trusted in your beauty, and played the whore because of your fame, and lavished your whoring on any passer-by'. Her lovers visit, strip her naked and set a mob to cut her to pieces. Only after this, when all passion (meaning rage) is spent, does God forgive and promise to remarry her. Leaving aside the metaphor of the moral failing of the Israelites forsaking their vows and making allegiances with the enemy, this is a remarkable tale of how sexual jealousy and rage can destroy a couple—any couple—and would have currency today. It is, in short, great literature.

In Chapter 23, Ezekiel—never one to let go of a good idea until he has flogged it to death—returns to the woman/whore analogy to a degree that can only be considered repellent. This time it is the sisters Oholah and Oholibah, representing Samaria and Jerusalem, who become whores with first the Egyptians, then the Assyrians. The graphic description is appalling, and the terminology cannot be described as anything but pornographic.

> Yet she became more and more promiscuous as she recalled the days of her youth, when she was a prostitute in Egypt. There she lusted after her lovers, whose genitals were like those of donkeys and whose emission was like that of horses. So you longed for the lewdness of your youth, when in Egypt your bosom was caressed and your young breasts fondled.

In the end, Oholah and Oholibah pay the ultimate penalty for their promiscuous behaviour, being brutally slaughtered, their nipples, nose and ears sliced off. This description is sadomasochistic to an extreme. Historian Charles van Onselen has pointed out the remarkable analogy with the modus operandi of Jack the

Ripper, who mutilated his victims in exactly the same way two millennia later.

In the text, there are no indications of Ezekiel's sexuality, and nor would we expect to find any, considering the biblical views on sexual deviance. All that is known is that he was married. The absence of any children is an intriguing hint of hyposexuality, but, as there could be so many other reasons for a barren union, nothing more can be made of this.

While there will always be different schools of thought about Ezekiel, a compelling case can be made for Geschwind syndrome. The result of his condition is not just a pile of scrolls or clay tiles detailing the daily minutiae of his life, but a great work of literature, history and the moral redemption of a people.

The Book of Ezekiel will remain an enduring item of the world's literary canon. It succeeds in conveying the anguish, confusion and disarray of a people uprooted from their land and the central focus of their religion. It does so in language that, despite the coarse and extreme intrusions, is extraordinarily eloquent: literature—and history—at its best. It provides the two foundations of Jewish life that are to sustain it for the next two thousand years: the importance of individual responsibility, and the establishment of the synagogue.

Ezekiel must have been impossible, intolerable, magnificent and utterly compelling to deal with. As a spiritual leader, he faced a challenge that had not been known by his people since the far-off days of the Egyptian exile. He would have been badly affected by the trauma of first defeat, then enforced exile. That his people were not persecuted by the canals of Babylon where they were abducted only made his mission more difficult. Whereas to the modern materialist mind, his visions are simply crazy, in the context of his time, they represent the highest moral precepts of monotheism. Despite the cacophony of visions, voices and extra-temporal episodes he experienced, in reality Ezekiel had one vision—but what a vision. He was the fountain through which flowed a unique theophany, that of the monolithic god and his chosen people. We will never know anything more of who he was, but this is hardly necessary. His magnificent book is all we need to know.

All of this stems from the man who, two and a half millennia ago, stood by the banks of a canal when something extraordinary came over him. So intense was the nature of the experience, as well as those that followed over the next two decades, that he was determined to make it a lasting feature of the cosmogony of his people. With the opening lines:

> *Now it came to pass in the thirtieth year, in the fourth month, on the fifth day of the month, that I was in the midst of the captivity by the river of Chebar; and the heavens were opened, and I saw visions of God.*

he tied us all to the moral history of his people.

LEONARDO DA VINCI

*I hope to show two things : (1) That both
halves (of the brain) are alike in so far that
each contains processes for words; (2)
that they are unlike, in that the left only is
for use of words for speech, and that the
right for other processes in which words
serve. The right half of the brain is for the
automatic reproduction of movements
of words, and the left side for their
voluntary reproduction.*

HUGHLINGS JACKSON

The Italian polymath Leonardo da Vinci is widely considered to
be one of the world's greatest painters and the most diversely
talented person ever. (In honour of this universal genius, we
can do no less than refer to him as 'Leonardo'.) The man who
invented model flying machines and painted the *Mona Lisa* was
a scientific pioneer whose paintings, drawings and writings still
engage teams of academics.

In 1482 Leonardo wrote a letter describing the many things
he could achieve in the field of engineering, also, in passing
(as a courtesy?), informing the Lord that he could also paint.
Could he just! Among his many skills, he was painter, sculptor,
architect, musician, scientist, anatomist, geologist, cartographer,
botanist, mathematician, engineer, inventor and writer. He was
involved in fields as diverse as anatomy, civil engineering, optics
and hydrodynamics. He designed models of a helicopter, a tank, a

solar power system, a calculator, the double hull and a rudimentary theory of plate tectonics, although few of his designs were constructed or even feasible during his lifetime.

Vasari, his biographer, described Leonardo in these terms:

> *In the normal course of events many men and women are born with remarkable talents; but occasionally, in a way that transcends nature, a single person is marvellously endowed by Heaven with beauty, grace and talent in such abundance that he leaves other men far behind, all his actions seem inspired and indeed everything he does clearly comes from God rather than from human skill. Everyone acknowledged that this was true of Leonardo da Vinci, an artist of outstanding physical beauty, who displayed infinite grace in everything that he did and who cultivated his genius so brilliantly that all problems he studied he solved with ease.*

A contemporary, Anonimo Gaddiano, wrote: 'His genius was so rare and universal that it can be said that nature worked a miracle on his behalf . . .' Art historian Bernard Berenson described him as:

> *the one artist of whom it may be said with perfect literalness: Nothing that he touched but turned into a thing of eternal beauty. Whether it be the cross section of a skull, the structure of a weed, or a study of muscles, he, with his feeling for line and for light and shade, forever transmuted it into life-communicating values.*

Leonardo believed we understand the world through our eyes. By giving priority to experience—especially visual experience—and experimentation, he led Western culture into a new era. From the sixteenth century to the nineteenth century, the development of science was intimately linked to vision, because the visible could be recorded: the mercury in a thermometer or a barometer, for example, makes the temperature or the air pressure visible and measurable. Art critic Kenneth Clark described Leonardo as the most relentlessly curious man in history.

Not content with observing and recording nature, Leonardo had to understand how it worked:

> *This is the true rule how observers of natural effects must proceed: while nature begins with reasons and ends in experience, we must follow the reverse [path], beginning with experience and with that investigating the reasons.*

By understanding how nature worked, man could then work as nature did. His thinking was based on two concepts: certainties could only be stated by mathematics, and every form of life could be stated in geometrical terms. His intuition was correct. After several centuries, almost all branches of knowledge, even biology, are defined in scientific, i.e., mathematical, terms.

Leonardo's words are simple and elegant, conveying his views on scientific and philosophical questions. A beautiful example is his description 'Of dreaming':

> *You will speak with animals of every species and they will speak with you in human language. You will see yourself fall from great heights without harming yourself. Torrents will sweep you along and mingle in their rapid course.*

Born on 15 April 1452 in the town of Vinci in the Florence area, the illegitimate son of Messer Piero Fruosino di Antonio da Vinci, a Florentine legal notary, and Caterina, a peasant, Leonardo had no surname; 'da Vinci' simply means 'of Vinci'. He spent his first five years in the home of his mother, then from 1457 lived with his father, who had married a sixteen-year-old girl named Albiera, who died young.

Leonardo was known for his 'outstanding physical beauty', 'infinite grace', 'great strength and generosity', 'regal spirit and tremendous breadth of mind'. His respect for nature manifested in his vegetarianism and habit of releasing caged birds—clearly he had not been to a country like Namibia where eating chicken is regarded as an act of treacherous vegetarianism.

Apprenticed to the painter Verrocchio, Leonardo was required to learn anatomy, drawing muscles, tendons and other anatomical features. In 1472, at the age of twenty, he qualified as a Master in the Guild of St Luke, the guild of artists and doctors of medicine—in those days, they understood that medicine was as much an art as science, a distinction lost in these days of techno-clones atrophied human sensibilities.

Leonardo drew many studies of the skeleton, muscles and internal organs, including the heart, blood vessels and one of the first scientific drawings of a foetus *in utero*. He was allowed to dissect corpses at hospitals in Florence, Milan and Rome, performing over thirty autopsies in his lifetime. From 1511 he prepared more than 200 drawings for a book on anatomy only published after his death. His drawings display the effects of emotion—notably rage—and age on humans, facial deformities and signs of illness. He also dissected horses, cows, birds, monkeys, bears and frogs, comparing their anatomical structure with that of humans.

After spending much of his working life in Milan, he later went to Rome, Bologna and Venice, spending his last years at Clos Lucé in France under the protection of Francis I. He died on 2 May 1519.

Twenty years after his death, Francis I said: 'There had never been another man born in the world who knew as much as Leonardo, not so much about painting, sculpture and architecture, as that he was a very great philosopher.'

Leonardo was closest to his pupils Salai and Melzi; he had no close friendships with women, except for Isabella d'Este. In 1476 Leonardo and three other men were charged with sodomy, but acquitted. His sexuality has been the subject of speculation ever since. Most famously, this prompted Freud to make the bizarre mental leap from a single comment from Leonardo about a dream of a vulture's tail feathers to claim that he had a lifetime of sexual inversion. Freud, admittedly at the late stage of a long life, had many things to worry him, but no one can exclude the likelihood that he still took the odd swig from a seven per cent cocaine solution bottle to facilitate this kind of delusion.

If we accept the account in the New Testament, Leonardo's friendships were no different to the relationship of Paul to his two closest apostles, Timothy and Philemon. If Leonardo was homosexual—who cares? What is important about this is a possible biological explanation that includes creativity, handedness and sexuality, which will be discussed below.

For Leonardo, painting was 'the sole means of reproducing all the known works of nature'. He always thought of himself as an artist and continued to paint until his hand became paralysed late in life. A handful of his works are regarded as among the supreme masterpieces ever created. His drawing of the Vitruvian Man, a study of the proportions of the human body, is reproduced on everything from the euro coin to T-shirts. The innovative techniques he used in applying paint, his detailed knowledge of anatomy, light, botany and geology, his interest in physiognomy and how humans display emotion, his stunning use of the human form in composition and the subtle gradation of tone and textures come together in his most famous works, the *Mona Lisa*, *The Last Supper* and *The Virgin of the Rocks*. Of these, the first two are the most famous, most reproduced and most parodied paintings of all time. The mysterious quality of the *Mona Lisa*—'la Gioconda' (the laughing one)—arises from her elusive smile, brought about by the subtle shadowing of the corners of the mouth and eyes, the shadowy quality known as 'sfumata' (Leonardo's smoke).

However, only something like fifteen of his paintings survive, the small number due to his experimentation with new techniques which led to some works disintegrating rapidly and his chronic procrastination, which led to some works never being finished. One critic noted:

> So much thought went into the conception of the Adoration that it is not surprising that there was not energy, or no interest, left for the labour of its execution. The physical completion of the painting must have seemed to Leonardo a problem of much lesser order than its ideation.

Leonardo's impatience with the practical difficulties of completing a work and his extraordinarily high standards explain in part why he abandoned many paintings. He also left an exceptionally large number of projects in unfinished states, ranging from drawings to detailed cartoons, as well as a full-size clay model of a horse—which never had a rider—for a gigantic equestrian monument. Leonardo's contemporaries often felt that he wasted his time on tricks and curiosities he devised.

Leonardo never managed to bring order into his collection of notes, jottings, drafts, excerpts and memoranda. Beside one of his drawings of a heart is the passage:

> Writer, what words of yours could describe this whole organism as perfectly as this drawing does? Because you have no true knowledge of it you write confusedly, and convey little understanding of the true form of things ... How could you describe this heart in words without filling a whole book? And the more minutely you try to write of it the more you confuse the mind of the listener.

And while discussing the design of machinery:

When you want to achieve a certain purpose in a mechanism, do not involve yourself in the confusion of many different parts, but search for the most concise method: do not behave like those who, not knowing how to express something in pertinent words, approach it by a roundabout route of confused long-windedness.

Leonardo's originality is most evident in his drawings of machines. In 1502 Leonardo travelled through Italy as a military architect and engineer with his patron Cesare Borgia. He created a map of Imola in the form of a town plan—a new concept. Leonardo also worked as an architect, ordnance designer and engineer, and his devices included musical instruments, pumps, crank mechanisms and finned mortar shells. He designed moveable barricades to protect Venice and proposed an impractical scheme for diverting the Arno River. So remarkable was his ability to visualise the most complex machines in three dimensions that he could make a finished drawing in perfect perspective.

Leonardo kept innumerable notebooks; of these at least 13,000 pages of notes and drawings survive, perhaps less than two-thirds of the total. The public will have seen selected pages, such as the exquisite drawing of the uterus bearing a foetus. For specialists, however, detailed study of these works is exacting. Kenneth Clark commented that Leonardo was too heavy and weighty for any scholar to bear, at least two Leonardists had gone mad, and several others had shown, in polite language, 'uncomfortable signs of nervous tension'.

A notebook written around 1508 in Milan has Leonardo's 'to do' list:

Describe how the clouds are formed and how they dissolve, and what causes vapour to rise from the waters of the earth into the air, and the causes of mists and of the air becoming thickened, and why it appears more or less blue at different times.

The notes were maintained daily. An account of Leonardo in Milan mentions 'a little book he had always hanging at his belt'. A compulsive notetaker, Leonardo would draw and describe anything he saw, often several times, record his thoughts, inscribe lists and write memoranda.

Friday the 6th of June at the stroke of the 13th hour I started to paint in the Palace. As I lowered my brush the weather changed for the worse and the bell began to toll calling the men to the courtyard. The cartoon was torn, water poured down ... Suddenly the weather became even worse and it rained very heavily till night-fall. The day turned to night.

The notes and drawings include lists of jokes, doodles, snatches of poetry, drafts of letters, household accounts, paint recipes, shopping lists, bank statements, people who owed him money, the human body and machinery, designs for wings and shoes for walking on water, compositions for painting, and studies of drapery, faces, emotions, animals, babies, dissections, plants, rock formations, whirlpools, war machines, helicopters and architecture.

In one of the anatomical folios, he wants to 'describe what sneezing is, what yawning is, the falling sickness, spasm, paralysis, shivering with cold, sweating, fatigue, hunger, sleep, thirst, lust.' Another note reminds him to 'describe the tongue of the woodpecker'.

His journals are full of small sketches and detailed drawings recording everything that took his attention. If he saw a person with an interesting face he would follow them around all day observing them. There are numerous studies of beautiful young men with the much admired 'Grecian profile'. Another often-reproduced drawing is a sketch showing the body of Bernardo Baroncelli, hanged in Florence in 1479 for murder, accompanied by detailed notes, such as the colours of the robes he was wearing when he died.

Many topics, for example, the heart or the human foetus, are covered in detail on a single page. Observations on optics, geology, anatomy, the behaviour of wind and water, the mechanics of pulleys and the geometry of intersecting circles, the growth of plants or the statistics of buildings are all mixed among drawings, absent-minded doodles, coarse fables and prose poems.

Leonardo's fascination with mathematics and geometry led him to fill many pages with calculations. On 30 November 1504 he wrote: 'Tonight I finally found the quadrature of the circle, as the light of the candle and the night and the paper on which I was writing were coming to an end.'

The journals appear to have been intended for publication. Why they were never published is unknown. Leonardo frequently noted how he had started a new book on some topic, but any scheme was always abandoned after a few pages.

Begun in Florence in the house of Piero de Braccio Martelli on March 22nd, 1508. And this is to be a collection without order, taken from many papers which I have copied here, hoping to arrange them later according to their proper place under the subjects of which they will treat. And I believe that before I shall be through with this, I shall have to repeat one and the same thing several times. Hence, reader, do not curse me, for the subjects are many and memory cannot hold them and say 'I do not want to write this, since I wrote it before.' And if I did not want to fall into this error it would be necessary for me always to reread all that had gone before I copied anything, to avoid repetition, particularly since

*the intervals are long between one time of writing and
the next.*

Leonardo's Brain

*His mind and personality seem to
us superhuman, the man himself
mysterious and remote.*

HELEN GARDNER

Leonardo was a healthy, energetic and active man, there is nothing
to indicate that he had physical or psychiatric difficulties until a
stroke paralysed his right hand (but not his speech) at the end of
his life. While he could be a lively and witty conversationalist, he
was also prone to long silences: 'Man has great power of speech,
but what he says is mostly vain and false; animals have little, but
what they say is useful and true.'

With this medical CV, albeit sketchy, indicating the absence
of any disorders during his life, can any conclusions be drawn
about Leonardo's brain? The answer is yes, and we can create a
picture that, while excluding any pathology, tells us much about
the human capacity for creativity.

Leonardo was a left-hander. He described the specific actions
of the right and left hand when he looked into a small cave:

*Bending my back into an arch I rested my left hand on
my knee and held my right hand over my down-cast and
contracted eyebrows: often bending first one way and
then the other, to see whether I could discover anything
inside ...*

His drawings were carried out with the left hand, the shading
or hatching typically sloping downwards from left to right, that

is \\\\, rather than in the more typical direction seen in drawings carried out by right-handers using their right hand, where the hatching slopes down from right to left, that is ////.

Almost every drawing attributed to Leonardo that is shaded from right to left is either unlike him in other respects or is demonstrably a copy'. From Popham we learn that 'there appears to be no instance of a genuine drawing which can be shown to have been drawn by Leonardo with his right hand'.

When viewed with a mirror, there is a striking resemblance between Leonardo's writing and that of his father, perhaps suggesting that the son learned writing from his father. A lawyer, his father, is not known to have been left-handed. The first dated note by Leonardo, written at age twenty-one, is done in mirror writing. This contradicts the view that his left-handedness was acquired after an accident in his earlier years or the stroke at the end of his life.

One of Leonardo's drawings is of a left hand holding a pen or quill, the posture in which the pen is held in the drawing is in the conventional posture employed by the majority of left-handers and nearly all right-handers. This drawing is interpreted as portraying Leonardo's own hand.

But his script was not just left-handed. All of Leonardo's writing, including his signature, was done in mirror writing. In this form of writing, as the name suggests, a person writes in the reverse direction to normal, with each letter reversed. Leonardo is the only known example of someone using mirror writing throughout his life. It was naturally written from right to left with margins on the right hand side of the page; that is, if read normally, it appears back to front, and can only be understood by being reversed when viewed in a mirror.

Vasari noted how Leonardo 'wrote notes in curious characters, using his left hand, and writing from right to left, so that it cannot be read without practice, and only at a mirror'. Pacioli described how 'he wrote in the reverse direction and left-handed, so that it could only be read when held to a mirror, or by looking at the paper from the reverse, against the light . . .'

Writing is a highly specialised motor activity integrally linked to language. Mirror writing was first described in 1688, but Buchwald listed it as a pathological phenomenon in 1878. A hundred years ago Allen made these observations: mirror writing is often a symptom of nerve disease; but the disease need not be the cause of the existence of the faculty, but only the cause of its discovery.

Mirror movements, symmetrical movements of the opposite side, occur in childhood, before there could be a conscious attempt to restrict this. When the right hand is used for writing, there will be a natural tendency for the left hand to perform these writing movements in mirror-fashion due to activation of muscles on that side. In most cases, mirror writing arises as a variant of the circumstances in which left-handedness emerges.

Mirror writing is almost always found in left-handers, and both left-handedness and mirror writing are more common in the intellectually handicapped because they have difficulty in converting innate mirror writing to script which can be read. Dyslexic children (who are more frequently male) not only have poorly established cerebral dominance, but word reversals and mirror writing of letters. It can also occur in normal children who are learning to write (either hand), people with congenital word blindness and left-handed individuals who have been taught to write with their right hand bi-manual writing (writing with both hands), forehead writing, writing on the under surface of a board, altered states of consciousness following a blow to the head, during hypnosis, in hysterical trance states, alcohol and drug intoxication, tremor and due to Parkinson's disease, spinocerebellar degeneration and mental abstraction; for example, telegraphists were known to jot down messages with their left hand in mirror-fashion, whilst their right hand was held on the key.

Abduction (away) or centrifugal (outward) movements are the most natural for both hands; if you go to the blackboard with a piece of chalk, you naturally draw a line from left to right when the chalk is held in the right hand. If the chalk is held in the left hand, the line will instinctively be drawn from right to left. Similarly, a circle drawn with the right hand is executed in a clockwise direction, if drawn with the left hand in an anticlockwise direction.

Why do all left-handers not write in mirror writing? This can be attributed to the powerful influence of education and Western culture in which left-to-right writing prevails. To this can be added the stigma of left-handedness, let alone that of mirror writing, until recent times. After an initial period of competition between conventional and mirror writing (and mirror writing is occasionally observed in most young children), the left-handed mirror-writing tendency will be replaced by conventional writing.

Why did Leonardo's writing not change during childhood to right-handed and conventional script? He had little education at the formative stage of his writing and pressure to do conventional writing would be less likely to have been applied. Also, his confidence and intellect would have already been sufficient to withstand pressure to conform. Finallly, as much of his work was not intended for public display, there was little necessity for him to be able to express himself in an easily understood fashion.

The notebooks reveal both mirror and conventional numbers. Leonardo would have learned his arithmetic at school when mirror numbers may have attracted criticism from his teacher, at a time of acquisition of new skills and when automatic movement may have been under greater voluntary control. This would explain why his numbers are often written in conventional form.

When a person writes in the conventional, non-inverted manner, the brain's language centre is opposite the dominant hand. In other words, that Leonardo was a left-hander since childhood, who held his pen in the conventional posture, favours the view that his language skills were situated in the right hemisphere, which is unusual for the majority of people.

Support for this view comes from an encounter that took place near the end of his life. On 10 October 1517, Leonardo was visited by Cardinal Louis of Aragon. Antonio de Beatis, the Cardinal's secretary, wrote that they saw 'three pictures.., all of them most perfect, but indeed, on account of a certain paralysis having seized him in the right hand, one cannot expect a more fine thing . . . Nevertheless he works at making designs . . .' Leonardo, his right hand paralysed by a stroke, was still able to use his left hand *and* retained his ability to speak. It is unlikely that de Beatis would have failed to remark on any speech disturbance if it was present. It is equally unlikely that, were Leonardo's speech localised to the *left* hemisphere, a stroke seriously affecting his right side should have spared the adjacent language centres.

Leonardo did not have any disorder or pathology of his brain until the stroke shortly before his death. In summarising the evidence, it seems clear that Leonardo had a dominant right hemisphere localisation for speech and language skills. This brings us to the central thesis of this book, namely that the degree of lateralisation of the brain is what determines the human capacity to express itself, in the process rendering some individuals susceptible to different problems and pathologies, but mostly providing for our superb and unique individuality.

Dyslexia, immune disorders and left-handedness are thought to share a common factor: elevated levels of prenatal testosterone. Creativity is frequently reported to be linked with left-handedness, more specifically in men. The proportion of left-handers also appears to be greater in gifted children.

And, added to this, is the theory that lateralisation affects sexuality. A word of caution: any venture into this highly fraught territory is best done by those who have written their intellectual wills, farewelled their loved ones, in addition to their wives and children, have lifelong tenure and a masochistic preference for being subjected to violent academic, public and intellectual abuse. It will therefore be taken as a given that what follows is a review of the current views, and confirmed proof is still pending, despite the intriguing nature of the theories.

It has been debated for a long time whether a person's sexual preference is innate, learned, or due to a combination of both causes. The frequency of left-handers among homosexual men is higher than in the general population. Older brothers increase the odds of homosexuality in right-handed males but not in left-handed males.

Research has shown that older brothers increase the odds of homosexuality in later-born males. This phenomenon has been called the fraternal birth order effect. The explanation for this proposes that the birth order of brothers reflects the progressive immunisation of some mothers to male-specific antigens by each succeeding male foetus and the concomitantly increasing effects of anti-male antibodies on the sexual differentiation of the brain in each succeeding male foetus.

The preference for using the right or left hand, and the direction in which scalp hair whorls have a common genetic mechanism. This suggests that sexual preference may be influenced in a significant proportion of homosexual men by a biological/genetic factor that also controls direction of hair-whorl rotation. Such a mechanism controls functional specialisation of brain hemispheres.

In the end, we are left with the genius of Leonardo, an individual who, like no one before or since, makes the word 'unique' seem somehow inadequate to describe his qualities. There is nothing to indicate he had any psychiatric condition, so often seen as the essential accompaniment to genius. Along with this went his homosexuality, indecisiveness, inability to complete projects, intellectualisation and a preoccupation with understanding the world to an extent that even the great Renaissance figures around him found beyond them. Just where this came from, remains a matter of speculation, but even the evidence is moving from mere theory to becoming testable facts. We have good evidence that his brain was differently lateralised. We see it in the left-handedness, the mirror writing, the phenomenal capacity to interpret dimension, form, shape and perspective. While there have been others of note who had this capacity, there have been none who were able to combine it with such an intuitive capacity to read the emotions of the subject—and it is unlikely there ever will be. Until then, we are left with Leonardo, of whom we never need another. His world and his work will be enough for us for all time.

ANTOINE LAURENT JESSÉ BAYLE

*Morality is a venereal disease. Its primary
stage is called virtue; its secondary stage,
boredom; its tertiary stage, syphilis.*

KARL KRAUS

The archaeologist Peter Mitchell says there are only three certainties: death, taxes and infectious diseases. Infectious epidemics, such as measles, influenza, plague, leprosy, anthrax and tuberculosis, have had a profound effect on society and changed the course of history. Hunter-gatherer groups were prone to the same infections as the primates around them but, after man settled in communities and population densities increased, the rate of transmission from animal carriers, particularly domesticated animals, to human hosts escalated dramatically. The organisms causing these infections arose in the tropical zones and followed the human vector into the temperate zones.

The Assyrian Codex and the Old Testament indicate that plagues have been a recurrent feature of settled society. However, no illness has had as much effect on society, culture and the development of medicine, to say nothing of a unique capacity to inspire fear and loathing, as syphilis. That it should do so is extraordinary: syphilis has never killed as many people as tuberculosis; it has never caused large pandemics like plague or influenza; it has only been present for 500-odd years.

The organism that causes syphilis, *Treponema pallidum,* is fragile and not easily transmitted. What makes the difference is the means of infection: sexual contact, and across the placenta. Furthermore, it not only has the capacity to invade every organ and tissue in the body, but affect the brain in a particularly insidious and horrible way.

While most infectious diseases originated in the remote past, syphilis is unique in that its emergence is documented. It first occurred in a world undergoing rapid change. By the late 1400s in Europe, the Catholic Church was old and corrupt; it believed it would rule forever. But it was losing its intellectual, cultural and, ultimately, moral grip. In the south of Europe, this would lead to the Renaissance, in which the old shibboleths were overthrown and there was an outpouring of artistic and creative genius. In the north, it would lead to a reluctant revolution, Protestantism, and the rise of capitalism. The growth and atrophy of empires was at a nodal point. Turkish forces came close to Vienna, but were held there. The great era of Islam was losing its drive, the Muslim forces would never get beyond the Balkans. But while they were there, they posed an obstruction to the land bridge through Istanbul to the East, essential for trade in spices and other commodities. It was partly in response to this, and partly the geographic convenience of being at the western end of Europe, that Spain and Portugal set out to find a sea route to the East. Henry the Navigator, a Portuguese prince, led the way down the east coast of Africa. By 1488, Bartholomew Diaz had sailed round the Cape of Storms (Cape of Good Hope), clearing the way for Vasco da Gama to complete the trip up the coast and across the Indian Ocean to Calicut in 1498.

But it was a Portuguese-based Italian, sponsored by the Spanish throne, who opened up the New World. As a result of Columbus' three journeys, expansion into the New World led to the destruction of pre-colonial societies and the rise of European empires. Columbus first set out in 1492, returning triumphant from the island of Hispaniola the following year. Having returned to Spain to report his finding to his Royal sponsors, he and his crew then sailed on to Naples, in turmoil from the war between France and Spain.

Charles VIII of France was as an exceptionally weak, if not misguided, monarch. He resolved to challenge the fading rule of the Spanish in Italy. The raising of large armies, movement through countries and resulting social disruption were ideal conditions for the transmission of a lethal venereal disease. His forces took Naples without a struggle, the victors celebrating with an orgy of unprecedented debauchery. They were then checked by the Spanish forces without much difficulty, straggling back to France and the other countries from which they had originated.

If the slow unfolding of history occurs with a murmur, then 1494 was distinguished by events that rumbled more than most. In a Europe inured to plague and pestilence, a most horrific plague struck. The victim broke out in an appalling pox with seeping ulcers, vast abscesses and rotting flesh, followed by a rapid death. It was rightly described as horrible, causing shock and repulsion, with such appalling manifestations that victims were even excluded from leper colonies.

It is at this point that the first episodes of the new disease are documented. The illness arose suddenly and had a dramatic impact. In a society familiar with the depredations of leprosy, it caused dismay, fear, loathing and disgust. Such was the impact of the illness that the nascent nation states perceived it as a form of biological warfare to be blamed on the enemy. That it had an obvious link with sexual activity scarcely improved the matter. Hence, as it spread to each new territory, it became variously the French pox, the English disease, the German fever, the Polish illness and so on.

The origin of syphilis has been the most enduring debate in medical history, lasting fully half a millennium, with the pendulum undergoing regular swings between the New World (for example, transmission by Columbus' sailors from the inhabitants of Hispaniola) and the Old World (caused by mutation of an existing organism or transmission from other regions opened up by exploratory voyages, such as slavery in Africa). Related conditions like yaws and bejel had existed in the tropics, but they only caused localised infections without the rampant spread found in syphilis.

Following the discovery in the Dominican Republic of pre-Columbian skeletons showing syphilitic bone changes in 2000, the balance of opinion favours a New World origin. The latest finding, based on DNA studies, confirms the widely held pattern of evolution. The *Treponemas* are widely distributed in nature, but a small group infected the Old World tropical primates. As a result, four subspecies passed on to the early hominids. At first, infections only occurred in children through the skin. With the move to temperate zones, the infections occurred via mucous membranes. As the environmental conditions became more difficult, and with the wearing of items of clothing, infection was more difficult but tenacious, and caused bone damage, which was evident in fossil specimens. With the spread of hominids through the Old World, the organism followed as a sort of microbial pilot fish, migrating across the Bering Strait to the New World. Here it remained in the native population, until the arrival of Europeans. They were not only fully clothed, but brought some cross-immunity from their exposure to other epidemics. In the colder climate of Europe, the organism mutated again, becoming the scourge that it is and soon spreading around the known world.

Syphilis, the name coined in a poem about a Greek shepherd by a fifteenth century Italian doctor, presented a familiar dilemma. Its association with debauchery was undeniable but the existing state of medical knowledge could find no cause for the illness and the approach was essentially a moral one. This segued easily into religious prohibitions, and sufferers were held responsible for their illness. Aside from moral injunctions for sexual abstinence, treatment followed along traditional lines: high doses of heavy metals, or herbal, natural or magical remedies of no effect whatsoever. Prolonged inhalation of vapours of mercury creams and salves produced horrendous side effects and many victims died of this long before the illness itself could kill them.

Over the next three centuries the organism and its host came to some kind of accommodation. While the disease retained its lethal capacity, it assumed a chronic nature. After the typical penile lesion, the chancre, the poxy secondary stage followed within a month or two. The disease then appeared to vanish—an illusion, because it slowly and silently attacked tissues in the body, causing death years later in a range of ways. It seemed to have a predilection for the heart, aorta and bones, but no organ was exempt.

The signs of syphilis were protean but frequently external and easily observed. The secondary poxy rash was unmistakable, other signs would develop, including hair loss (giving a moth-eaten look), crumbling ears and collapse of the nasal bridge. For this reason, wigs were worn in Europe long before they became a fashion accessory. Congenital syphilis had its own collection of stigmata—such as notch-incised peg teeth, hearing and visual difficulties—marking the unfortunate victim for life.

It was in the early decades of the nineteenth century that the next significant change occurred in the interaction of syphilis with society. The Enlightenment gave the world the metric system, the Code Napoléon, stunning advances in science and medicine and the expansion of empires to connect the circular globe. Captain Cook's voyages opened up the South Pacific, but his ship also carried Joseph Banks to examine the botanical wonders they encountered. It was a rich irony that a South Pacific Eden such as Tahiti soon lost its primeval innocence and succumbed heavily to syphilis. Following the French Revolution and the Napoleonic wars, Europe had been through the equivalent of a continental war. But the turmoil did not not just lead to social upheaval, but a change in the mind of man. The nature of man was not to be determined by the church, but regarded as a product of rational thinking.

Accompanying these upheavals was the arrival of a new psychiatric illness first described in Paris. It was a dramatic disorder associated with grandiose thinking, disorganised behaviour, emotional outbursts and flights of wild fantasy culminating in some sort of grand collapse, followed by a rapid dementia and paralysis with death in close attendance. By the second decade of the eighteenth century, there was a near epidemic and psychiatric wards rapidly filled up with patients. It was not clear what caused the new illness. The condition became known as general paresis of the insane (GPI).

It is fitting that cases of the disease were first reported in Paris, the centre of the Revolution and French culture, a city associated with hedonism, indulgence, creativity and apostasy. But where was syphilis?

In France, the psychiatric profession was in a cultural war and the new disease became the focus of the debate. The leader of the debate was Philippe Pinel, who made his name by liberating imprisoned mad wretches from their chains in the jails. He believed in an illness model of symptoms and treatments. The treatment of psychiatric illness was by support, care and encouragement— moral treatment. Moral treatment aimed at relieving symptoms. Pinel, in short, was an environmentalist.

Pinel was determined to break away from what he saw as the cloying adherence to the anatomico-pathological model of disease, which sought the cause of disease in observable changes in the body and, in his opinion, produced few results and less answers for patients. His pioneering role should not be understated. It led to the rise of the asylum, a development that institutionalised psychiatry and began the process of organising its practitioners into a professional discipline.

Pinel's environmental doctrine was maintained by his disciple Esquirol. Esquirol, too, was not interested in post-mortem findings. He firmly maintained the view that GPI was the result of insanity, rather than the cause of it.

This doctrine was challenged by one of the most original and unusual characters in the history of psychiatry: Antoine Laurent Jessé Bayle. Bayle came from a medical line; his father and uncle were physicians, his uncle an adherent of the (temporarily) discredited anatomico-pathological model. Furthermore, as royalists they were distinctly unfashionable, subject to the political vagaries of the time and candidates for persecution, or at the very least, exclusion from the zones of medical hegemony.

Bayle did his medical training under René Laennec, the inventor of the stethoscope. Unusually for a Frenchman, Laennec objected to having to put his ear on the perfumed (but often unwashed) breasts of his patients to listen to their breathing and devised this iconic devise to provide an objective distance for himself and the rest of the profession. Laennec was a firm adherent of the anatomico-pathological view. We do not know why Bayle went into psychiatry at the Charenton asylum in Paris, but he may have thought it would provide access to post-mortem material.

And so it did. For his doctoral thesis, at the tender age of twenty-four, Bayle described six autopsy cases of GPI. The brains had gross thickening of the meninges (the tissue-like linings of the brain and spinal cord) and inflammation of the blood vessels. GPI, he stated, was due to chronic meningo-vascular arachnoiditis. The significance of his findings, ignored at the time by his peers, cannot be understated. It was the first time the cause of a psychiatric disease had been demonstrated and deserves to go down in history as the *fons et origo* of the scientific roots of the discipline. This discovery was made by a young man at the equivalent of what today would be regarded as internship—truly prodigality unleashed.

Bayle, undeterred, went on to review several hundred cases, claiming that *all* psychiatric illness was due to meningeal inflammation. This time the response from his peers was caustic, if not personalised. He was accused of being immature, impertinent and having a rash nature. Much of this not only reflected rearguard action by the defenders of Pinel's environmental paradigm, realising that they were being outflanked. The environmentalists, in full cry, won the battle. But it was a short-lived victory; the war was lost.

Bayle's reaction to the attacks on his work is not known but at the age of twenty-seven he walked away from psychiatry, seemingly without regret. Having proved his point, he became an archivist and never went back to his early work. The only comparable example in cultural history is the decision of Arthur Rimbaud to give up poetry in his early twenties and go to Africa to become a trader.

Bayle sank into obscurity, but the medical profession saw the rise of a new kind of expert: the syphilologist, a specialist in all aspects of an illness that showed a remarkable capacity to affect every organ and tissue in the body and produce symptoms resembling other illnesses. With GPI, psychiatry found its grand cause, its defining illness, and it was not until the middle of the twentieth century that it ceased to play a part in the daily life of doctors in psychiatric wards. But why did GPI arise in this period? By then syphilis had spread not just through the Old World, but to the New World as well. The likely explanation is a mutation, producing a neurotropic strain of intense virulence to the nervous system. Once again the organism had demonstrated its lethal versatility.

GPI was almost exclusive to upper-class men, the list of affected artists, writers and musicians was extensive and it was widely believed that it was associated with creativity. It was widely believed that the final stages of lucidity represented a creative peak for the doomed artist, Nietzsche being cited by many as the classic case.

But this is a good example of the tendency to slap diagnoses like syphilis on the rich, the famous and the especially talented.

It has now been shown that Nietzsche did not have syphilis, but rather a fronto-temporal dementia.

Something of an obsession with congenital syphilis was reflected in the literature of the time. Guy du Maupassant regarded it as virtually a rite of passage to have syphilis, and his sense of elation when the secondary phase cleared is palpable. In Oscar Wilde's *The Picture of Dorian Gray* and Emile Zola's *Nana*, syphilis was a metaphor for corruption. Through all of this coursed an especially malignant idea: hereditary syphilis. This myth of hereditary syphilis had remarkable persistence; it ran and ran. How could a third generation of a family be so afflicted unless the disease was inherited? A young man, restricted to visiting prostitutes until he became financially established, would pass it on to his wife; their daughter would show the characteristic changes of congenital disease and, in theory, pass it on to her own children.

Arthur Conan Doyle, the inventor of the greatest detective in history, Sherlock Holmes, graduated as a doctor in 1881. For his MD thesis Conan Doyle chose the topic of complications of tertiary syphilis. In 1894 he wrote a short story, *The Third Generation*, illustrating how syphilis could run through several generations of a family, leaving havoc in its wake.

Hereditary syphilis fitted perfectly into the theory of degeneration and coursed through psychiatry, like a septic stream, into the twentieth century. It was to catch the attention of an obscure youth living in Vienna. Coming from a rural background rife with intermarriage, mental handicap and ancestor confusion, Adolf Hitler was convinced that hereditary syphilis, spread by the Jews, would destroy the German race, his obsession fuelled by the persistent rumour that he had a Jewish grandfather. Typical of much of the sludge that dominated Hitler's thinking, he did not understand the difference between congenital syphilis (the organism can cross the placental barrier, which distinguished it from other sexually transmitted diseases) and hereditary syphilis. Years later, in Landsberg Prison, he was to devote fully thirteen pages in his autobiography *Mein Kampf* to showing how the syphilitic 'taint' spread by Jews passed down the generations.

As the twentieth century loomed, the syphilis organism showed its adaptability to the tides of history. By 1900, it was estimated that five to twenty per cent of the population of Europe and the United States had, or would have, syphilis. In 1914, there were over 100,000 new cases and three million cases of syphilis in Great Britain alone, a prevalence of seven per cent. Syphilis occupied such a dominating role in the pantheon of diseases that it was accorded 113 pages in the 1893 *Index Catalogue of the Surgeon General*; tuberculosis, a condition that was more prevalent and had a greater morbidity, was given a mere fifty-five pages.

Was there something in the air, a change in human nature? Human nature was under scrutiny as never before. Jean-Martin Charcot, the father of neurology, was obsessed with hysteria, believing it to be a condition stemming from sexual repression and relieved by hypnosis. Interest in multiple personalities abounded. German romanticism provided the ideal nidus for an idea whose time had come: the unconscious. The young Sigmund Freud, seeking an opportunity to make his name and become a scientific conquistador, wrote gushing letters to his fiancé Marthe Bernays from Paris about the wonders at Charcot's clinic.

Advances in technology, surges in population and the decline of rural life led to the growth of huge cities. By 1850, for the first time in history, the urban population of England was greater than the rural population. Large crowded populations, social disorder and unemployment created ideal conditions for transmission. The syphilis organism (and by implication, the disease) became milder and less virulent: GPI went egalitarian. Previously an illness of upper-class men, it went downmarket, affecting women as much as men. Grandiosity, the characteristic feature of GPI that was such a dramatic feature of turn-of-the-century psychiatry, vanished, to be replaced with depression, apathy and dementia.

By 1910, technological and scientific advances bore fruit. *Treponema pallidum* was recognised as the organism that caused the disease; the Wasserman blood test made it possible to demonstrate its presence; Noguchi and Moore demonstrated its presence in the brain in 1913; and the development of Salvarsan by Paul Ehrlich promised that the lethal consequences of mercury treatment could be avoided. The 'Silver Bullet' did not quite deliver the goods. There were intense side effects and only a small percentage of cases made a full recovery—but it was a start.

The desperation that stalked psychiatric wards should not be underestimated. Bayle had held out some hope that understanding the pathology of paresis would lead to a cure. Therapeutic bleeding, he hoped, would reduce the 'terrifying mortality'. But GPI did not respond to mercury treatment and people were prepared to consider any idea that promised some hope.

The hunt for psychiatry's biggest prize, the cure for GPI, shifted to Vienna. In 1917 Austrian psychiatrist Julius Wagner-Juarreg developed the first physical psychiatric treatment, inducing malaria to treat syphilis. Wagner-Juarreg, a man of aristocratic origins, had that essential adornment for the man of medicine, a truly impressive moustache—he looked like an Upper Austrian woodcutter.

Interest in the role of fever, both as a cause and a cure of disease, went back to the Greeks. The first recorded case of inducing an infectious disease for treatment was by Alexander Rosenblum in Odessa, using malaria, typhoid and relapsing fever on psychotic patients in 1876. His findings were reported in an obscure journal and consequently ignored, but Rosenblum deserves credit for being the first to appreciate the curative effect of fever on the psychoses.

After thirty years of experimentation, Wagner-Juarreg tried malaria infection. His statement illustrates how the war had changed attitudes towards care of the individual:

We were already in the third year of the war, and its emotional implications became more manifest from day to day. Against such a background a therapeutic experiment could stir me little ... in comparison to the thousands of able-bodied and capable men who died on a single day.

On 14 June 1917 patient TM, a thirty-nine-year-old actor with GPI, was injected with vivax malaria-infected blood, obtained from a shell-shocked patient with 'a slight injury of the nerves' who had served in Macedonia. By injecting infected blood intramuscularly, the patient's liver was bypassed to avoid malarial recurrences, and the attack was ended with quinine. Eight other patients followed. Six had 'extensive remission' and in three the results proved enduring.

What led to the cure? Wagner-Juarreg suggested that vivax infection might produce anti-syphilitic toxins. It was not the fever, but an intense response around blood vessels affecting the infected cells.

The use of fever treatment spread widely, to the Netherlands and South America (1921), Britain, Italy and Czechoslovakia (1922), and Russia, Denmark and France (1923), with good results claimed. Wagner-Juarreg was awarded the Nobel Prize in 1927 for his work.

Malariotherapy did not cure GPI, but it restored a virtually normal life to patients who otherwise faced a demented death within a short time. Compared to the days when the diagnosis of GPI was a death sentence within three years, malariotherapy was an enormous advance, 'an epochal moment' in psychiatry. Malariotherapy engaged doctors and nurses alike. The patient became the focus of a process that aimed to cure or, at the very least, relieve suffering. When both patients and psychiatrists could agree on the therapeutic course to be followed, this led to the expectation of hope, a quantity in distinct absence in psychiatric hospitals before then. If neurosyphilis could be cured, then there was no end to the possible result with other psychiatric conditions.

The discovery of penicillin was a caesura, the end of malariotherapy. Penicillin was first used to treat syphilis in 1943. Mercury, arsenicals and fever treatment seemed to be relics of the distant past—although malarial therapy still continued to be used until the sixties in some countries. Syphilis declined as a public health problem and it was assumed the condition was destined for the museum. Reports of the death of syphilis, however, proved premature. By the 1960s, the incidence began climbing, and the sexual incidence once again changed. By the time of the Vietnam War, there was growing resistance to standard antibiotic preparations. In Africa and Asia, there was rampant escalation of syphilis from female prostitutes living in tropical areas.

During the 1960s and 1970s, the increasing episodes of syphilis epidemics across US cities was documented. Just when syphilis was again becoming of clinical interest, it was overshadowed by an awful new epidemic: AIDS. By the time the dust settled, two issues were evident. Firstly, there was a remarkable symmetry between the perceptions and stigma associated with neurosyphilis and that of AIDS. Secondly, the syphilis organism, displaying the adaptive volte-face that characterised its survival over millennia, was a fellow-traveller with AIDS. Syphilis is returning in new forms in tandem with the AIDS epidemic, occurring alongside infectious diseases, such as tuberculosis, spreading without restraint in immuno-compromised hosts. What future form it will take remains to be seen, but its mutability and capacity to run in carriage with human society cannot be denied.

Since 1494, syphilis, more than any other illness, has been intertwined with human history. It has been associated with intense moral condemnation and, paradoxically, linked to creative brilliance. It has arguably had a greater effect on the development of medicine and psychiatry than any other illness. Of all those involved in its investigation and treatment, there are many heroes and more than a few villains. Among these, Antoine Laurent Jessé Bayle stands out for his creative, fearless and intuitive approach, making him the first psychiatric pioneer. The message is that by ignoring the past, we are becoming prisoners of the future. Endlessly written-off by its obituarists, syphilis abides.

JOSEPH LIS

Joseph Lis was an arsonist, bank robber,
barber, bigamist, brothel-owner, burglar,
confidence trickster, detective's agent,
gangster, horse-trader, hotelier, informer,
jewel thief, merchant, pickpocket, pimp,
policeman, rapist, restaurateur, safe-cracker,
smuggler, sodomist, special agent, spy,
storekeeper, trader, thief, widower,
wigmaker and white slave trafficker.

CHARLES VAN ONSELEN

During World War II, the grim-grey Przymysl military fortress was
a central point on the front between the Austrian forces ranged
against the Russian Army. A few weeks before the end of the
protracted war, a prisoner was led out of his cell for execution. A
shadow of his former self, the prisoner was riddled with syphilis.
With clumps of his hair missing, his face scarred by an ugly rash,
he walked with the characteristic high-stepping gait caused by
spinal degeneration. It is doubtful how much he understood of
what was happening. As the officer commanded the firing squad
to cock their rifles, we might imagine that before him flashed a
few images of a turbulent past, a criminal career of extraordinary
ruthlessness leading to a reign of terror.

Their task done, the firing squad threw the lifeless body
into an unmarked grave. They neither knew nor cared who they
had just shot. After all, in a war in which millions were obliter-
ated in the trenches by cannon shell and machine-gun fire, who

cared about another Jewish smuggler and intelligence peddler? The prisoner's file was closed with the cryptic note that 'This matter has been dealt with'. The body lay in the grave and history closed in.

In the latter half of the nineteenth century, an ominous new activity became a bellwether for the alienation of individuals from society. On 31 August 1888, serial killing, the perfect manifestation of vicarious terror, was launched in Whitechapel, London. In what became known as the Autumn of Terror, five women were brutally murdered over ten weeks, the ferocity of slaughter and mutilation escalating until the ghastly debouching of Mary Jane Kelly.

On the morning of Friday, 9 November 1888, Kelly, a prostitute 'possessed of considerable attractions', aged twenty-five, was found lying on her bed in the room she rented in Miller's Court, off Dorset Street in Spitalfields. Undisturbed in the victim's room for several hours, the killer had severed the nose and ears, eviscerated the abdominal cavity, mutilating the rest of the body and then burning the heart. Kelly lay naked with 'her head turned on the left cheek, the legs were wide apart, the left thigh at right angles to the trunk'.

Dr Bond, the medical officer who examined the body, stated:

> *The whole of the surface of the abdomen & thighs was*
> *removed & the abdominal cavity emptied of its viscera.*
> *The breasts were cut off, the arms mutilated by several*
> *jagged wounds, & the face hacked beyond recognition*
> *of the features.*

The eviscerated body parts were scattered or arranged around her body, 'viz. the uterus & kidneys with one breast under the head, the other breast by the right foot, the liver between the feet, the intestines by the right side . . . the pericardium was open below & the heart absent'. It may have been burned in the fireplace, which bore evidence of a 'fire so large as to melt the spout off the kettle'.

George Hutchinson, an acquaintance of Mary Jane Kelly, saw a man go into Miller's Court with her shortly after 2 a.m. The man wore a long dark coat with the collar and cuffs 'trimmed astracan' (*sic*), and a dark felt hat, and his moustache was 'curled up each end'. Though of 'respectable appearance' he was 'very surly looking' and 'walked very sharp'.

A neighbour, Julia Venturney, told police that Kelly was very fond of a 'man named Joe', who sometimes gave her money, but also 'often ill-used her'. At Little Paternoster Row, a woman came forward to say that one of her lodgers, called Joe, had acted suspiciously around the time of the murder, pacing around in his upstairs room all night, and disappearing immediately after it. This man was Joseph Isaacs, who was shortly afterwards arrested; newspaper reports state that he matched the description given by George Hutchinson, down to the Astrakhan coat. Isaacs, who had been imprisoned as a thief, was brought in for questioning but never charged.

The trail went cold and the murders ceased. The effect of the Ripper Murders, as they became known, on the public perception cannot be understated. The murders occurred shortly after a version of Robert Louis Stevenson's *Dr Jekyll and Mr Hyde* appeared on the London stage, a perfect metaphor for the time. To the Victorian mind, there was a pure virtuous and hygienic public life, coexisting with a raft of government, church and voluntary agencies to save the lost souls and redeem them for society. Hence Lord Gladstone's frequent tours to the demi-monde to 'lecture' fallen women. Beneath Victorian public life was a dark sinister underside, an affliction of the soul as it were, which could be projected onto any agencies regarded as hostile, marginal or just foreign. Hypocrisy ruled supreme; a vast hoard of prostitutes existed for the sexual purposes of the Victorian upper-class male. The Jews of Whitechapel were a perfect target of this disdain. The Ripper suspects were either unlikely members of the British aristocracy or establishment, alternately hapless Jews in Whitechapel who happened to have criminal problems of their own.

The Ripper Murders not only represented a hitherto unique form of gynaecide, but seemed to epitomise the social prejudices of the era. The killer was obsessed with mutilation of the female reproductive organs. There was intense suspicion that the killer was a butcher, barber or tailor, common occupations for men in that area. That the victims (the 'Canonical Five') were all prostitutes raised the possibility that the offender blamed them for something, infection with syphilis being very likely. This raised the possibility the killer had syphilis. Blaming prostitutes, as representatives of all women, for spreading the infection has been a recurrent theme of serial killers over time.

The Ripper became a tantalising chimera, able to materialise in any form that historians, writers or artists conjured up. The speculation never ended; each new generation interpreted the Ripper according to its values; the list of candidates would grow to include royalty, members of the aristocracy, society painters, leading doctors, spies and mad foreigners. But while the search for the Ripper's identity became an extended parlour game, no convincing candidate ever emerged. It had long been believed that no new historical evidence was going to emerge and the identity of the Ripper would remain hidden forever.

Segue to Johannesburg 1898, a mining camp exploding like dynamite into a city in the middle of the African veldt, a city the writer Olive Schreiner described as the epitome of evil on earth. In this raw excrescence of capitalism at its worst, sly grog houses, gambling dens and prostitution flourished. *Uitlanders*—foreigners—poured in to exploit the fantastic wealth garnered by the huge population of male miners. A Polish-Jewish brothel-owner known as Joe Silver (one of a host of *noms-de-plume*) attracted attention as the most outrageous, if not ruthless, of the crime figures. He ran the American Club, a 'trade union' of Polish-Jewish pimps who would communicate with their agents in 'coded, telegraphic and postal communication' as far afield as Russia, Argentina and the United States. Silver boasted that he had been a 'special agent' with the Society for the Prevention of Crime in New York City. At the same time as he was writing outraged letters to the newspaper about controlling the city's vice, he was busy informing the police about his opposition.

Silver posed such a threat to social order in the mining town that Jan Smuts, the new South African Republic State Attorney, set up a special force to contain him. Caught and jailed, the tides of history, as they so often did, were running Silver's way. As the British Army, driving the Boer forces before them, approached the Rand, all prisoners were freed and he made his way to the Cape and freedom to continue his criminal activities.

Silver continued his career of criminal mayhem, travelling to Windhoek, the infant capital of German South West Africa, followed by prison and a spell of safebreaking and bank robbery in Europe, more time in the United States, the United Kingdom and then South America.

Silver's trajectory was forgotten and would have remained so until historian Charles van Onselen, writing a history of early Johannesburg, studying the clash of social forces in the infant mining city, was paging through the *Standard & Diggers' News*, when his attention was caught by an item about an outrageous character named Joe Silver. Intrigued, Van Onselen looked further afield to learn more of the man who started life as Joseph Lis. Like a ball of string, once he started pulling, it kept unravelling; the result was a search extending to four continents over several decades. Van Onselen's research revealed a psychopath, police informer, sex slaver, safecracker, thief, spy and serial murderer. He was mostly known as Joe Silver, the alibi derived from his mother's name of *Kwekzylber*—meaning quicksilver or mercury, a wholly apt moniker for a man who epitomised everything that was ephemeral about human nature. Just a few of his many aliases were Joe Eligmann, James Smith, Joseph Schmidt, Charlie Silver, Charles Greenbaum, J. Cosman and Abraham Ramer Ludwig.

Joseph Lis (*Lis* means *fox* in Polish and Russian) was born in Kielce, Poland, in 1868, one of nine children of a Jewish tailor and petty criminal, Ansel Lis. His grandfather and father were low-life criminals, his slatternly mother had a son to another man. On 14 August 1884, Lis, then fifteen, got a passport to travel to England, arriving in London the following year. The typical route for emigrants was by ship from Hamburg to Hull, then by train across to Liverpool for a passage to London where the inevitable destination was Whitechapel in the East End.

Covering scarcely a few square kilometres, Whitechapel was the most crowded area in Europe, containing some 30,000 to 40,000 people; it was a dumping ground for Jewish migrants fleeing Tsarist persecution, a convenient focus of blame for all that was wrong in a capital city that spawned at least 75,000 prostitutes. Teeming with life, its inhabitants did what they could to keep going and, where they could, recreate the *shtetl* life they left behind. Synagogues, kosher butchers, barbers and tailors abounded. There were welfare societies, Yiddish theatres and serious-minded socialist clubs, debating utopian realities such as Theodor Herzl's *Judenstaat (Jewish State)*.

In this environment, a faultline between the establishment and marginal worlds, burglary, fencing of stolen goods, illicit liquor and other underworld activities all flourished. The chief activity was prostitution or, as it came to be known, white sex slavery. This was an organised business run by Jewish criminal gangs, often made up of close relatives. The gangs harnessed the available industrial and technological developments to their advantage. These were fast and cheap steamships for moving around the Atlantic, and the telegraph for rapid transmission of information. In what was essentially a franchising operation, using coded messages to avoid scrutiny, at its best, the organisation could meet any need on request provided the cost was met. The best example of this was the six-week period it took to provide a teenage virgin from the Pale of Settlement (in Russia) to a client in Johannesburg. Considering it was in the closing years of the nineteenth century, this was a remarkable turnover, the appalling nature of the criminal activity notwithstanding.

The transatlantic steamers and long-distance trains carried thousands of young women—mostly Jews from Eastern Europe fleeing the depredations of Russian oppression to the faultlines between the Old and New Worlds. Travelling alone and vulnerable, they were easy pickings for ruthless operators. They were seduced, traduced, conned or simply abducted and brutalised to become prostitutes, then sent around the Atlantic to work in brothels as far afield as Valparaiso, Kimberley, New York and Santiago. The Peruvians (as the slavers became known) were organised, ruthless, contemptuous of authorities and victims, and prepared to go to any lengths to maintain their trade against all opposition. They paid off the police, informed on their colleagues and used force to remove anyone who challenged their territorial rights or tried to escape their clutches.

Silver, as I shall call him now, would trawl around Whitechapel to find the newly arrived young Jewish women and ingratiate himself with them. His means of 'breaking in' the young women who fell into his clutches was an extraordinary process of sadistic brutality. Encountering one of the *arrivés*, he would pretend to be a charming and well-established man of the world with a respectable family seeking a companion and begin courting, showering them with gifts and meals for a week or two, the epitome of good behaviour. The women, who had mostly come directly from small *shtetls* where they knew no one except their own family and the other people who lived there, were completely taken in.

Silver would then invite them around to meet his family to discuss wedding plans. The unsuspecting young woman would be taken to what appeared to be a small hotel run by the family, who were all very welcoming and appropriate. On some pretext, she was taken to one of the rooms whereupon Silver's polite demeanour dropped. She would be violently raped and beaten, then locked in the room. Over the next few weeks, she would be subjected to repeated violence and sexual abuse until she was utterly broken and completely dependent on her jailer. When she had lost all will and ability to fend for herself, she would then be put to work as one of his prostitutes, giving everything she earned to him.

Sex slavery and the organised criminals who ran it bewildered and embarrassed the Jewish establishment. They reacted with denial and condemnation, establishing social and welfare organisations. The Austrian welfare worker Bertha Pappenheim became a leading activist for the cause, making risky voyages to crime centres in Eastern Europe to investigate and publicise what was occurring.

Silver had a spell as a tailor, then frequented the barber shops, boxing rings and brothels of Whitechapel, jammed with Jewish refugees from Russia. He took to thieving and prostitution with remarkable aptitude, organising a gang of relatives to run Jewish prostitutes, running a brothel near Waterloo Station. Violence, threats and intimidation were his stock in trade and whores were brutally beaten and raped to enforce his demands. He was acquitted of a rape charge on a technicality and jailed for petty larceny in Pentonville and Wormwood Scrubs prisons.

In late 1888 Silver went to New York City, where he operated as a low-grade thief, thug, jailbird and police informer. Convicted of stealing a couple of dollars and a silk shawl on the Lower East Side, he was jailed for two years in Sing Sing. The receiving clerk noted that his face was 'full of pimples' and 'pitted' with small scars—the facial lesions associated with secondary syphilis.

Silver traduced police, government officials, pimps and prostitutes. He was a criminal entrepreneur, housebreaker, jewellery thief, police informer, gangland enforcer and terroriser of prostitutes. He led a charmed life, moving with ease between continents and countries on the steamships, organising his criminal activities by coded telegraphic messages and defying the authorities. He used the Atlantic Ocean as his backyard, moving with casual abandon to New York, South African diamond and gold mining towns, Windhoek, Paris and Brussels. He robbed a jewellery store in France and financial institutions in Belgium before heading to Valparaiso, Buenos Aires and Santiago (where he was known as José Silva or José Silves).

Constantly moving, Silver frustrated and infuriated legal authorities on four continents, gliding from one jurisdiction to another, driven by urges that made sense to nobody, juggling social chaos and fortunes of war to his advantage. Like a dog going back to its vomit, he kept coming back to London. Spells in prison were no more than an occupational hazard and failed to interrupt his criminal path. Silver was transported under armed guard from German South West Africa to Germany to serve a three-year jail sentence.

Four surviving photographs chart his progress. Around twenty, he had a jaunty look with a flower in his buttonhole. In police records in Paris (1909) and Santiago (1912) he looks like a thug with bad skin. The last photograph, taken in New York around 1914 for a passport, shows him straining for upmarket status with a waxed moustache, rounded collar, tie-pin, smart jacket and waistcoat—beneath a sneering, sinister glare.

In his travels, Silver was mostly accompanied by his half-brother Jack. He paid no attention to his daughter Bertha, seventeen, until he returned to London and promptly put her to work for him as a prostitute. All her life Bertha lived in terror of her father and only gave out the most limited amount of information when interrogated by the police. Later, showing that she too adhered to the Lis family tenet of caring for no one but their own, she had two children to Jack.

In a business dominated by brute force and coercion, Silver's violence was extreme, an expression of his psychopathic personality. He routinely assaulted the women who worked for him. An indication of the aura of danger that he projected occurred in Johannesburg in 1899, when Silver threatened Lillie Bloom, a prostitute who was going to give evidence against him. The presence of policemen notwithstanding, Silver hissed at her in Yiddish that if she betrayed him he would 'open up her belly'. On another occasion, he plotted to punish a prostitute by chloroforming her and inserting 'blue vitriol' (hydrated copper sulphate) into her vagina.

At least three wives, all of whom worked for him as prostitutes, were held in his physical and psychological thrall. Two of them—Hannah Opticer, whom he married in London, and Hannah Vygenbaum alias Annie Alford, were made to 'disappear' once they were of no use to him. A third, Rachel Laskin, born in Poland about 1880, was raped and broken down by Silver in London, and brought with him to South Africa. She died in 1945, having spent the last forty years of her life in mental hospitals, known only by the name he had given her, Lizzie Silver.

In the middle of World War I, Silver went from South America to Przymysl, near his home town of Kielce, on the Eastern Front between the Austrians and the Russians. He was arrested in 1916 and executed six weeks before the end of the war. But for the curiosity of a historian about a newspaper entry in a dusty archive room of the Johannesburg Public Library, he would have disappeared off the map, lost to memory.

What would make a criminal opportunist return to Poland in the middle of World War I? The attraction was home: Kielce, where Silver's mother Hannah lived, presented an opportunity to resolve the ineluctable conflict that had driven him all his life. Silver, like all serial killers, was haunted by extreme ambivalence towards his feckless, seductive mother. Hannah Kwekzylber Lis had a bastard child, providing the betrayal so often experienced by the serial murderer. Ansel Lis, his father, was an inadequate role model, constantly failing at minor crime. By the time he was twenty, Silver had syphilis. A prostitute was carrying his daughter. Echoes of his mother's seductiveness collided head-on with fears of intimacy, commitment and betrayal. It was August 1888 and the Autumn of Terror was to commence.

Why, van Onselen asked himself, did Silver go to such efforts to hide the fact that he had been in London from 1885 to 1889? Could he have been the Ripper? Silver was not only in Whitechapel at the time, he was living in the very heart of the area where the killings occurred. Following the Kelly killing, police suspected a Joseph Isaacs. From three days after the murder until April 1889, Isaacs/Silver was in custody on theft charges. The description of Isaacs fitted that of Silver, known to be a thief of jewellery and clothing, to a tee. Freed from custody, Isaacs immediately disappeared; at the same time, Silver sailed to New York and was in Sing Sing Prison from October 1899 to October 1891. This neatly removed the Isaacs/Silver character from the ensuing investigations, let alone the scrutiny of Ripper historians.

Some time after 1881, a Lewis Lis set up business as a 'general dealer' in Plumber's Row, just south of the Whitechapel Road, and close to the zone of the Ripper murders. It is an unusual name, and it would be surprising if he were not a relative of Joseph Lis. He was still in business there in early 1888, when his daughter married his clerk, Moses Gourvitch. Around the same time, one Haskel Brietstein alias Adolph Goldberg, described as a 'chronically unsuccessful actor and burglar', was involved in a break-in at a warehouse directly opposite the Lis family's store. This Goldberg was later a close associate of Joseph Lis in New York, and is the only actual source—admittedly not a very trustworthy one—for Lis' presence in London. He stated in a New York courtroom that he had known Lis in London in the early months of 1889.

Van Onselen believes that Mary Jane Kelly's 'Joe' was indeed the agitated lodger Joseph Isaacs; that Isaacs was none other than

Joseph Lis, employing one of his aliases; and that all these Joes, when properly arranged, lead us to Jack.

Joe Silver's life was the product of massive social forces: persecution, marginality, migration, the opening up of the Atlantic Ocean by steamship and telegraph, transfer of massive wealth from gold and diamonds, the inability of government agencies, especially police, customs and immigration, to regulate movement and crime, and the constant need of society, whether in London, New York, Kimberley or Johannesburg, for illicit services such as prostitution provided by those who operated on the margins.

Joe Silver's Brain

The three cardinal factors in Joe Silver's peripatetic life of crime, mayhem and destruction are psychopathy, serial killing and syphilis. That Silver was a psychopath cannot be doubted. He was utterly immoral, constantly and superbly deceptive, going to any lengths to gratify his immediate needs or whims, and utterly remorseless in exacting revenge on anyone who crossed him without consideration of the consequences. The only time he appeared to show any distress was when he was jailed, and much of this was confected to ensure sympathy.

Lacking the inner regulating controls that most of us have, psychopaths have a remarkable faculty for being what their interlocutor wants them to be. This enables them to manipulate, inveigle and bamboozle people by making their victim feel reassured, if not special. In this regard, Silver was a remarkable con man, perhaps one of the greatest con men of all. Along with this went a remarkable ability for adopting new aliases, disguises and presentations to suit his circumstances.

This can be seen in Silver's most regular activity. As an indication of his superior psychopathic abilities, he always ran the sex slaving operations, using a squad of like-minded relatives, if not people from his home region, as lieutenants. He maintained discipline by violence, having no hesitation in resorting to stupe-fying drugs, rape or murder if necessary.

The recurrent question in forensic psychiatry is whether psychopaths are born or made. While it is accepted that psycho-paths have a structural abnormality in their brains, there is as yet no real consensus on what this is. It does not take much dealing with utterly remorseless, highly manipulative and completely hedonistic psychopathic criminals to come to the conclusion that they are born that way, and will be so forever.

Anatomy, however, is modified by reality. Firstly, there are many individuals who have a parent who is obviously psycho-pathic, but go on to lead perfectly ordinary and blameless lives. Being born with a psychopathic brain, it seems, requires certain experiences, modelling and influences during the formative years to express itself. But this is not always immediately evident or obvious. Consider the case of Harold Shipman, the English doctor found to have killed at least 256 (a possible figure is 400) of his patients, having started early in his career. On the surface, Shipman seemed to have had an ideal upbringing as the second child of four in a hard-working and close working-class family; the only setback in his life was the death of his beloved mother from cancer when he was seventeen. But on closer scrutiny, the picture becomes fragmented. Shipman's parents were very differ-ent and led quite separate lives. His relationship with his mother, from an early age, was pathological and he slept in her bed while his father did night duty until he was thirteen and already sexually mature. He was shattered by his mother's death and had a patho-logical reaction, not telling anyone at school what had happened, but for remembrance, her sigh of relief each afternoon when the doctor came round to give her a pain-relieving injection.

Silver came from a family of low-grade criminals, including both his father and grandfather. His mother was a louche char-acter who had an affair, leading to the birth of his half-brother Jack, when he was thirteen. This would have been highly unusual (and widely frowned upon) behaviour in the Jewish community of Kielce. His criminal activities started before he left Kielce at the age of sixteen for Whitechapel, where he soon burrowed into the demimonde, hanging around barber parlours, working at times as a tailor and doing some professional boxing to toughen up—good training for a future enforcer, not to say knife slayer. From there it was a natural progression to prostitution.

Why did serial killing begin in the late nineteenth century? It was a phenomenon of crowding, dislocation, alienation and isolation. There have been a myriad of theories, the writer Colin Wilson going as far as to suggest that the invention of the typewriter took women off the streets as prostitutes to become secretaries, thereby leading to a shortage of paid women for sexual abuse. Considering the flourishing of prostitution by the end of the century, this can hardly be valid. Could it have been a Malthusian perversion? As the population expanded exponentially, the percentage of psychopaths, emotionally numb, morally defective individuals, increased to a point where they could no longer wander the countryside undetected or expend their murderous energy in one or other war. Europe, after all, had been through the longest period of peace in its history, and war had always been a great means of mopping up the explosive energy of psychopathic individuals for what was perceived as the social good—of the side they fought for, at any rate.

In 1970, forensic psychiatrist Robert Brittain described sadistic serial killers as obsessional, narcissistic, insecure lonely men with rich fantasy lives. They started young, killing by the age of twenty. Their fathers were often abusive. They were troubled by their mother's promiscuity. Other symptoms include alcohol or drug abuse, callousness, sadistic sexual fantasies and homosexual experiences. Yet they seldom presented as brutal, unkempt, disorganised or angry; rather, they were polite, quiet and neat, frequently obsessional and with a capacity to present themselves at their best to people when it suited them.

Prostitutes are a recurrent target of the mission killer: someone who has a target against a particular group of people, justifying their killing with a rebarbative pseudo-morality. The Ripper murders showed the *modus operandi* of a sadistic mission killer: frenzied attacks on prostitutes with overkill, displaying their mutilated bodies in lewd positions to shock onlookers. Add to that factors such as sexual ambiguity, extreme misogyny, trophy collection, extreme vengeance fantasies and the die was cast. The positioning of his victim's body with splayed legs was one of the Ripper's signatures, a common feature of mission killings. The aim was to show the despised prostitute at her lewd worst, as well as cause the greatest shock, if not distress, to the viewers.

The ripping out of the Ripper victims' organs (including the burning of Mary Jane Kelly's heart), known as the harvesting of body parts, was associated with extensive mutilation of the face and genital areas. During his Jewish education Silver was inculcated with the work of Ezekiel, (see earlier chapter) who swore punishment on the whores of Israel and Babylon, threatening to excise jewellery, fingers, noses and ears as punishment for venery, hubris and perfidy. The savage precepts attack the 'filthiness' of a woman who has 'committed whoredoms', and the vengeance to be visited on her: 'They shall deal furiously with thee. They shall take away thy nose and thine ears; and thy remnant shall fall by the sword . . . Thus will I make thy lewdness to cease from thee.'

There is a very good case for Silver being a serial killer. He left bodies wherever he went. The Ripper murders aside, he was associated with a number of other killings; at least two wives (in reality, prostitutes forced to marry him so they could not testify in court) were disposed of once the litigation was finished. He plotted to insert blue vitriol into a prostitute's vagina and threatened to 'cut open' several others. His history of sadistic violence shows that murder meant no more to him than a morning shave.

The Ripper victims were street prostitutes of a certain age, the only exception the younger and less shop-worn Mary Jane Kelly, whom Silver/Isaacs visited before she died. The killer had skill with a knife such as a tailor, barber or butcher would have. Silver, in addition to honing his violence in the boxing booths, worked for some time as a tailor and a *feldscher* (barber–surgeon).

Silver raped prostitutes at will, and hated women. He caught syphilis from a prostitute and his daughter Bertha was born in April 1888, a traumatic event for a man with deeply conflicted feelings about his sexuality and all women, especially his mother. For the rest of his life, he bore a hatred towards women, especially street prostitutes, going to great lengths to exact sadistic revenge at every opportunity.

He was sexually ambivalent. He almost certainly had a relationship with Adolph Goldberg, with whom he was in jail for two years, and sodomised a black prisoner in Johannesburg Gaol.

He was amazingly confident, able to talk almost anyone around. There are numerous accounts of his meticulous, obsessional nature, both in regard to dress and appearance, and his organised criminal work.

And, if serial killers slip up, it is often because they cannot resist the temptation to wallow in adoration, if not ecstasy, over their sadistic work. They keep trophies, diaries and records, return to the scene of the crime and even link up with the authorities on the grounds of being helpful so that they can gloat over their success. Despite fleeing to the United States, Silver (as Isaacs had morphed into) kept returning to Whitechapel to both relive his killing spree while doing everything he could to obliterate any connection with the events in 1888.

Somewhere around Przymysl, Joseph Lis lies in an unmarked grave among the bones of hundreds of soldiers. From the five sad graves of the Whitechapel victims to the Hebrew section of Potchefstroom cemetery where lies Rachel Laskin, and any number of places in between, rest the bones of Silver's victims. In those awesome words, how anyone could ever imagine unquiet slumbers for the sleepers in that quiet earth?

JEAN-BAPTISTE-ÉDOUARD GÉLINEAU

> For two years since the age of 36, the
> patient had experienced sudden and
> repetitive 'sleep attacks', preceded by a
> feeling of 'deep heaviness … of a heavy
> load on the forehead and deep in the eyes'.
> As the attack commenced '… his thoughts
> are shadowed and he sleeps'. Once in the
> Jardin des Plantes '… around the monkey's
> cage, rendezvous of the curious, the maids,
> the soldiers … he just fell asleep with
> everyone around him laughing'.
>
> JEAN-BAPTISTE-ÉDOUARD GÉLINEAU

Since the dawn of time, humans have gazed upon the face of the moon in awe and wonder. Our nearest planetary neighbour has provoked endless speculation about its origin, composition and influence over our lives. Some of the moon's secrets were revealed after the invention of the telescope but, despite improvements in the technology over succeeding centuries, the rotation of the orb ensured that fully forty per cent of its surface—the dark side—was never visible to the inhabitants of earth.

Never seen, that is, until 1959, when the Russian Lunar 3 probe succeeded in reaching an orbital position to view the dark side. While, to considerable disappointment, nothing unexpected was revealed, publication of the photograph was an epochal moment for mankind in understanding the universe in which we occupy such a small and lonely part.

The hero of this chapter, Jean-Baptiste-Édouard Gélineau, was born on 23 December 1828 in the Bordeaux region of France. A brilliant student, he did his medical studies at the Naval Medical College. While still a student, he received praise for his work during a cholera epidemic in La Rochelle in 1849. He developed that tendency of medical men of a certain sensibility who write about life and produced work on a range of topics, starting with clinical cases, before going on to other issues. As a naval surgeon, he spent time in Réunion and the Comoros Islands. Here he collected data on the incidence of various illnesses which he later used for a doctorate. He wrote about colonial life, waxing lyrical about the beauty of the Creole women, and describing psychiatric cases, such as puerperal psychosis, in a fictional setting.

Leaving the navy, Gélineau set up as a general practitioner in the Rochefort area of France. In 1870, he served with distinction as a Surgeon-Major in the army during the Franco-Prussian War of 1870. Finding that health problems made it difficult to keep up with the pressures of his practice, he moved to Paris and practised as a specialist in nervous diseases.

This was at the time when neurology was becoming established as a speciality and Charcot's work at the Salpêtrière attracted doctors from all over the world. Gélineau did not join a university or medical school, and admitted his patients to a private hospital. He used his time to write prolifically, publishing nine books. Among his activities was serving as a director of a friendly society for doctors and their widows, and founding the French Society of Health Spas and Mineral Waters. He also had a nice little earner, known as Dr Gélineau's Tablets, a mix of bromide and arsenic for the treatment of epilepsy and the neuroses. This provided the nest egg for his retirement.

Gélineau was an astute observer, prepared to listen carefully to his patient's complaints. In 1880 a thirty-eight-year-old wine barrel merchant saw him with a distressing tale of an unusual problem that was not only affecting his business, but leading to great embarrassment. For the last two years, he would be overcome with uncontrollable sleepiness under any circumstances, even when serving customers. These attacks were irresistible. They lasted between one and five minutes and occurred up to 200 times per day.

In addition, the patient had attacks of muscular weakness, leading to collapse which could be precipitated by emotion, such as laughing when making sales, at cards or in public. This caused consternation in those around him, if not considerable embarrassment. The most humiliating episode occurred at the monkeys' cage in the Jardin des Plantes when he fell asleep in front of the cage, the onlookers comparing him to the cage's inmates.

In an article published in *Gazette des Hôpitaux*, Gélineau designated the abrupt onset of sleep attacks and muscular collapse as a unique new disorder in the neurosis category. The new condition, which he called narcolepsy, could occur independently or secondary to other illnesses. He referred to the neuromuscular collapses as astasia. The term narcolepsy (the English version of the French word *narcolepsie*) is derived from the Greek words *narke* (numbness, stupor) and *lepsis* (attack, to seize).

Gélineau went on to analyse fourteen cases, writing them up in a book in 1881. He tried various treatments, including bromides, strychnine and amyl nitrate, with little success. He speculated that narcolepsy was a form of normal sleep, distinct from epilepsy. This received scant attention from Charcot and his colleagues, who were dismissive of the possibility that anyone could have such brief attacks of sleepiness and then get up and carry on.

Undeterred, Gélineau stuck to his guns, but that was where the situation stayed for some time.

Which brings us to the role of sleep and the human story. Dreams and dream states have had a profound role in our development as a modern species. Shamans, witchdoctors, diviners, mystics, thinkers, philosophers and physicians have tried to penetrate the mystery of the state that comes over us as night falls. Sleep-talking, sleepwalking, dreams and nightmares are aspects of a state that seemed to many to be a parallel dimension of consciousness, a state when the gods, the devil, the cosmic ether, could take over our waking nature.

From the very earliest times, dreams were perceived to be of singular importance—messages of prophesy, good will or portents from the gods. The narratives of religion and mythology detail how visitations from gods, devils or angels would occur during sleep, for example the Dream of Joseph in the Book of Genesis. The person who had vivid dreams and the ability to relay them in a graphic and meaningful fashion to others was seen as a divine vessel, specially chosen by fate, the gods or circumstance to be a relay between the gods and mortals.

Sleep used to be seen as a passive condition, an essential but inert state to allow for rest and recuperation of the body and the mind. The problem with this view becomes obvious if you observe someone sleeping: sleep is anything but inert. It includes a range of phenomena, both perceptual and behavioural, that variously cause disturbance, distress or delight.

Dreams, the most common example of a natural psychotic state, are only one phenomenon that illustrate the dynamic nature of sleep. They are the window through which we can all view altered states of consciousness—in this sense, Freud's description of dream symbols as the 'royal road to the unconscious' is closer to the truth than realised.

The nature of dreams and sleep continued to trouble the minds of thinkers over the millennia. By the nineteenth century, it was not just Freud, tormented by strange dreams of loss after the death of his father (to say nothing of the cocaine he was sniffing), who ventured in the domain of night, but many other neurologists and psychiatrists were looking thoughtfully at the demimonde. Sleepy or dreamy states were common among the hysterical, neurotic or epileptic patients of the Salpêtrière Hospital, as Charcot demonstrated at his case presentations. In the asylums, where there was a renewed focus in classifying mental illness, it was evident that disturbance of sleep was a common feature of psychiatric disorders.

For all our scientific advancement, until the last fifty years—a mere pinprick in time— we knew as much about sleep as we did of the far side of the moon. According to psychoanalysts, dreams were a disguised symbolic expression of repressed unconscious memories, an idea that has repeatedly been shown to be incorrect. In 1931 psychoanalyst (and former neurologist) Ernest Jones said that an understanding of sleep phenomena would have 'momentous' consequences for the understanding of religion itself—a nice thought, but nothing new as anthropologists had been saying the same thing for the previous century. The critical breakthrough, opening the door to the secrets of sleep, was the discovery of the electroencephalogram (EEG), showing changes in the waves of the waking and sleeping person. The EEG became the essential tool for examining the sleeping brain.

Like all other organisms, chronobiological cycles play a significant role in human physiology, for example, the onset of puberty, twenty-eight-day menstrual cycle, nine months gestation of a baby. Our most important chronobiological activity, sleep is something we can never get enough of. It consumes fully one-third of our lifespan. Wakefulness is only the period during the diurnal cycle dominated by alertness. While the earth rotates on its axis every twenty-four hours, our body clocks, established aeons ago under different cosmic circumstances, are set at a cycle of close to twenty-seven hours. Add to that the pressures of modern life and the insatiable demand to conform with schedules based on economic and social factors, rather than the cycles of nature, we are always trying to catch up on that missing hour or two of sleep we lose every night.

Sleep is defined as the period of non-wakefulness, with lack of awareness of the external world. Between sleep and wakefulness are drowsy, non-alert phases when alertness is reduced, consciousness is slipping away and perceptual changes can arise. At the interphase between consciousness and sleep—the hypnagogic state—the usual orientation in time and space becomes vague and meaningless. Drifting into sleep, there is a natural process of first slowing, then deepening, of consciousness. Familiar objects can assume different qualities and are usually perceived as a threat. Sleep itself is not homogenous, but divided into REM and non-REM phases. Once sleep is assumed, the subject goes deeper and deeper from waking consciousness until Stage 4. In this state, the brain waves have progressively slowed; there is complete muscular paralysis.

After 90 to 120 minutes, there occurs REM sleep. The term is derived from rapid eye movement, which will be observed in the eyes of the sleeper. REM sleep is a state of dreaming and mental regeneration when the day's debris is cleaned out of the memory banks and dream images, stirred up from all the cerebral nooks and crannies, will flutter, flitter, surge and occupy the inner self with an astonishing array of events. The sleeper is in a sub-cognitive state; the rational and material world we inhabit in the day is gone. In its place is a physiological whirlpool, akin to a showground roundabout. Wild fluctuations of pulse, blood pressure and respiration occur. Bladder and bowels contract and relax. And, in males, the penis is erect. The state of muscular paralysis continues. If this protective mechanism breaks down, the subject can act out the content of the dreams, in some cases with lethal consequences.

As sleep progresses, REM sleep cycles wane and, at the end of the night, the sleeper rises to shallow levels before waking.

The state of sleep includes a range of phenomena, both perceptual and behavioural, that variously cause disturbance, distress and delight, but not always in that order. There are dreams and dreams. As a rough guide, dreams that are remembered occur in REM sleep; non-REM sleep dreams tend to be forgotten.

Sleep paralysis is a transient, conscious state of involuntary immobility occurring immediately prior to falling asleep or upon wakening and is classified as a parasomnia associated with REM sleep.

Sleep paralysis creates a state of consciousness onto which cultural loading and personal belief will produce images that conform to the subject's expectations or fears. This converts ordinary experiences from dreams, psychoses and mirages into spiritual experiences. Another way of saying this is that the content of nightmares is influenced by culture but the physiological expression has a measurable physiological basis.

The vivid dreams, as well as hypnagogic (while falling asleep) and hypnopompic (while waking) hallucinations were responsible for such diverse folk myths as the Succubus devil and the Old Hag phenomenon, spirit possessions, old hag attacks, ghostly visitations and alien abductions. As far back in history as the Assyrian Codex and the Bible are documented the disturbing nocturnal events we now know as sleep paralysis, the term for what most of us call a nightmare. A wide range of terms have been used to describe it, confirming its ubiquity in history and culture. The Anglo-Saxon term 'merran' (to crush) describes the crusher who comes in the night. 'Mare', the Saxon word for pressure, refers to the characteristic sensation of pressure on the chest.

Sleep paralysis can occur in fully forty per cent, if not more, of normal individuals, as well as those with physical and mental disorders. The individual wakens suddenly from a deep level of sleep with muscular paralysis, unable to move, pressure on the chest, experiencing a sense of suffocating. This is associated with a sense of falling, floating, drowning, being held down or throttled. The person is unable to open their eyes and subsequently report events in their surroundings during the episode.

Sleep paralysis is associated with an acute sense of a monitoring 'evil presence', combinations of auditory and visual hallucinations, as well as intense out-of-body sensations, interpreted as time or astral travel. The affected person may not see a spirit, but experience the sense of being a spirit.

Sleep paralysis is classified into three stages:

1 Intruder states consist of the sense of a presence accompanied by visual, auditory and sometimes tactile hallucinations. Vivid visual hallucinations may include human intruders, witches, demons, monsters and extraterrestrial abductors, associated with footsteps, whispering, animal sounds, verbal threats as well as being grabbed. These events stem from a hypervigilant state to detect danger.

2 Incubus states consists of pressure on the chest, breathing difficulties and pain due to changes in respiration.

3 Vestibular-motor hallucinations arise from activation of the neuromatrix consisting of sensations of floating, flying, spinning and falling. These are associated with out-of-body experiences, erotic feelings and feelings of bliss, related to physically impossible experiences generated by body position, orientation and movement.

For the majority of people, sleep paralysis is taken as a kind of spiritual experience because of the presence of a non-physical 'threatening presence' as part of the event. In others, sleep paralysis is associated with the experience of alien encounters, alien abduction and astral travel. In recent years, this has had sensational forensic consequences as a result of an assumed connection with childhood sexual abuse.

There is a tendency to assess sleep in terms of the changes that occur during sleep—this is incorrect. In fact, the changes induced by sleep disturbances can present at any point during the twenty-four-hour cycle. Most of us regard the commonest disturbance of sleep as insomnia, meaning a state of lacking sleep. Common as this is, it is the alternative state, excessive sleep, or sleeping at the wrong times, that has a profound effect on a number of conditions and has led to intense speculation as to its cause and meaning.

Narcolepsy is the most dramatic disorder of sleep. It arises from the failure to segregate the different stages of sleep from each other, leading to their intrusion on consciousness.

Narcolepsy has a hereditary basis, affecting 1 in 200 of the population, but can occasionally arise from head injuries. It is estimated that there are up to three million sufferers worldwide, an incidence of 0.7 per cent of the population. This makes it as common as well known disorders such as multiple sclerosis or Parkinson's disease.

Narcolepsy, which affects men and women equally, mostly starts in adolescence or early adult life. Children may have poor school grades or reports that they are always sleeping in class. It presents with sleep paralysis, hypnagogic and hypnopompic hallucinations, hypersomnia and cataplexy, the rarest of the four. The latter symptom, described as being 'struck down' by a supernatural force, is an emotion-induced muscular weakness, leading to sudden collapse with emotions like anger or laughter. Many patients do not have all the symptoms, and only twenty to twenty-five per cent have all four.

The diagnosis of narcolepsy is complicated by the fact that the condition can lead to a range of emotional, behavioural, psychiatric and forensic disorders and may not be detected until much later—often up to fifteen years. It is often confused with other sleep disorders, epilepsy or effects of medication.

Despite Gélineau's work, neurologists and psychiatrists in the nineteenth and twentieth centuries were dubious about accepting narcolepsy as a sleep disorder. This left it open to any interpretation, a gap into which the psychoanalysts surged. They regarded it as an unconsciously determined condition, an escape from inner conflict—an explanation which received far more attention than it deserved for lack of any other explanation. It took decades before there was any progress. Suggested causes of the condition were epilepsy, degenerative conditions or third-ventricle tumours.

But Gélineau had been right. It took the discovery of REM sleep on the sleep EEG in 1953 to confirm that narcolepsy arose from a breakdown in the control of deep sleep and alertness. Further investigations led to the development of the multiple sleep latency test (MSLT) for diagnosing narcolepsy.

This was a start, but it still took a long time. Narcoleptic patients, like epileptics, are frequently arrested and harassed when they collapse or fall asleep in public. The condition is associated with a range of behaviour problems, psychiatric difficulties, and relationship and work problems. Families, courts, doctors and judges often refuse to accept that strange, confused or difficult behaviour could be caused by a sleep disorder, particularly one that only lead, at worst, to very brief periods when sufferers are not conscious.

Narcolepsy has one advantage that facilitates research—it occurs in several dog breeds, making them useful for study. The most recent discovery was the critical role of the pituitary hormone orexin (hypocretin) in mediating sleep and wakefulness. Narcolepsy arises when there is a shortage of orexin. All over the world, white-coated researchers are beavering away in their laboratories to synthesise orexin or do gene splicing to prevent the shortage from arising, glaring at their captured Labradors, Dobermans or dachshunds when they refuse to wake up on command. Until they succeed, we use amphetamine-like drugs to treat the disorder, mostly achieving excellent results once the underlying condition is recognised.

In 1900, in the grand French tradition, Gélineau retired to his castle in Blaye at the age of seventy-two, happily making award-winning wines. In addition, he published several historical memoirs of Blaye and wrote a play entitled *After the Ball*. He died on 2 March 1906.

Largely forgotten to history, Jean-Baptiste-Édouard Gélineau is an all-too-rare example of the truly talented individual who goes into medicine and uses his ability to make a finding—based only on observation and intuition—that changes the face of the discipline. Recognition may have been a long time coming, but narcolepsy has been an important window on sleep, the biological phenomenon that plays such an important part in the daily function of the brain. For this we shall be ever grateful to Gélineau.

VINCENT VAN GOGH

*How can I convey to you that here every
being—a being of every tree, every yellow
strip or green field, every fence, every
hollow tunnel in the stone hill, a being of
the pewter pitcher, the earthenware plan,
the coarse chair,—rose up to me as if
newborn out of the frightful chaos of
non-life, out of the abyss of non-being.*

HUGO VAN HOFMANNSTHAL

In 1901 Hugo van Hofmannsthal, with Arthur Rimbaud, one of
the great lyrical poets of the late nineteenth century, went to a
small exhibition in Paris by a little-known artist. He was taken
aback by the sheer intensity of the pictures: 'They seemed to me
harsh and disturbing, quite raw,' he wrote as he adjusted to the
impact. He saw in them something sublime: 'The human spiritual
power that Nature had formed . . . the essential thing, I lost the
whole, so that I lost the sense of myself in these images, and came
back powerfully and was lost again.'

The painter, whose name was Vincent van Gogh, van
Hofmannsthal later wrote, had invented a pictorial language
capable of rendering the sense of the unity of one's consciousness in the mute, inanimate world. The harmony, sensuousness
and magical atmosphere of traditional painting was gone, to be
replaced by the sheer physical weight of the unremitting intensity
of the colours. The paint on the canvas was not an illusion of the

scene, as in traditional painting, but a physical substitute for it, using colour for purely emotional effect.

Regarded as the quintessential tormented artistic genius, Vincent van Gogh produced some of the greatest paintings ever. Museums around the world pay millions of dollars for his works, blockbuster exhibitions are sold out and his paintings have become postmodern icons, regarded by the public as cultic for their expression of emotion through vivid colours. Van Gogh's short life lasted from 1853 until 1890 when he shot himself in the chest. A late entrant to painting, van Gogh produced over two thousand artworks in the last ten years of his life, an extraordinary output by any standards. The year he painted *Starry Night*, he was producing a new painting, watercolour or drawing every thirty-six hours.

In addition to his paintings, van Gogh's greatest legacy has been his letters, now released in an unabridged six-volume edition with extensive annotations, translation and references. Considering the short period in which they were produced, his letters offer a unique insight into the mind of a great artist and constitute an extraordinary contribution to the artistic canon. Written daily— sometimes up to three a day—they provide a detailed account of van Gogh's daily activities, thoughts, mood and artistic progress. The majority of the letters are written to his brother Theo, the only person who could tolerate him and was unstinting in supporting him through thick and thin.

Vincent van Gogh, the first of six children, came from a Dutch family of clergy and people involved in the art business. His father was a Dutch Reformed Church minister. Biographers are unanimous that from an early age van Gogh was an extraordinarily difficult individual who, until his death, fell out with everyone except Theo. His behaviour was regarded as obsessive and eccentric. He was moody, impulsive and prone to irrational behaviour or explosive outbursts. Even Theo, who cared deeply for him, found Vincent intolerable to live with and they had a far better relationship communicating by letter.

*I do know that there is a release, the belated release.
A justly or unjustly ruined reputation, poverty, disastrous circumstances, misfortune, they all turn you into
a prisoner. You cannot always tell what keeps you
confined, what immures you, what seems to bury you,
and yet you can feel those elusive bars, railing, walls.
Is all this illusion, imagination? I don't think so. And
then one asks: My God! will it be for long, will it be for
ever, will it be for eternity?*

Leaving school at fifteen, van Gogh, spent some time in London,
failed any courses of study he attempted before working in the
family art business and teaching, both with equal lack of success.
His career as art salesman was only notable for the fact that
he abused customers for their poor taste. None of these failures
was due to lack of application, but rather his inability to find an
outlet for the constant, insistent drive within him for emotional
expression.

*The work is an absolute necessity for me. I can't put it
off, I don't care for anything but the work; that is to
say, the pleasure in something else ceases at once and
I become melancholy when I can't go on with my
work.*

People invariably found van Gogh's intensity overwhelming. This
intensity was coupled with a near-complete inability to understand
other people's feelings, while being outraged that they could not
cope with *his* passion. A letter to his boss at Goupil's Gallery after
the death of the man's daughter is peppered with Biblical quota-
tions, and reads more like a sermon than a note of condolence,
indicating the extent of van Gogh's religious fervour.

When his father died, van Gogh sent Theo a telegram baldly
stating '*Sudden death, come, van Gogh*', showing his inability

to understand the effect of his actions on other people, to say nothing of the confusion it would have caused his brother since it was unclear who had died.

Van Gogh's relationships were rancorous. He tended to idealise painters he admired, but this was inevitably followed by a bitter falling-out, mostly because the recipients could not tolerate his obsessive intensity: 'People are often unable to do anything, imprisoned as they are in I don't know what kind of terrible, terrible, oh such terrible cage.'

His attitudes towards women was no different; he saw them either as saints or whores. Besotted with his cousin Kee Voss, who refused to return his affections, he resisted all refusals to allow him in her house until he was threatened with jail. The situation culminated in a dramatic episode when he held his hand over a lamp flame in an attempt to persuade her father to allow him back.

> *Love is eternal—the aspect may change, but not the essence. There is the same difference in a person before and after he is in love as there is in an unlighted lamp and one that is burning. The lamp was there and was a good lamp, but now it is shed.*

Later van Gogh formed a dysfunctional relationship with Sien, an older prostitute who gave him gonorrhoea (and may have had his stillborn child). He was also reported for forcing himself on an artist's model.

Making no progress in his career, van Gogh returned to Holland and, after failing several theology courses, went to serve as a trainee minister to a poor community in the Borinage district of Belgium. Here he insisted on accompanying his parishioners down the coalmines, living in rough housing, wearing shoddy clothing, sharing his food and giving away his possessions. This behaviour, added to ferocious attacks on the establishment in his sermons, so alarmed the church authorities that he was stood down for bringing the ministry into discredit.

> *That God of the clergymen, He is for me as dead as a doornail. But ... I love, and how could I feel love if I did not live, and if others did not live, and then, if we live, there is something mysterious in that. Now call that God, or human nature or whatever you like, but there is something which I cannot define systematically, though it is very much alive and very real, and see, that is God, or as good as God. To believe in God for me is to feel that there is a God, not a dead one, or a stuffed one, but a living one, who with irresistible force urges us toward aimer encore; that is my opinion.*

Disillusioned by the hypocrisy of organised religion, van Gogh determined to become a painter. He had been drawing for some time, but threw himself into the task.

> *Then I feel like a weaver who sees that his threads are tangled, and the pattern he had on the loom is gone to hell, and all his thought and exertion is lost.*

Compared to his previous attempts at study, he became extremely knowledgeable about current developments in painting, from England to Japan. Many of his letters are covered with his illustrations of the paintings he studied, as well as discussions of the books he read.

> *Try to grasp the essence of what the great artists, the serious masters, say in their masterpieces, and you will again find God in them. One man has written or said it in a book, another in a painting.*

With Theo's support, he went to Paris, mixing with many of the most famous Impressionist and Post-Impressionist painters.

Van Gogh's attitude to painting had all the elements that he had brought to work, relationships and religion: a deeply spiritual attitude going well beyond dedication. He wrote how the spiritual aspects of painting connected the artist to God: 'When I have a terrible need of—shall I say the word—religion then I go outside in the night to paint the stars.' No one who sees the art of Vincent van Gogh can avoid becoming aware of the powerful feelings motivating the artist. It was a consuming obsession infused with apocalyptic elements, a prism through which the entire world was viewed.

From 1880, van Gogh produced works of art at an astonishing rate. In the ten years until his death, he produced an extraordinary 800 paintings, in addition to drawings and sketches, continuing to work until the day of his death. Despite times when he had to forgo food to buy art materials or was unable to work due to illness, he kept painting.

Just slap anything on when you see a blank canvas staring you in the face like some imbecile. You don't know how paralysing that is, that stare of a blank canvas is, which says to the painter, You can't do a thing. The canvas has an idiotic stare and mesmerises some painters so much that they turn into idiots themselves. Many painters are afraid in front of the blank canvas, but the blank canvas is afraid of the real, passionate painter who dares and who has broken the Spell of 'you can't' once and for all.

In his work, van Gogh wanted to go beyond mere representation. He saw developments such as Impressionism and Post-Impressionism as only a means to an end, providing the technical facility for what he saw as the most important issue: the expression of emotion. By the end of his life, he had settled on the means to do so: colour. For this reason, Vincent van Gogh is the father of Expressionism.

> *I can very well do without God both in my life and in my painting, but I cannot, suffering as I am, do without something which is greater than I am, which is my life, the power to create.*

In the last year of his life, his mental state deteriorated alarmingly. Despite hospitalisation, he struggled to continue. His last paintings (notably *Crows Over a Wheatfield*) were ominous. The situation blew up when he saw his doctor. He threatened him with a pistol, left the office, and shot himself in the chest. He died two days later with Theo at his side. To complete the tragedy, Theo died of syphilis within six months and it was left to Theo's widow to market the paintings and later ensure that the letters were published.

Vincent van Gogh's Brain

In spite of his wretched life, van Gogh produced art regardless of the travails he was going through. These would have overwhelmed anyone under the best of circumstances, but he was indifferent to his material welfare and only stopped working when his mental state made it impossible for him to continue. In the wake of his death, something of a minor medical industry has arisen, attributing van Gogh's problems to a variety of conditions; among the many cited are porphyria, absinthe toxicity, digitalis poisoning, epilepsy, borderline personality disorder, manic-depression and schizophrenia. Some of these diagnoses—notably porphyria and digitalis toxicity—do not stand up to scrutiny and belong in the wilder realm of speculation. The intention here is to consider a neurological basis for van Gogh's behaviour, while remaining neutral about a specific disease, physical or psychiatric.

Van Gogh had hypergraphia. His production of paintings surpasses that of major Renaissance and Baroque artists who, in addition, had teams of students and assistants included in their projects. His explosion of creativity in Arles (1888–89) generated 200 paintings and 200 drawings and watercolours. Aside from his output of paintings, his letters are the most superb example of the thoughts and work of any painter. Every night, after painting for fourteen to sixteen hours, he would write to Theo, the shortest letter six pages. The volume and output, let alone the detail, is astonishing. Written in a neat script, they fill the pages, often overflowing on the margins, with inserted comments and added pictures. The paragraph below is an example. Note the overwriting and repetition of 'idler':

There is a great difference between one idler and another idler. There is someone who is an idler out of laziness and lack of character, owing to the baseness of his nature. If you like, you may take me for one of those. Then there is the other kind of idler, the idler despite himself, who is inwardly consumed by a great longing for action who does nothing because his hands are tied, because he is, so to speak, imprisoned somewhere, because he lacks what he needs to be productive, because disastrous circumstances have brought him forcibly to this end. Such a one does not always know what he can do, but he nevertheless instinctively feels, I am good for something! My existence is not without reason! I know that I could be a quite a different person! How can I be of use, how can I be of service?

There is something inside me, but what can it be? He is quite another idler.

In addition to hypergraphia, van Gogh had all the features of Geschwind syndrome. He had an unconventional sexuality, alternating between periods of hyposexuality and hypersexuality, liaisons with women and men including, it seems, Paul Gauguin. There are many examples of social clinging, inability to understand social boundaries, insensitivity to the feelings of others, tendency to moralise, criticise and make impossible demands, pedantry and obsessiveness, intense religiosity, tendency to derive spiritual meanings from his paintings, and viscosity of thinking.

The stormy relationship with Gauguin illustrated not only his mental stickiness but also his aggression. Gauguin bemoaned the difficulty of ending conversations with van Gogh. The affair culminated in the painter's famous auricular self-amputation: during a heated argument, a voice in his ear whispered, 'Kill him', so he attacked Gauguin with a razor; then he turned the blade against his own ear and went to a brothel to present the severed earlobe to a favoured prostitute.

Van Gogh had Geschwind syndrome—but what of the cause? Geschwind, when giving a lecture on Fyodor Dostoevski (a much-studied case of temporal lobe epilepsy) was asked for his opinion on van Gogh. Epilepsy, he replied without hesitation— just like Dostoevski. But was he right?

Van Gogh had several seizures and was diagnosed with epilepsy during his lifetime. This led a number of writers to diagnose temporal lobe epilepsy, most notably Dietrich Blumer. Ronald Pickvance (organisers of the 1984 *Van Gogh in Arles* exhibition at the Metropolitan Museum of Art) claimed that the painting *Over the Ravine* shows signs of a seizure during composition: brush strokes actually tore the canvas. This explanation must be strongly questioned, taking into account van Gogh's aggressive nature and moodiness, to say nothing of any number of other explanations, including the neglect of his paintings due to his disorganised lifestyle.

Neurologist Shahram Khoshbin believes that tertiary colours consistently appear in the artwork of those diagnosed with epilepsy, describing van Gogh's *Self-Portrait in the Fog* as an outstanding example. Khoshbin studied van Gogh's work to determine the link between his use of colour and emotion, noting that van Gogh would pair certain colours—such as blue-violet with yellow-orange—to evoke emotions. As he said in his letters:

> It often seems to me that night is still more richly coloured than the day, having hues of the most intense violets, blues, and greens. If only you pay attention to it you will see that certain stars are citron-yellow, others have a pink glow, or a green-blue and forget-me-not brilliance.

While the intuitive response to the evidence is for temporal lobe epilepsy as the cause of his Geschwind syndrome, the case for cannot be sustained. John Hughes, in an elegant and critical appraisal, reviewed the evidence and was unable to confirm its presence. In those days, the diagnosis of epilepsy was applied to any seizure, if not a range of other symptoms. The only mention of ictal (seizure) activity is late in van Gogh's life when he had withdrawal seizures from alcohol and thujone, the toxic ingredient of absinthe. These are, in other words, secondary seizures, not indicative of a primary epileptic disorder.

As noted, the many other causes cited for van Gogh's illness are either wildly speculative and untenable, or merely symptomatic, rather than representing the primary diagnosis. Therefore, in Hughes' words, van Gogh's Geschwind syndrome was 'an orphan in search of a parent'. What that was will remain unknown. What we can say with some confidence is that the overcharged output from the temporo-limbic region was the driving force in a life that was emotion incarnate. Tormented, tortured, maddening, impossible, often messianic, at times deluded, van Gogh oscillated from the heights of elation to the depths of despair but he never gave up until he was overwhelmed by his inner demons, leaving us a legacy of the graphic illustration of human feelings that will never be surpassed.

> *Well, right now it seems that things are going very badly for me, have been doing so for some considerable time, and may continue to do so well into the future. But it is possible that everything will get better after it has all seemed to go wrong. I am not counting on it, it may never happen, but if there should be a change for the better I should regard that as a gain, I should rejoice, I should say, at last! So there was something after all!*

BERTHA PAPPENHEIM

*Neurosis: an illness of fantasy and
a fantasy of an illness*

PETER SWALES, FREUD, BREUER AND THE BLESSED VIRGIN

Well over a century ago in *fin-de-siècle* Vienna occurred one of
the strangest episodes known in medicine. In the plush surroundings of a comfortable middle-class home, a twenty-one-year-old
woman shrieked, had visions of black snakes, spurned water,
threw fits, shuddered in agony and cried. She developed a squint,
disturbances in hearing and vision, and had prolonged absences
(altered states of consciousness while awake). She became paralysed down one side and lost the ability to speak her native
German, using English instead. Her personality oscillated between
one living in the present and one living 365 days earlier.

Her father became ill with a tubercular abscess while the
family were staying at their holiday home in the Spa of Isle (today
Bad Isle). A surgeon attempted to drain the abscess, but her father
remained unwell and steadily relapsed. The patient, who had a
'passionate love for the father who pampered her' (according to
her analyst), would nurse him at night. For the two months before
he died, she was not allowed to see him and was lied to about the
seriousness of his condition. Consequently, his death came as a
shock, she felt 'robbed' and fell ill herself.

From December 1880 to June 1882, she was attended by
Josef Breuer, who had been the family physician for several years.
A dedicated physician and brilliant researcher, Breuer discovered
the role of the vagus nerve in breathing and the semi-circular

canals in balance. Described by physicians in Vienna as 'the doctor's doctor', he had a special interest in the fashionable speciality of neuropathology.

Breuer described the patient's personality, noting 'the sexual element was astonishingly undeveloped in her'. Despite early reservations and doubts—at one time, he wondered whether she had tuberculous meningitis—he diagnosed hysteria. Breuer's patient was a surprising candidate for an illness that continues to baffle, intrigue and raise questions to each new generation.

At a loss to help, Breuer suggested hypnosis; intuitively, his patient took the lead. Each afternoon, she fell into a somnolent state; in the evening they did 'chimney-sweeping' sessions, discussing the symptoms of the day to make them disappear. She called this her talking cure. Inexorably drawn into the case, Breuer spent two hours a day with his patient. She in turn became dependent on his care, and would invariably relapse when he was away for a few days. Treatment was brought to a close when she reproduced a frightening hallucination of a black snake. After this, reported to have 'regained her mental health entirely' she remained well.

Breuer discussed the case on numerous occasions with his brilliant young protégé, Sigmund Freud. Freud had visited Jean-Martin Charcot (the 'Napoleon of neurologists') in Paris. Establishing a school and inspiring a generation of neurologists, Charcot devoted the last years of his career to studying hysteria, a condition he believed could be cured by hypnosis. Freud returned to Vienna singing the praises of his new mentor—and named his first son after him—convinced the cause of hysteria lay in hidden psychological trauma.

Although his heart was in research, Freud went into private practice as a neurologist to enable him to finally marry his fiancé, Martha Bernays. Freud did not find private practice easy and it took a while to get established. He saw a series of female patients with hysteria. He used the conventional cures of the day—including faradism (electrotherapy), warm baths, magnetic cures—but had little success. In desperation, he tried hypnotism. He was not a natural hypnotist, patients refused to go under and he began to eliminate the rituals instead, getting patients to talk about the first thing on their mind. From there, he developed the 'talking cure', convinced the cause of hysteria lay deep in the unconscious: the repressed memory of sexual abuse. But all this was to come later.

By the 1890s Freud had collected four cases of hysteria and wanted to get into print, making a concerted effort to persuade Breuer to write up the case that had made such an impact on him over a decade earlier. Freud's rush to get *Studies on Hysteria* out in 1895 was to ensure that French neurologist Pierre Janet did not get credit for discovering the psychological treatment of hysteria. Breuer, however, had reservations about going into print. His involvement with the patient had played havoc with his working and home life and he swore never again to subject himself to such an ordeal. Furthermore, as he and Freud were both aware, the case had turned out to be far from successful—this troubled him far more than it did Freud.

The patient was admitted to a psychiatric hospital where a significant effort was made to cure her of morphine and chloral hydrate addiction. This may have led to criticism from colleagues that Breuer's conduct was 'less than exemplary'—a reference to his tendency to freely dispense morphine to his patients.

Finally, Breuer reluctantly gave in to the urging of his protégé. To ensure anonymity—a dubious enterprise, considering the close-knit circles of middle-class Jewish Vienna—the patient's name was given as Anna O., an alias that was to go down in psychiatric history. Breuer's case history was written from 'incomplete notes'. Early in the discussion, he used the term 'repress', the first documented mention of the central tenet of psychoanalysis. The case became the centrepiece of Breuer and Freud's book *Studies on Hysteria*.

The book received a less than modest response. Freud, who regarded himself as the prophet in the wilderness, accused colleagues of being too timid to accept his shocking findings. The truth was less exciting. In the Vienna of Krafft-Ebing, sexual perversion was nothing new, nor the idea that neurosis stemmed from childhood abuse.

The drama of the case enveloped its protagonists. While Breuer accepted there could be a sexual element in hysteria, he doubted whether this was the only cause. He cautioned Freud against being too dogmatic, but did not get a warm response. Freud drew away, and later rejected Breuer. In Freud's view, Breuer was not 'Faustian' enough to accept the truth of the daring hypothesis that became the *leitmotif* of psychoanalysis: that repressed sexual trauma was the cause of hysteria.

The Anna O. case was read and re-read, repeatedly cited as a reference and recognised as the first case to be treated with psychoanalytic methods. Freud's biographer Peter Gay described it as 'the founding case of psychoanalysis'. Swiss psychoanalytic historian Henri Ellenberger described the story as 'a unique case of which no other instance is known, either before or after her'. From these beginnings came psychoanalysis, Freud's vision of the unconscious world of man.

Yet, despite the intention of her keepers, Anna O. was never destined to rest in a museum. Freud discussed the undisclosed ending of the case with people around him, including Carl Jung, the man designated as the crown prince of psychoanalysis. In 1925, by which time the two had gone their own ways and Jung had few reasons to keep silent, he stated that the case had been far from the success the authors claimed and could by no means be regarded as a cure.

In 1932, Freud told his friend the writer Stephan Zweig a story about Breuer's final contact with his patient. Some time after he ended his active treatment with her, he received an urgent call to the house, where he found Anna O. lying on the bed, writhing in pain. 'Now comes Dr B's child,' she cried. Recognising a pseudocyesis (hysterical pregnancy), Breuer hypnotised her to remove the symptoms, and fled the house. He took his wife on a hastily arranged second honeymoon to Venice, as a result of which his daughter Dora was born. The story was emblematic: Breuer, lacking the steel of the true conquistador, blinked at the crucial moment, refusing to recognise the erotic element in the transference. Freud, by contrast, had held his gaze and had gone on to discover the truth at the basis of psychoanalysis.

The sniping did not end there. Freud, perhaps suffering from a guilty conscience, made a footnote reference to the 'reconstruction' of a memory in which Breuer had confirmed the hysterical pregnancy, communicated by his daughter after Breuer's death. Freud's 'reconstruction' was no more valid than any other recovered memory and has been firmly discounted by researchers. There the matter would have rested, Breuer being only the first of a long line of apostates that Freud banished, allowing his acolytes to gossip about them as much as they wished. Little of this passed beyond the insular world of psychoanalysis.

Freud's authorised biography was published in stages after 1953 by one of his most loyal followers, Ernest Jones. Jones' attitude to the case may be judged from the comments of Breuer's biographer, Albrecht Hirschmüller, who described him as 'having a certain fixed attitude which would bear closer examination. His account should be treated with some caution by the historian.' The biography, or rather hagiography, was a careful work of censorship designed to ensure the legend of the founder of psychoanalysis was maintained intact, free of blemishes and awkward events. In conjunction with Anna Freud, the master's daughter and chief intellectual heir, Jones ensured that any number of embarrassing documents were excluded from the text. But, perhaps to divert attention from the numerous elisions, Jones produced one rabbit from his hat, a drastically altered version of the Anna O. case. For the first time, the name of the patient known as Anna O. was publicly disclosed, to the fury of her family and surviving relatives.

Anna O. was Bertha Pappenheim, who had gone on to be a pioneer social worker and feminist advocate. Never marrying, she worked in Jewish welfare and lobbied against Jewish prostitution in Eastern Europe. She established women's refuges and wrote plays and children's poetry. She wrote on a wide range of topics and corresponded with some of the leading philosophers of her day.

Now that Anna O. had a real name, there was a flurry of interest but little was done. The Jewish community of Austria had been wiped out in the Holocaust or fled Europe. To refute Jones' claims, a modest biography was published by Dora Edinger, but it never had wide distribution.

If that was Anna O., who was Bertha Pappenheim? Her paternal grandfather, Wolf Pappenheim, a descendant of the famous Rabbi Nathan, came from the town Pappenheim in Bavaria; the family name was derived from there. Later he inherited a fortune from his wife and lived in the Pressberg ghetto. He had two sons, Kalman and Siegmund, Bertha's father. Siegmund Pappenheim settled in Vienna as a wealthy grain merchant. A practising Jew, he contributed to the Schiffshul synagogue building fund. He was appointed guardian of Freud's future wife, Martha Bernays, after the death of her mother in 1879, and she became friendly with Bertha.

Recha Goldschmidt, Bertha's mother, was born in Frankfurt am Main. Her prominent family had connections to many well-known Jewish families, including the Hombergers, Warburgs and Rothschilds. Among her antecedents were the poet Heinrich Heine and the acclaimed diarist, Glückel of Hameln.

The Pappenheim marriage in 1848 had been arranged, as was customary at the time. The family lived in the Leipoldstadt Jewish Quarter before moving to Liechtensteinstrasse in 1880. Recha Pappenheim never enjoyed living away from her family in Vienna. There are claims the marriage was unhappy and Siegmund Pappenheim frequented brothels, but no evidence exists for this.

Breuer described Recha Pappenheim as 'very serious'; Jones, less respectfully, as 'somewhat of a dragon'. She lost two daughters; Flora died three years before Bertha was born, and Henriette died of tuberculous meningitis when Bertha was eight. Pappenheim's brother Wilhelm practised law in Vienna. He was described as an accomplished gentleman with the most complete library on socialism in Europe. The siblings were estranged, Bertha claiming he bullied her unmercifully during childhood.

Born on 27 February 1859 in Vienna, Pappenheim went to a Catholic school, there being no Jewish day school in Vienna at the time. Despite her father's orthodoxy, she had a liberal upbringing. According to Breuer, she was 'thoroughly unreligious', had a powerful intellect with great poetic and imaginative gifts. She could speak English well, in addition to French and Italian.

While Breuer said she led a monotonous existence as a 'superior young lady', this is at odds with the picture of a lively young woman in riding habit. As was common for women from her background, she went horse riding, did needlework, played the piano (until late in life) and went to the theatre; she especially enjoyed Shakespeare.

After discharge from the Sanatorium Bellevue, Pappenheim stayed with relatives in Germany for some months and attended a nursing course at the Union Clinic in Karlsruhe. Returning to Vienna in 1883, she relapsed and had three long stays at Inzerdorf Sanatorium. By 1888 she had recovered and moved with her mother to Frankfurt, Germany where her career in social work began.

Pappenheim founded and directed a home for orphaned Jewish girls for twelve years. After her mother's death in 1905, she lived at the orphanage. In 1904 she founded the League of Jewish Women, followed in 1907 by a teaching institution affiliated with the organisation. She led an international campaign against prostitution, described as 'White Slavery,' involving young Jewish women from Eastern Europe and the Near East.

She travelled widely in Eastern Europe and the Middle East, often experiencing hardship, if not danger, to inspect brothels.

Her work, although not always free of controversy, was regarded as a beacon for others. Her dedication was legendary and she is considered the founder of social work in Germany. She wrote extensively: fairy stories, Jewish prayers, and a play depicting female characters who were exploited by men. She maintained a wide correspondence, much of which was lost during the war, including an exchange with the philosopher Martin Buber.

By all accounts, Pappenheim was a lively, engaging personality, free of psychological problems. She lived alone and never married. She had a good sense of humour, loved good food and had a fine collection of glass, porcelain and tapestry.

Pappenheim returned to Vienna in 1935, dying of cancer on 28 May 1936, heavy with foreboding at the tragedy she predicted for European Jewry. Her grave lies in the Jewish cemetery of Frankfurt. Her death was commemorated with a forty-page special edition of a journal she had founded.

In 1954 Bertha Pappenheim was honoured as a pioneer social worker with the issue of a stamp by the West German Republic.

Bertha Pappenheim's Brain

Henri Ellenberger, author of a definitive history of psychoanalysis, *The Discovery of the Unconscious*, believed Freud had picked up ideas that had been around since ancient times. In the eighteenth century, the rise of 'magnetic cures' rekindled interest in the unconscious, and further developments occurred after Charcot became interested in hypnosis.

Ellenberger had good reason to question the official version of the Anna O. case, stating that Jones' version 'is fraught with impossibilities . . . based on hearsay and should be considered with caution'. He obtained a picture of the young Bertha Pappenheim in 1882, showing an attractive, healthy-looking young woman in a riding outfit—an image markedly at odds with Breuer's description. In an ingenious piece of detective work, the picture was screened under special light in the forensic laboratory of the Montreal City Police to reveal the name of the photographic studio and therefore the origin of the picture.

After one false lead, Ellenberger tracked down the Sanatorium Bellevue at Kreuzlingen, Lake Constance, where Pappenheim was admitted for treatment. Allowed to investigate the hospital records stored in a dusty basement, he found Pappenheim's file, including Breuer's handwritten account of the case. Ellenberger's excitement as he sat down to read the file can only be imagined; in his hands he was holding the case notes of the most famous patient in psychoanalysis.

The notes, however, revealed an outcome he could scarcely have expected. Far from being the cure and recovery that Breuer had claimed, Pappenheim had been admitted to the psychiatric hospital in a wretched state, addicted to morphine and chloral hydrate. She followed a long and stormy course with periods of confusion and psychosis. She continued to have trances, hallucinations, convulsions and severe facial neuralgia. On one occasion, she tried to hang herself from a tree. She improved, was discharged and had to be admitted again. During this time, Dr Holländer, one of her physicians, fell in love with her, prompting her removal from the hospital.

It took seven years before Pappenheim had fully recovered and was able to return to her family. No more was known of her medical history after that but, in view of her active career, it was assumed she remained well.

Ellenberger published his findings in 1972. He summed up the case with the arch comment that the famed prototype of a cathartic cure had been neither cathartic nor a cure. Later Hirschmüller, Breuer's biographer, was able to discover additional documents related to the case. From this followed a minor cataract of writing about the case.

Ellenberger's findings were taken up by Elizabeth Thornton, a medical librarian at a London hospital, who wrote a book on Charcot's hysterical patients, noting that many of the women were coached and only allowed to stay on in hospital if they put on a good display at presentations. Many of the cases of hysteria had temporal lobe epilepsy. Breuer, it will be recalled, diagnosed Anna O. with hysteria, a diagnosis that had far wider application than today.

Thornton came up with the intriguing hypothesis that Anna O. had tuberculous meningitis, the infection presumably coming from her father whom she had nursed before he died. Her sister had also died from tuberculosis. Although tuberculous meningitis was usually fatal, Thornton pointed out that there were records of non-fulminating cases that had recovered in the pre-antibiotic era. Breuer had considered whether Anna O. had tuberculous meningitis, but dismissed the possibility, just as he had the opinion of an ophthalmologist who explained Bertha's convergent squint as due to paralysis of the abducens nerve (which controls some eye movement) – which most physicians would regard as an organic condition.

Thornton's challenge provoked others to review the case. Psychoanalysts uncritically accepted the Breuer/Jones version, with Ellenberger's findings only considered to a limited extent, if at all. In the 1950s, the high-water mark of psychoanalysis, several writers claimed Anna O. was suffering from schizophrenia, a diagnosis lacking any real evidence. Several decades later, this was resurrected as first borderline personality, then multiple personality disorder, one author stating Breuer 'unwittingly encouraged and amplified' Anna's dissociations.

English psychiatrist Lindsay Hurst suggested cerebral sarcoidosis, an illness which can cause a plethora of neurological symptoms associated with spontaneous remission. Sarcoidosis can lead to cerebral complications, and often lasts for twelve to twenty-four months. Another diagnosis Hurst considered was 'spontaneous acute disseminated encephalomyelitis', a condition which could cause drowsiness, ocular palsies and paralysis. Support for the latter came from epileptologist Pierre Flor-Henry, who believed Anna O. probably had subacute encephalitis.

Andrea Orr-Andrawes, a psychoanalyst with experience in neurology, came to the conclusion that Anna O. had temporal lobe epilepsy complicated by iatrogenic dependence on chloral hydrate and morphine. The oscillation of her moods and behaviour from day to night was typical of a delirium induced by drug withdrawal. She had the rare form of reflex epilepsy (an explanation Thornton had found for some of Charcot's cases), exemplified by Breuer's ability to induce trances by holding up an orange. Less convincingly, Orr-Andrawes claimed that Anna O.'s subsequent career was indicative of epileptic personality (or Geschwind syndrome).

Segio de Paula Ramos concluded that the diagnosis should be chloral hydrate and morphine dependence, with primary or drug induced mood disorder. He noted that Anna O. was using extremely high doses of chloral hydrate (5 grams a night) and morphine (100–200 milligrams per day. Such doses would be potentially lethal for the ordinary person and could only be used in someone with a high tolerance. Many symptoms, including negative and pseudo-hallucinations, altered states of consciousness, periods of confusion and agitation, weight loss and severe pain were consistent with addiction and withdrawal states. This view is supported in a letter written by Pappenheim to the hospital director after her discharge, in which she writes: 'You will realise that to live with a syringe always at the ready is not a situation to be envied.'

Another view on Anna O.'s illness comes from psychiatrist Harold Merskey, reflecting a swing from neurological to psychiatric diagnosis. Merskey has devoted a distinguished career to the study of pain and hysteria. In an extensive review of the case, taking into account all the organic and psychological explanations, he found that Anna O. had a severe depressive illness, typical of major depressive disorder with melancholia. After a protracted illness, she recovered and had gone on to an energetic and active career in social work, the product of a cyclothymic temperament (a temperament prone to elevated or depressed mood swings).

A last word on the case—for now, at any rate—comes from Freud researcher, Mikkel Borch-Jacobsen. Breuer was ambivalent about the case, to say the least. His wife was not happy about the time he devoted to his patient, and he later visited Anna at the sanatorium as a friend, not her doctor. Afterwards he vowed 'never again to submit himself to such an ordeal'. Borch-Jacobsen finally scotches Freud's claim of pseudocyesis, showing that Breuer did not flee to Venice for a second honeymoon. His daughter Dora was born three months *before* he ended his involvement with the case.

But what of Anna O.'s symptoms? Ellenberger had little doubt about the origin of the illness, describing it as 'analogous' to the great cases of magnetic illness in the first half of the nineteenth century in which the patient dictated to the physician the therapeutic devises to use, prophesied the course of the illness, and announced its terminal date. He noted the striking resemblance between similar cases such as Anna Emmerich and Friedericke Hauffe. Added to this list is Louise Lateau, the Belgian 'stigmatic', demonstrating that Anna O.'s illness was 'shaped, if not inspired' by the suggestive power of such famous illnesses.

Carl Hansen, the Danish stage hypnotist, had given well-publicised performances in Vienna in early 1880—Anna O.'s illness started at the end of that year. The Breuers, Freuds and many others in their circle had seen his induction of paralysis, anaesthesia, amnesia, prolonged muscular spasm, hallucinations and other bizarre behaviour. The performances were a sensation, provoking intense controversy; Hansen filed a lawsuit in his defence, but police closed down the show. It is inconceivable that Anna O. could have been unaware of Hanson's performance and, drawn into an intense relationship with her physician after her father's death, she gave an almost-exact repetition of his stage cases. In the great tradition of magnetic patients, she 'led all the way and her doctor followed'.

Beyond Anna O. beckons the chimera of Bertha Pappenheim, mostly luculent, sometimes wavering and cryptic. What Bertha Pappenheim thought about Anna O. cannot be known as she is alleged to have destroyed any documents pertaining to her childhood or youthful illness. Dora Edinger, her biographer, disclosed that while she never discussed the illness with relatives, she was always scathing about psychoanalysis. Some indication of her attitude is gleaned from the one of her doctors at Bellevue Sanatorium who noted her 'disparaging judgements against the ineffectiveness of science in regard to her sufferings'. As Borch-Jacobsen rather archly summed it up, the game goes on. But the last word, surely, must go to Bertha Pappenheim: 'If there will be justice in the world to come, women will be lawgivers, and men [will have] to have babies. Will Saint Peter keep his job?'

EUGEN BLEULER

*Insanity ... provides us with the proper
scale for comprehending the numerous
intellectual, moral, religious, and artistic
currents and phenomena of our social life.*

EMIL KRAEPELIN

On Thursday 24 April 1908, Swiss psychiatrist Eugen Bleuler, Director of the Burghölzli Asylum Hospital in Zurich, at a meeting of the German Psychiatric Association gave a lecture with the title, 'Die Prognose der Dementia Praecox (Schizophreniegruppe)'. This gave the world the name that has become the leitmotif for psychiatry: schizophrenia, defined as a disease 'characterised by a specific type of alteration of thinking, feeling and relation to the external world'."

What is schizophrenia? The most severe psychiatric illness, it has been recognised since antiquity. There are credible descriptions in the Mesopotamian Assyrian Codex. However until the nineteenth century, psychosis was regarded as merely another form of lunacy. A significant change arose after the French Revolution. The Enlightenment led to a new attitude towards the mentally ill, which took shape in the ideas of that fervid revolutionary, Philippe Pinel, who established the basis of the modern discipline of psychiatry.

Pinel was Medical Superintendent at Bicétre and Salpêtrière hospitals. A supporter of the Revolution, Pinel made his name liberating imprisoned mad wretches from their chains. Pinel was determined to break away from what he saw as cloying adherence to the anatomico-pathological model (for example, infection or trauma) of disease, which produced few results for patients. He believed in an illness model of symptoms and treatments; science (meaning anatomy) could follow at its own pace. Psychiatric illness was treated with support, care and encouragement—moral treatment. Moral treatment aimed to care for the mentally ill by relieving symptoms, based on the rationale that the root cause of all mental illness lay in the environment.

Pinel, in short, was the first psychotherapist and devoted his career to this end. His pioneering role should not be understated. His work, taken up in England, led to the rise of the asylum, a development that institutionalised psychiatry and began the process of organising its practitioners into a professional discipline.

Admirable as its intentions were, Pinel's doctrine of moral treatment was to fall victim to the shifting scientific tides and the anatomico-pathological model ruled supreme after that. Within decades the centre of psychiatric gravity moved westwards and the baton was taken up in the Germanic world.

Capitalism had played a decisive role in the rise of German medicine. The German dye industry spun off new technology in all directions. New chemicals to stain tissues led to the first changes in morbid anatomy since the autopsy, a process unchanged since Hippocratic days. Progress was facilitated by the invention of compound-lens microscopes, a huge step forward on the old single-lens devices, the lead taken by Carl Zeiss of Jena who established his workshop in 1846. Permanent fixing of tissues was established by 1870 and colour staining by 1880. Rudolph Virchow established the discipline of anatomical pathology, putting forward the magisterial cellular theory, a hypothesis that proved the equivalent of Newton's *Principia* until the development of subcellular and molecular technologies. Robert Koch was Virchow's microbiological equivalent, establishing the criteria for defining infectious diseases and initiating the 'golden age of bacteriology'.

It was an exciting time for German medicine, and psychiatry was not exempt from the optimism. It was an indication of the age that the two most important figures in twentieth century psychiatry—Emil Kraepelin and Sigmund Freud—were born in 1856, and Eugen Bleuler the following year.

German psychiatry, strictly speaking, originated in Vienna but was first taken up in Prussia, and later the newly united Germany. Psychiatrists made their names by describing psychiatric symptoms and syndromes. They studied the brains of patients in the hope that a cause would emerge. But the available techniques produced few results; furthermore, any discoveries were captured by neurology—a hegemonic struggle that continues today.

Psychiatry was practised by academicians who perceived themselves as scientists and regarded their patients as research material. As it turned out, this was a Faustian pact of the most ominous nature. In it lay the seeds of the total moral collapse of German psychiatry under the Nazis that led them to gas their own patients on eugenics grounds. While there were those who were as caring, compassionate and kind as any of their psychiatric colleagues, it is remarkable how often biographies describe the leading figures as unsympathetic towards their patients, if not completely detached.

In this setting arrived the meticulous man with the magnificent moustache who single-handedly created modern psychiatry—Emil Kraepelin. He was born in Neustrelitz, capital of the Grand Duchy of Mecklenburg-Strelitz, in northern Germany, into a nominally middle-class background teetering on the edge of respectability thanks to his father, a feckless, heavy-drinking actor, opera singer and music teacher who deserted the family. His older brother Karl, showing that the urge to classify ran deep in the family, foreshadowed Kraepelin's later activities by developing a system for classifying mollusc species. Kraepelin became interested in medicine when a family friend, a doctor, took him on his rounds.

Kraepelin, unusually, always wanted to do psychiatry; for many doctors at the time, it was seen as a low-status discipline only undertaken as a last resort. Qualifying in medicine at the University of Leipzig in 1878, he looked for a suitable academic position. Poor eyesight prevented him from doing microscopic work, saving him from the blind-alley followed by so many of his colleagues. His research strategy was directed towards investigating the symptomatology, family history and long-term course of disease entities. Like Koch and Pasteur, he hoped to derive the organising principle of the disease entities from the study of illnesses like neurosyphilis.

Kraepelin's philosophical underpinning was based on degeneration and eugenics. A warped social Darwinism, degeneration was extremely influential at the time, so Kraepelin was no great exception in his adherence to this. Among the races and classes, he believed that Gypsies, who were viewed as swindlers and poets, were prone to hysteria, while Jews also had a psychopathic nature.

Kraepelin's initial experiences in psychiatric wards were deeply upsetting. He wondered if he could continue, but steeled himself to do so. His prediction that he would be a professor before he was thirty was realised when he was appointed head of the psychiatric hospital at Dorpat (Tartu) in Estonia, then a Russian province, in 1886. The patients spoke Estonian or Russian, neither of which he understood (and a telling indication of his lack of interest in talking to patients). Furthermore, his German nationalism ran headlong into the heavy-handed Russian administration. After five years, Kraepelin happily returned to German soil when he was appointed to the chair at Heidelberg, where his star continued to ascend. He moved to Munich in 1903 where he stayed until he retired in 1922. In 1917 he founded the German Institute for Psychiatric Research, a model research institution.

Kraepelin, an aloof and withdrawn personality, was extremely private. He was devoted to his family, abstemious to a fault and seemed free of inner turmoil. Like Freud, Kraepelin had to defer his marriage until he was more established. He developed a lucrative private practice, was able to purchase substantial properties and build a villa in Italy. To his colleagues, he was someone to respect but not to admire, keeping his distance. He did not relate well to his patients and often contradicted himself by making subjective or judgmental findings.

Kraepelin had deeply bureaucratic instincts and established a comprehensive basis for a modern speciality. He developed training programs, lobbied the government for mandatory syphilis testing and constantly planned trips to exotic locations to see how psychiatric illness manifested in other cultural settings.

Kraepelin regarded alcohol use and sexual promiscuity as degenerate activities that could only lead to disease, holding fanatical views on drinking and sexual abstinence. It turns out that he wrote poetry to express his inner yearnings. The poems are littered with terms about race, stock and nation. He was shattered by Germany's loss of World War I and later expressed disturbing ideas, described as proto-fascistic.

He may not, however, have been entirely devoid of a sense of humour: 'There are two sorts of psychiatrists, those by inclination, and those by chance; those entering psychiatry by chance are sometimes reasonable.'

In the last year of his life, Kraepelin studied Buddhism and was planning a trip to visit shrines when he unexpectedly died from viral pneumonia in 1926. Hitler would have been unknown to him. But how would he have reacted after 1933 when the German medical profession, including almost all psychiatrists, threw in their lot with the Nazis?

To improve his income, a publisher persuaded him to write a psychiatric textbook in 1883. In the first textbook, Kraepelin announced that he intended to classify illnesses on the basis of etiology—meaning somatic causes—derived from the principles of experimental psychology and bacteriology. The textbook soon expanded into an encyclopaedia with regular and ever-expanding editions (growing from 385 pages in the first edition to 2425 in the ninth) that announced the latest developments in his classification. His book on general paralysis of the insane, re-published in a new English edition, is a classic.

Kraepelin gave us some of the best descriptions of psychopathology ever. Consider the following passage on hallucinations:

> *The patients ... see mice, ants, the hound of hell, scythes, and axes. They hear cocks crowing, shooting, birds chirping, spirits knocking, bees humming, murmurings, screaming, scolding, voices from the cellar ... The voices say 'filthy thing', 'all conceivable confused stuff, just fancy pictures', they speak about what the patient does ... They say: 'That man must be beheaded, hanged', 'swine, wicked wretch, you will be done for ...'*

His discoveries did not arise in a 'Eureka' moment. He methodically studied cases, recording their details on special *zahlkarten* (hospital or ward record cards). He would take the cards in a rucksack with him to weekends at Lake Starnberg, seeking a pattern that would help him understand the psychoses.

The 1908 edition of his textbook confirmed the great distinction that has dominated psychiatric practice ever since. As a result of his finding that one group of patients did not recover, Kraepelin made a distinction between the two great psychoses: dementia praecox and the circular, or manic-depressive psychoses. Dementia praecox meant an irretrievable descent into madness, while manic-depressive episodes were self-limiting without the accompanying breakdown of personality.

The clumsy term 'dementia praecox' (precocious dementia, of early youth), is derived from Latin, means a privation of the senses and is therefore a static condition. It could not be used in an adjectival fashion. Kraepelin was never clear what he meant by the term dementia, except that it was the outcome in the majority of cases. Praecox was chosen because the majority of cases presented in the teenage years or shortly thereafter. The terminology did not seem to trouble Kraepelin—let alone the implications of such a diagnosis for a patient or their family.

To his credit, Kraepelin had no hesitation in changing his ideas or stating that he had made incorrect conclusions. At the end of his life, he pointed out that a significant percentage of his dementia praecox cases did recover: 'We cannot satisfactorily distinguish between the two diseases. The suspicion remains that we are asking the wrong questions.' The unavoidable implication of this statement is that the duality concept was unviable. Had Kraepelin lived another ten years, it is possible he would have fully recanted his classification.

German psychiatry was one thing; then there was Swiss psychiatry. Its practitioners came from all classes, doing military service like the rest of the male population, were employed in the public system and had close contact with their patients. This was in marked contrast to the German system where the doctors came from privileged backgrounds, were supporters of the establishment, mostly did research and saw private patients.

Eugen Bleuler was born in 1857 in the farming village of Zollikon, an hour from Zürich. While his father was a merchant, the family arose from generations of peasant stock with a deeply ingrained respect for rugged individuality and mutual assistance. Bleuler decided in high school to become a psychiatrist, made aware by his parents that the village canton was unhappy with the treatment of the locals at the Burghölzli University Psychiatric Hospital Clinic by academics who were only interested in research and could not speak Züri-Tütsch, the local dialect. As a student, Bleuler saw that when a young girl from his village had a severe mental disorder, her management was complicated by the clinic psychiatrist's lack of understanding. He studied psychiatry in Paris, London and Munich under the leading psychiatrists of his day.

In 1886 Bleuler became Director of the Rheinau Clinic, a former Benedictine Monastery on the Rhine. During the twelve years that he was there, Bleuler dedicated himself to the health and welfare of not just his eight hundred and fifty patients, but the hospital staff and the people of the village too. He ran a regular theatre list and treated them during epidemics. He was completely involved in the lives of his patients, going hiking with them, participating in amateur theatricals and looking after their savings.

In 1898, with some reservations, he accepted the appointment as Director of the Burghölzli Hospital. Bleuler had wanted to work at the Burghölzli, not least because it meant that he could live close to his ageing parents. The professorial mantle brought a large teaching workload that cut into the time he could spend with patients. Open to ideas, he encouraged colleagues to try new methods and tests. He attracted outstanding psychiatrists to work with him, including Carl Jung, Herman Rorschach, Ludwig Binswanger and Karl Abraham. With Jung, Bleuler was one of the first psychiatrists to look to psychoanalysis to explain mental illness, applying psychoanalytic concepts to his understanding of schizophrenia (although he steadily drifted away from this for the rest of his career).

Bleuler, a man of considerable modesty, lacked interest in status and material acquisition; the contrast with Kraepelin and his affluent private patients is notable. Bleuler lived in the hospital and mixed with his patients. Determined to regard his patients as individuals, he taught his juniors to regard each patient as unique. He was prepared to take as much time as necessary to understand their language. In contrast to Kraepelin's *zahlkarten*, Bleuler made thousands of notes of conversations and observations of his patients which he incorporated into his book on the schizophrenias.

Bleuler wrote the first paper using the term schizophrenia in 1910, following up with his textbook in 1911. After a century, it is almost impossible to think of the practice of psychiatry anywhere in the world without schizophrenia.

But the devil is in the detail. Schizophrenia is without doubt a wonderful term: evocative, capable of adjectivalisation and essentially descriptive. But 'schiz' was seized on by the public, facilitated it must be said by many psychiatrists, leading to the belief in the splitting of the personality, not the functions of the mind. Bleuler had meant a 'splitting of the senses' not a split personality, but it made little difference. The metaphor of 'splitting' has its origin in nineteenth-century culture, most distinctly in Robert Louis Stevenson's book, *The Strange Case of Dr Jekyll and Mr Hyde* (1886) — a book that came to haunt its author and soon passed into popular mythology.

Bleuler introduced the term schizophrenia for several reasons. The word was derived from Greek; *schizein* meant splitting; *phren* originally denoted the diaphragm, later 'soul, spirit, mind'. The semantic distinction between Kraepelin's dementia praecox and Bleuler's schizophrenia was critical; Kraepelin used a term derived from the Roman Empire; Bleuler, in preference, found a name derived from classical Greek with its focus on the nature of man. The schizophrenia that Bleuler described was not free of problems. The secondary symptoms were difficult to define, open to misinterpretation and fostered a purely psychological view of the condition.

Coming from, on the one side, asylum psychiatry and, on the other, university psychiatry, the two men inhabited different cultural universes. Bleuler wanted to widen Kraepelin's definition of dementia praecox. He conceived of schizophrenia as a genus, rather than a species; hence his book title *The Group of Schizophrenias*. His list of secondary symptoms, largely derived from psychoanalysis, implied an aetiology (cause). This was a critical difference from Kraepelin's concept: the disturbance or exaggeration of normal psychic function was light years away from the categorical distinction between psychosis and sanity.

Kraepelin's findings became the dominant paradigm of twentieth-century psychiatry. No other psychiatrist was as influential, and in the rapidly changing world that he lived through, the consequences of these attitudes were extreme. Kraepelin has to take credit for the catastrophic effect of the theory of degeneration on German psychiatry—ultimately the lowest point that psychiatry reached in its history. A successor, Robert Gaupp, stated that Kraepelin's work comprised nothing less than *the foundation of all Nazi racial hygiene laws*. In this grotesque vision, the doctor was the final agent in the Nazi myth of therapy via mass murder. More than any of his colleagues, Kraepelin had the intelligence and vision to see that degeneration was an ultimately doomed and immoral proposition.

Could Kraepelin have sanctioned the gassing of psychiatric patients? We shall never know, but his poems leave some disturbing ideas. Within seven years after his death, the German psychiatric profession, in a state of complete moral disarray, embarked on gassing their patients, a trajectory that led ineluctably to Auschwitz.

For a century, it was held as a canon in psychiatry that you cannot be 'a little bit' psychotic. You either had a psychosis or you did not. Schizophrenic patients had a negative outcome and responded to antipsychotic medication; manic-depresssive patients mostly recovered between episodes and responded well to lithium. As the first century of schizophrenia passed, acceptance of the dualism of the psychoses started to move to the perihelion and a grudging recognition arose that the time of the dualistic classification has passed. It was clear that manic-depresssive patients did well with antipsychotic medication and schizophrenia is no longer considered an illness with inevitable deterioration.

One who challenged this rule was German psychiatrist Ernst Kretzmer. In the nineteenth century, it was strongly held that syphilis was associated with creative brilliance. Kretzmer took this further, studying the association of madness and genius, a topic of great fascination. He believed that psychosis was merely the extreme end of a spectrum of behaviour ranging from the normal. One of the few doctors prepared to stand up to Hitler, Kretzmer made the observation that whereas in the past they had treated psychopaths, they were now ruled by them—and was lucky to get away with his life. Psychiatry however remained under the influence of Kraepelinian dogma and Kretzmer's views were regarded as incorrect but harmless.

To see who has picked up the baton after Kraepelin and Bleuler, we look to the Oxford psychiatrist Professor Timothy Crow who, for several decades, has pursued a controversial, if not lonely, path to find the cause of schizophrenia. According to Crow, schizophrenia arises from a genetic mutation—proto-cadherin XY—that determined the extent of lateralisation of the early hominid brain.

Humans go into the world with their brain lateralised to the dominant side to a varied degree. The genetic change in which our species originated is the speciation event, enabling humans to expand into almost every ecological niche and eliminate other species in the process. The laterality gene results in a range of profoundly human capabilities. These include intellectual ability, creativity, emotionality, psychosis and a range of phenomena variously referred to as schizotypal, eccentric or magical traits. Schizophrenia and schizotypy are linked with increased creativity and increased right hemisphere dominance. Those who lie between the extremes of normal and schizophrenic tend to be schizoid, artistic, creative, eccentric or just plain different, but not psychotic, individuals.

It is thought that creativity and schizotypy result from the freeing up of right hemisphere processes, allowing their involvement in tasks in which the left hemisphere normally specialised.

Lateralisation permitted the previously symmetrical brain to do something unique in nature: develop a language centre on the dominant side. Why is this important? After all, birds chatter away, baboons hunt in packs and chimps seem to communicate quite well.

Language is the material component of symbolism, the component that separates us from our immediate primate predecessors. As the professor said to Darwin, 'If I met a talking pig it would ipso facto cease to be a talking pig and be a human being.' Symbolism meant an exponential increase in the capacity of the enlarging primate brain; by definition, symbolism is the means to store and transport information outside the material capacity of the brain.

Language manifested with several modalities: speech; spiritual and creative activity, such as rock art, engraving and sculpture; and complex stone tools, requiring the ability to conceptualise three-dimensional forms and instruct another person in its manufacture. But why do the language centres need to be on the dominant side of the brain when it is clear that facilities on both sides of the cerebrum are needed for language?

The answer comes from information technology: processing speed. The two halves of the brain perform different but coordinated functions with regard to language. To make sense of the received message and convert it to a signal to the motor centres to put out as speech—the brain cannot afford the delay of sending the signal across the bridge between the two halves, the corpus callosum—so the expressive and receptive centres are in close proximity. A range of related facilities cluster around the language centres and it is here that most of the centres that constitute our personality originate.

Lateralisation is distinctly lopsided; over eighty-five per cent of people are left-dominant (meaning right-handed), eight to twelve per cent are right dominant, leaving a small group between the two. Some brains are poorly lateralised, what is known as hemispheric indeterminism. Here, the brain literally does not know if it is left- or right-dominant and these children have more reading, social and behavioural problems—later on, they are more likely to develop schizophrenia.

Crow was one of the first to confirm what had been suspected for well over a century. Schizophrenic patients lacked brain tissue, especially around the language centres. Further examination showed that the brains of schizophrenic patients lacked lateralisation; in other words, the basic fault was a failure to lateralise as effectively as non-schizophrenic people.

Another feature associated with reduced lateralisation is the capacity for altered states of consciousness. Such individuals are more likely to have trance states, either naturally or as result of epilepsy or schizophrenia. The neurological components of creativity, spirituality and the capacity to develop trance states include religiosity, hypergraphia and enhanced emotional reactions.

In what may be the most important psychiatric news of the new century, a large Swedish study has shown that schizophrenia and bipolar affective disorder (manic-depression) share the same genes. This may not seem to be of much interest to anyone outside psychiatry, but the implications affect all humankind. Now that all psychoses are shown to arise from the same genes, it is clear that there is another cause responsible for the different symptoms. And that cause is lateralisation—the extent to which the human brain is rotated from the anterior/posterior axis to establish the dominant language centre.

Schizophrenia is more, much more, than a name for the emblematic psychiatric disorder. It sums up the history, culture and social attitudes of the different worlds in which its progenitors lived. For its first century, schizophrenia ruled psychiatry much as the internal combustion engine ruled the twentieth century, a testament to the energy and vision of the man who classified it. A century later, Bleuler would have good reason to be pleased with his creation.

Schizophrenia endures, and will remain—in one form or another—as the ürword for psychiatry. To quote Tim Crow, 'Schizophrenia is not just an illness of humans, it may be *the* illness of humanity.'

VASLAV NIJINSKY

> *I started to go down a dark road, walking
> quickly, but was stopped by a tree which saved
> me. I was on the edge of a precipice. I thanked
> the tree. It felt me because I caught hold of
> it; it received my warmth and I received the
> warmth of the tree. I do not know who most
> needed the warmth. I walked on and suddenly
> stopped, seeing a precipice without a tree.
> I understood that God had stopped me
> because He loves me, and therefore said:
> If it is Thy will, I will fall down the precipice.
> If it is Thy will, I will be saved.*

VASLAV NIJINSKY

In December 1917, Vaslav Nijinsky, the most celebrated male dancer in the Western world, moved into a villa in St Moritz with his wife Romola and their three-year-old daughter, Kyra. With the war on, his association with the Ballets Russes ended, he and his wife decided to wait for peace in neutral Switzerland. By 1919, however, Nijinsky was going insane. From 19 January to 4 March 1919 he wrote a diary, the only on-the-spot written account by a major artist of the experience of entering psychosis.

Nijinsky, who made his reputation in Imperial Russia, remains one of ballet's most enduring legends: the faun who leaped into the air and stayed there until he decided to come down.

He was born in Kiev in 1890. His parents were Polish dancers who worked in theatres and circuses around Poland and Russia;

his sister Bronislava Nijinska was later a choreographer. His father, Thomas Nijinsky, who had a somewhat wayward nature, was astonishingly talented. He performed throughout Russia, his mastery of classical and character (national or folk) dancing a source of awe wherever he went. It was from his father that Nijinsky learned to regard all dancing as fundamental to Russian life.

At seven Nijinsky made his debut in a circus in Vilna. When his father abandoned the family the following year, his mother moved the three children to St Petersburg. At nine, Nijinsky entered the Imperial Ballet School, to be followed later by Bronislava. He was a poor student, but his talent was evident from the start, and it did not stop at dancing. He learned to play the accordion, the clarinet, the flute, the mandolin and the balalaika without taking a lesson. When he went to the opera, he could come home, sit down at the piano and play through what he had heard. He went to great lengths to train and develop his physical skills.

This did not endear him to his classmates, who taunted him: 'Are you a girl, that you dance so well?' They set him up to jump over a heavy wooden music stand, soaping the floor and grabbing his ankle at the crucial moment. He fell, hit his head on the floor, and was taken to the hospital in a coma. It is said that he was unconscious for a week.

On his return to the school, he continued his astonishing progress as a dancer. By the time he appeared in school productions, the press was calling him a prodigy. When Thomas Nijinsky, making a rare visit in vacation time, was taken to the Imperial Ballet School by his son and daughter, he spontaneously danced a variety of pieces, showing them (in Bronislava's words) 'one dance after the other of a technical difficulty I had never seen before. To this day I cannot understand the mechanics of some of his dancing movements'. If Nijinsky's phenomenal talent was inherited, there was little doubt where it came from.

In 1900 there was a family tragedy. When Vaslav was ten, his older brother (Stassik) Stanislav fell out a fourth-storey window.

Later he 'went off his head' and was committed to a mental institution. There is the suggestion that Stassik had behaved strangely before the fall.

Nijinsky, continuing to astonish everyone with his prowess, was soon given a string of leads. When he graduated at eighteen, he was taken into St Petersburg's Imperial Ballet as a coryphée of the corps de ballet, a higher rank than the usual starting position of member. He immediately became a star.

Nijinsky started a sexual relationship with thirty-year-old Prince Pavel Lvov with the blessing of his mother, well aware of the sexual trade that occurred in the ballet and proud to see her son with a wealthy prince. Lvov gave him a gold ring set with a large diamond and twelve pairs of shoes handmade by the best shoemaker in St Petersburg.

However, Lvov soon tired of Nijinsky's bouts of depression and religious hysteria. In 1908, after catching a dose of clap from Nijinsky, he introduced him to Sergé Pavlovitch Diaghilev by telephone. Diaghilev hired him on the spot, they became lovers on the same day (it is unclear who seduced who) and Nijinsky exchanged the gold ring for a massive Cartier platinum sapphire ring.

Diaghilev was a leading figure in the St Petersburg art world, a celebrated and highly innovative producer of ballet and opera who promoted Russian art abroad, particularly in Paris. No artist himself, Diaghilev had an uncanny ability to sense the artistic mood and to spot and promote new talent. Western Europe was reluctant to recognise Russian talent, leaving what amounted to virgin territory for him to exploit, and he made annual visits, usually to Paris. In 1906 Diaghilev presented an exhibition of Russian painting and sculpture; in 1907, a series of concerts of Russian music; in 1908, the first production in the West of Modest Mussorgsky's *Boris Godunov*. In 1909 Diaghilev took Nijinsky with a company of Russian opera and ballet stars to Paris. Their success led Diaghilev to create his company Les Ballets Russes.

New ideas and movements were erupting everywhere. Matisse led the Fauves, Picasso and Braque created Cubism and Leger celebrated the machine. There were the Expressionists in Germany, Frank Lloyd Wright in the United States, Marcel Proust in his cork-lined room, the Irish theatrical Renaissance and Louise Blériot flying the Channel.

In historian Barbara Tuchman's words, the Ballet Russes captured all the 'fever and fecundity of the hour'. The company oozed talent: dancers included Tamara Karsavina, Anna Pavlova and Lydia Lopokova; for stage design, there was Léon Bakst; choreography was by Michel Fokine; scores were by Igor Stravinsky. It was a period in the history of dance that has yet to be surpassed for creativity. Classical dance had become mired in the past, predictable and sedate. The Ballets Russes blew this away with emotional spectacles oozing sex appeal. A sensation, setting trends in art, dance, music and fashion, they were easily the most influential European theatrical enterprise during the pre-World War I period, and until the 1920s. Above all, the fame of the Ballets Russes arose from Nijinsky's dancing.

Nijinsky progressed from being a star to a great artist. He was celebrated for his virtuosity and for the depth and intensity of his characterisations. An extraordinary actor, strongly sexual if not androgynous, he had the capacity to put himself into the spirit of any character he portrayed. In *Scheherazade*, he appeared as the Golden Slave in brown body paint, wound around with pearls, oozing perversity, androgyny, enslavement, violence. His leap out of a window made people say that he was of the air, not the land. The effect was outrageous, riveting, incredible and ultimately stunning. Hugo von Hofmannsthal said that Nijinsky was 'the greatest miming genius on the modern stage (next to Duse and, as a mime, greater than Duse)'.

Physically, an unprepossessing figure, Nijinsky was barely 1.6 metres (5 foot 4 inches) tall. His only distinguishing characteristics were his hypertrophied thigh muscles, the dynamo for his seemingly gravity-defying leaps. His athleticism was astonishing. Bronislava described how his great leap in *Le Pavillon d'Armide* was regarded as a miracle, the audience never having seen a dancer do such a thing. He appeared to have the capacity to seem to almost hover before he landed.

Throwing his body up to a great height for a moment, he leans back, his leg extended, beats an entrechat-sept, and, slowly turning over onto his chest, arches his back and, lowering one leg, holds an arabesque in the air. Smoothly in this pure arabesque, he descends to the ground ... From the depths of the stage with a single leap, assemblé entrechat-dix, *he flies towards the first wing ... With each* relentissement *in the air the audience holds its breath.*

Nijinsky developed a supreme coordination and synchronisation of movements, achieving a perfect balance of the body, thus rendering himself literally 'weightless', high above the stage. His sister described how he set a new standard for male dancing. He trained to improve his muscular drive, strength and speed, working at the *barre* and floor exercises to complete in forty-five to fifty minutes what would have taken another dancer three hours. To perfect his characteristic fluttery wrist-and-finger movements, he constantly clenched and unclenched a black rubber ball in his hand.

Parisians referred to him as *le dieu de la danse*, the papers describing him and Tamara Karsavina as the 'most exemplary artists of the time'. Dancing with Anna Pavlova in London in 1911, Nijinsky astonished the London audiences with his *variation* of the *coda*, introducing a new step, *pas volé*, never done before by a male dancer.

Nijinsky's glamour was enhanced by the atmosphere of scandal that enveloped him. Living openly as Diaghilev's lover, he became the subject of fantastic fables, for example, that he had girdles of emeralds and diamonds given him by an Indian prince. People stole his underwear from the dressing room during performances.

On stage a magnetic presence, off the stage, Nijinsky appeared to have no social skills, completely lacking in charisma, and coming across as naive, shy and distant. Most people who knew him were struck by his social incompetence. The dancer Lydia Sokolova said that 'He hardly spoke to anyone, and seemed to exist on a different plane.' His muscular development made him look chunky and ill at ease in conventional dress—he was described as looking like a coachman on his day off. It was said that Diaghilev took him around like an ocelot on a leash. In company, he barely said anything, picking nervously at his cuticles until they bled. The dancers called him 'Dumbbell' behind his back.

But Nijinsky was not merely a mechanical dancing robot, albeit one of phenomenal ability, he was focused on dancing to an extent that has never been seen before or since. He wanted to change the whole notion of what could be done on a stage. Between 1912 and 1913, Nijinsky choreographed three ballets—*The Afternoon of a Faun* (1912), *Jeux* (1913) and *The Rite of Spring* (1913)—that revolutionised ballet, ushering in modernism and making him a worldwide celebrity.

These works were so different that to produce them was to enter a world alien to classic dance. Nijinsky had to invent and carry through three entirely different new idioms at a time when he was performing one arduous role after another. This was done in the face of intense opposition from the dancers, his composer Claude Debussy, critics and audiences. The dancers moved in profile, slicing the air like blades (*The Afternoon of a Faun*), or hunched over, hammering their feet into the floor (*The Rite of Spring*). His approach was described as 'analytic', the appearance as 'ugly', the emotions it aroused in the audience as disconcerting.

Faun, an eleven-minute ballet, required over a hundred hours of rehearsal. To induce classically trained dancers to move like figures in an antique frieze or aborigines around a camp fire required great communication skills—abilities Nijinsky conspicuously lacked. In the final tableau of *Faun*, the lead character mimed masturbation with the scarf of a nymph, leading to accusations of obscenity. The first performance caused an uproar. A riot broke out and the police had to be called. Despite the chaos, the company danced the ballet over again.

The following year, *The Rite of Spring* reached a climax never seen before or since. In Tuchman's words, it was 'the Twentieth Century incarnate, the equivalent of Beethoven's *Eroica* in the nineteenth century. It abandoned structure, melody and harmony'. During the premiere on 28 March 1913 the uproar in the theatre was so great that the dancers could not hear the music. Nijinsky stood in the wings, screaming the score in frustration. People felt they were witnessing a blasphemous attempt to destroy art and responded in kind. 'Listen first, hiss afterwards,' screamed the theatre manager. Several members of the audience traded blows. Only when repeated the following year was it recognised as an apotheosis in modern music that would dominate future generations.

Nijinsky paid no attention to the controversy, only that the piece had reached the state of desired perfection:

> *I know what* Le Sacre du printemps *will be when everything is as we both want it. For some it will open new horizons, huge horizons flooded with different rays of sun. People will see new and different colours and different lines, all different, unexpected, and beautiful.*

At the same time as he launched his career as a choreographer, Nijinsky's relationship with Diaghilev was collapsing. Bronislava recalled that he was in a 'heightened state of nervousness 'as if . . . a net was being woven around him'.

In response, Nijinsky got married.

In the summer of 1913, the Ballets Russes embarked on a tour of South America. Romola de Pulszky, a twenty-two-year old Hungarian, attached herself to the company with the intention of snaring Nijinsky. After four weeks, barely having exchanged more than a few words (they had no language in common), they married in Buenos Aires. Devastated by the defection, Diaghilev fired Nijinsky, effectively meaning he could not perform his extended roles with the Ballets Russes. Banished from the company, Nijinsky was replaced by Léonid Massine.

Nijinsky undertook a two-month engagement in London the following March, but his mental state crumpled. He couldn't sleep, was beside himself with anxiety and went into screaming rages. The contract was cancelled after two weeks. His mood changed for the worse after the birth of his daughter Kyra in June 1914. The family travelled to Budapest to visit Romola's mother. World War I broke out, the Hungarian authorities convinced themselves that he was an enemy alien and he was placed under house arrest for a year and a half, having to report to police headquarters once a week.

He began to speak and act irrationally, his reaction to his mother-in-law verging on the paranoid. Romola helped to work out a reconciliation with Diaghilev. After international intervention, the Hungarian authorities released him for a season in New York and they sailed there in 1916. He choreographed *Till Eulenspiegel*, received by audiences as a triumph — as it turned out, this was his last public success. Diaghilev and Nijinsky were quarrelling, but Ballets Russes was engaged for a second New York season, to be followed by a four-month journey, stopping in fifty-two cities, with over a hundred dancers and musicians directed by Nijinsky.

Nijinsky came under the influence of two members of the company who followed novelist Leo Tolstoy's philosophy. He took to wearing peasant shirts, became a vegetarian, preached non-violence and tried to practise 'marital chastity'. He gave lesser-known dancers leading roles, including his own, without announcing the cast changes to the public. He told Romola that he wanted to return to Russia to plough the land—an announcement that prompted her to abandon the tour. Nijinsky went on to perform for a few months with the Ballets Russes in Spain and South America. On 30 September 1917, at a Red Cross benefit in Montevideo, Nijinsky came onstage after midnight and performed some steps to Chopin. This was Nijinsky's last public performance. He then moved with his family to St Moritz.

During the first year in Switzerland, Nijinsky planned new ballets, made drawings and worked on his notation system. Then, in January 1919, he closeted himself in his studio all night long, furiously drawing nothing but eyes. One day he went down the street wearing a large gold cross, telling people to go to church. He drove his sleigh into oncoming traffic and threw Romola (holding Kyra) down the stairs.

Romola had become friendly with a Dr Hans Frenkel, who worked at one of the resort hotels. During his medical training in Zurich, Frenkel had attended Eugen Bleuler's lectures and was familiar with Jung's theories. Frenkel visited Nijinsky daily, gave him chloral hydrate (a sedative used at the time), and had him do word-association tests. To no avail. Nijinsky spent his time in his study drawing staring eyes or writing his diary. Probably as a result of the chastity Nijinsky was practising, Romola was conducting a love affair with Dr Frenkel, providing some substance to the metaphor that just because you are paranoid, it doesn't mean you don't have enemies.

The affair with Romola later ended. Frenkel, unhappy over Romola's refusal to divorce Nijinsky, attempted suicide in 1920 and became addicted to morphine, dying in 1938.

On 19 January 1919 Nijinsky gave a final performance before an invited audience at a local hotel. Sitting in a chair, he stared silently at the audience for half an hour before performing a bizarre gyration over a velvet cross unrolled on the floor. On that day, he began writing his diary. Famous for his jump, Nijinsky seemed to pause in the air before coming down. Now, it seemed, he had declined to come down.

Frenkel wrote to Bleuler, who agreed to see Nijinsky. Romola's mother and stepfather came from Budapest to help her take Nijinsky to Zurich. On 4 March 1919 they left for Zurich, the diary ending abruptly as Nijinsky was waiting for the cab to take them to the railway station.

At the Burghölzli, Bleuler first saw Romola, making the endearing statement that 'The symptoms you describe in the case of an artist and a Russian do not in themselves prove any mental disturbances.' When he saw Nijinsky the next day, Bleuler changed his mind after ten minutes. Nijinsky was 'a confused schizophrenic with mild manic excitement'. He told Romola that her husband was incurably insane. When she returned to the waiting room, Nijinsky looked at her and said: '*Femmka* [little wife], you are bringing me my death-warrant.'

That night Nijinsky locked himself in his hotel room. The police had to be called and they took him to the Burghölzli Hospital. Three days later he was sent to the Bellevue Sanatorium at Kreuzlingen, run by Ludwig Binswanger. After three months, Nijinsky was hallucinating, tearing his hair out, attacking the attendants, declaring that his limbs belonged to someone else. He was often mute and helpless; he could not brush his teeth or tie his shoelaces.

From 1919, Nijinsky spent the rest of his life in and out of psychiatric hospitals and asylums. When he was more settled, Romola would take him home. He saw many of the most famous psychiatrists of the day. He was assessed by Alfred Adler, who felt he could be saved with psychotherapy, but could not see him as a patient. He spent long periods having psychotherapy with first Binswanger, and then a Russian-speaking psychiatrist, but to no avail. It is reported that he was assessed by Sigmund Freud, but there is no information on what occurred. Others included Professor Julius Wagner-Juarreg and Manfred Sakel.

The latter put Nijinsky through a marathon series of insulin coma treatments, the therapy that he had been responsible for developing. He had over 200 treatments. The result was that he was no longer agitated or violent, but he was virtually mute for the rest of his life. When he appeared to be calmer and even a little more responsive, Romola told the press that a recovery was imminent and he could return to dancing again. This was not to be. Despite the high hopes, the coma therapy had no curative effect, only causing hypoxic brain damage (caused by lack of oxygen), hence his passivity and loss of speech.

Romola had to take on the role of guardian of Nijinsky's reputation, which she did in her own inimitable fashion. A highly redacted version of his diary, excising the more lurid comments about his health and sex life, and portraying her caring role in a elevated light, was published. Contradicting the image of herself as a devoted wife, she went to the United States and had several lesbian relationships in Hollywood. Romola made regular announcements to the press of Nijinsky's imminent recovery, but eventually this, too, stopped.

They moved to various locations in central Europe, including Vienna and Budapest. During World War II, Nijinsky's situation became extremely dangerous as the Nazis were exterminating psychiatric patients (which they called 'euthanasia') and he had to be kept in hiding on a farm in the Hungarian forest. The arrival of the Russian forces at the end of the war led to a happy interlude. Russians had been raised on the myth of Nijinsky, and gave him as much support as they could, even offering to take him to Moscow where he was certain to recover with the help of Soviet psychiatry—an offer wisely refused. He mingled happily with the soldiers and to everyone's amazement, began speaking in Russian, a language he had not used for several decades. He became more animated when the soldiers had their dancing parties and even joined in for a while.

But, for the rest, Nijinksky was a stocky silent man taken

around where he had to go, cared for by a succession of male nurses, developing health problems as he aged. At the end, they were living in England when kidney failure became progressive.

Nijinsky's thirty years' death-in-life came to an end in London on 8 April 1950. At the autopsy, hoping to account for Nijinsky's amazing leaps, the medical examiner cut open Nijinsky's feet to see if it was any different from the feet of an average male. He discovered nothing unusual. In 1953 Nijinsky's body was reburied in Montmartre, Paris.

Since then, the myth that surrounded him has grown to epic levels. A founding figure of modernism, he became one of the most famous men of the century. His illness only seemed to confirm his immortality. Much of his reputation rests on the diary, described by one reviewer as 'a huge suicide note'. His dancing survived only through rumour and anecdote; the artistic evidence comes from posed photographs of him in costume, because no film exists of him dancing—Diagelev refused to allow performances to be filmed, a decision to some extent justified by jerkiness of the motion pictures of the time. Attempts have been made, with varying degrees of success, to reproduce Nijinsky's ballets but, if anything, the absence of visual recordings has ensured that he remains forever elevated, soaring like one of his magnificent leaps.

Vaslav Nijinsky's Brain

Nijinsky's family was predisposed to psychiatric illness and there are early signs that he had problems. His grandmother starved herself to death on being widowed. Stassik was mentally unsound and hospitalised as a teenager. Nijinsky may have suffered brain damage as a result of a fall at age twelve. During his first season in the Imperial Ballet at eighteen, he stopped dancing one night in the middle of the Act I of a ballet and began taking bows while the orchestra was still playing.

Nijinsky may have started the diary to document his sanity and his ascension to what he believed was a higher plane. He was bringing a message from God to the world: people should not think, but feel. This was the cause of the war. David Lloyd George, the British Prime Minister, operated by intellect, while Woodrow Wilson relied on feeling. Nijinsky believed the entire world was being laid waste, industrialists were despoiling the planet, the shops were robbing the poor, his servants were having sex with animals. His relationship with Diaghilev is described in conflicted and bitter terms. As the diary proceeds, the list of enemies lengthens; he believed the novelist Emile Zola was gassed to death, the English would send people to shoot him and the manufacturers of his fountain pen would have him imprisoned. Bodily processes— particularly digestion and sex—were constantly on his mind. He already refused to eat meat and now regarded sex with revulsion.

Interspersed among this are grandiose elements. He wanted to build a bridge from Europe to America, had a cure for cancer and planned to invent a new kind of fountain pen—which he would call 'God'. He was now God, and going to convert the world by the diary. He intended to have it published and wanted it reproduced in facsimile because the live manuscript would transmit feeling to readers.

Halfway through the diary, there is a break; he signs off as 'God Nijinsky'. The last lines of the first notebook are: 'My little girl is singing: Ah! Ah! Ah! Ah! I do not understand the meaning of this, but I feel its meaning. She wants to say that everything, Ah! Ah! is not horror but joy.' Book II, 'On Death', starts with an apocalyptic theme: 'I am not God, I am not man. I am a beast and a predator.'

Preoccupied with the belief that his death was imminent, which he accepted, the arrival of his mother-in-law, followed by the trip to Zurich to place him in an institution, threw him into a panic.

He knew that something extraordinary was going on in his brain, but he does not know whether this means that he was God or a madman abandoned by God.

Nijinsky sensed he was going mad: 'I am standing in front of a precipice into which I may fall. My soul is sick . . . I am incurable.'

His fear of being hospitalised, as his brother was, remained a constant theme: 'I will be put in a lunatic asylum, because I dance very well and give money to anyone who asks me.'

At times the diary reads like a novel. While lying in bed with Romola, it records how he hears phones ringing, people running, Romola weeping somewhere with Frenkel comforting her.

Many parts of the text are repetitious, obsessional and boring, but also searing and apocalyptic: 'The earth is the head of God. God is fire in the head. I am alive as long as I have a fire in my head. My pulse is an earthquake. I am an earthquake.' The last lines in the notebook are mordant, ironic: 'I will go to my wife's mother and talk to her because I do not want her to think that I like Oscar more than her. I am checking her feelings. She is not dead yet, because she is envious'.

Nijinsky left a fourth notebook in which he wrote a series of erratic, if not incoherent, letters to various people.

Nijinsky makes bizarre puns, or writes long poems in Russian and begins writing in the voice of God. The form of Nijinsky's thoughts shows the characteristic schizophrenic loosening of associations. The text has clang associations, the connecting of words on the basis of sound (often rhyme) rather than sense, and perseveration, or persistent repetition. Also present is the derailment of schizophrenic thinking. Nijinsky says that he is an Indian, a sea bird, Zola and God; then he says that Dostoevski is God too.

Nijinsky's diary seems to confirm that he was heterosexual by inclination, but immersed in exploring the boundaries between male and female. Romola stated how good he was at impersonating female dancers: 'He was able to place himself in the soul of a woman'. As late as 1912 he said to his sister that if he ever married, it would be with one of Gauguin's girls from Tahiti, so that their children would have beautiful brown skins. The impression is left that he was only passive and acquiescent in his relations with men.

Nijinsky did not appear to suspect the affair between Frenkel and Romola, who he accuses of being 'death'. He liked her nose; he wanted to walk with her; he wanted to save their relationship.

The diary endlessly reiterated his belief that he was God began with being called a god by the Parisian audiences. He repetitively drew circles and arcs, forming eyes and also fish (the sign of Christ) and the female genitals. At times, he believed the eyes were watching him.

There are delusions of grandeur, of persecution, of control (one's actions are being manipulated by an outside force), of reference (environmental events are directed specifically at oneself) and somatic delusions are present: he believes that the blood is draining away from his head, that the hairs in his nose are moving around. He is hallucinating. He feels someone is in his studio, staring at him behind his back. God speaks out loud to him.

On this evidence, and taking into account the long, sad, relentless slide into nothingness, there can be no arguing with Bleuler's assessment: schizophrenia. The illness first took Nijinsky to artistic heights that are unlikely to be scaled again in our time. For this he paid a terrible price, but he left us a legacy that will enrich humanity.

HANS BERGER

We see in the electroencephalogram
a concomitant phenomenon of the
continuous nerve processes which
take place in the brain, exactly as the
electrocardiogram represents a concomitant
phenomenon of the contractions of the
individual segments of the heart.

HANS BERGER

If putting a current through a frog's leg nerve got the muscle to contract, could one *read* the brain's electrical output to get the soul to reveal its secrets? Measurement of the electrical impulse in a single animal nerve in a laboratory is one thing; measuring the electrical discharge of the living human brain beneath the skull is entirely different, and was well beyond the capacity of the available technology in the nineteenth century.

Within a few years of the onset of the twentieth century, this situation changed drastically. Willem Einthoven's invention of the ECG in 1910, allowing electrical measurement of the heartbeat, provided a huge stimulus to medicine. However, those working with the brain were dismissive of the likelihood that the electrical output of such a richly complex organ could be measured and their endeavours stayed focused on making traces of individual neurons. Brain neurophysiology shifted to the sidelines, becoming marginalised, if not disregarded.

This was the state of affairs when Hans Berger commenced his professional life. Berger, born on 21 May 1873 at Neuses near Coburg, Bavaria, came from a middle-class familly; his father was the medical superintendent of a country asylum. Berger had no interest in studying medicine, opting for mathematics and astronomy. The choice is interesting. Astronomy requires a perspective on the largest issues known to man combined with a detailed understanding of the huge technical problems.

However, Berger did not continue along this path. He opted to do military service and, at nineteen, had a near-death experience when he came off his horse during manoeuvres. Shaken by the experience, he then got a telegram from his father who had been contacted by his sister, living some hundreds of miles away, struck by a sudden intuition at the same time as the accident that her brother was in danger. Amazed at the veracity of this telepathic experience, Berger resolved to study psychology.

This meant a career in medicine and psychiatry, the only way he could have access to clinical material. He completed his studies at various medical schools, a common practice at the time, and commenced at the University of Jena hospital in the German state of Thuringia. He became an assistant to one of the most famous psychiatrists of his time—Otto Binswanger. Patients from all over the world flocked to the charismatic Binswanger. Berger was to stay at Jena until 1938, aside from three years' service with the Axis forces during World War I.

While Berger was conscientious to a fault in his work, there are good indications that his heart was not in psychiatry and he may have even disliked it. He considered himself a specialist in organic brain disease and his neurological skills were excellent. It would seem he was interested in organic nervous diseases, rather than psychiatry. Berger did not hold psychology in high esteem and considered Freud to be outside the bounds of true science.

Berger married and had four children. A shy and reticent man, he hid a sensitive and humane personality behind a facade of sternness and self-discipline. (His clinic was run with quasi-military discipline.) His colleagues regarded him as unimaginative and would hardly have classed him as an innovator. There were comments that he spoke as seldom as possible directly to his patients. According to his assistant, Ginzberg, Berger was pathologically secretive, never discussing his work with anyone and his approach to the day-to-day problems of the psychiatric hospital 'did not suggest genius.'

Germany's defeat and the revolution of 1918–19 marked a critical period in Berger's life. The fall of the Kaiser's Germany meant his achievements and irreproachable record as an obedient and loyal German professor had come to naught. Worse still, Binswanger, for unknown reasons, left Germany. The hospital lost its chief, and Berger his protector. However, he pressed on with his work and his research, the lack of results notwithstanding.

Berger's scientific path was hardly stellar. His publications before 1929 were few, scarcely making any impact. He maintained a rigid distinction between clinical and laboratory work, working on his own in the late afternoon and early evening. The studies were conducted during the early evening hours in the seclusion of his laboratory.

Berger's neurophysiological approach was based on the graphical measurement of physiological output. He believed in the mind–brain duality. A key feature of this theory was the principle of conservation of energy; that is, brain activity in one part would lead to a change in metabolism indicating the energy that had been used for this process. At the time, the idea of measuring the electrical output of the brain itself was ignored, if not derided. Agreeing that it was not worthwhile to attempt to trace electricity from the brain, physiologists and investigators of Berger's time simply passed by an almost obvious phenomenon. Despite what would seem such a massive disincentive, Berger's approach from the start was focused in this direction.

His early studies included intracranial blood circulation, the bodily manifestations of psychic states, and psychophysiology. Now he attempted to assess the brain's activity through its blood flow. This was done with plethysmography (measuring pressure with balloons) on patients with skull fractures, which provided access to the underlying tissue.

After well over eight years, Berger finally accepted the futility of trying to get a meaningful result by examining the brain blood flow and metabolism, turning to the task of measuring the electrical output of the brain. That he succeeded at all is evidence of his remarkable tenacity. In order to record the tracing, he used three different galvanometers, each one more sophisticated and sensitive, but even so, considering the measurements required and compared to what is available today, appallingly crude instruments.

Using a vacuum tube amplifier with electrical needles giving a 100 times magnification of the electric current, it took until 1924 to get a minute readable electrical tracing from the surface of the brain of Patient K, who had a head injury.

Having got an electrical tracing from the brain, Berger was prepared to let others into his laboratory. He asked Ginzberg to volunteer as a subject. Later he used other colleagues, in addition to his son and daughter. The procedures involved no danger.

Berger would inject Novocaine into the scalp and put the electrode into the periosteum (the tough white lining of the skull) of the skull. Later, presumably when the recording technique had improved and he was more confident, he simply attached the electrode to the scalp in the same way it is done today.

As the quality of the readings improved, his discoveries escalated. Berger made the distinction between the alpha and beta rhythms, showing how they reflected different aspects of the brain's activities. He was able to show the distinction between the brain waves at rest, and the altered wave (to be known as the alpha wave or Berger's wave) when the subject performed an intellectual task such as calculation. He was able to show how there was complete cessation of electrical activity in the area of a brain tumour and the changes that distinguished the sleeping from the thinking brain. One of his achievements was to show the presence of a brain tumour with his new device. He was unable to succeed in his ambition of recording a grand mal fit, but got good readings of a typical petit mal tracing.

It is a measure of Berger's caution, reticence and probable fear of failure or criticism, that he took a further five years before publishing his readings. It is difficult to avoid the conclusion that his pathological secretiveness also played a part in this, although it is not clear why it was in his interest not to get recognition of his discovery.

Berger called the new procedure electroencephalography (*electroenkephalography* in German), or EEG, in preference to the Russian term electrocerebrogram. His publication met with an indifferent response, particularly in Germany and, to a lesser extent, elsewhere in Europe. He was unknown to most of the major players in neurophysiology; to those who knew him, he was a scientific low-flyer and an indifferent clinician who had only obtained his position through political influence. Most of all, his secretive style undermined his credibility.

If Berger was upset by the lack of response, he gave no indication, publishing until 1938 a total of fourteen papers. It is a measure of his meticulous approach that each paper had the same name, only that they were numbered between one and fourteen.

At the time, the leading neurophysiologist in the world was Edgar Adrian of Cambridge, who won the 1932 Nobel Prize for medicine. Adrian was deeply sceptical of Berger's findings and, in 1934, got his team to do tests with the intention of discrediting Berger's claims. To their surprise, they immediately got accurate tracings, replicating the distinction between alpha and beta waves. To his credit, Adrian immediately published his findings, supporting Berger. This led to a surge of excitement, and workers began to develop and use EEGs. The EEG became a diagnostic mainstay in neurology and psychiatry, receiving most recognition in America where the equipment was the most advanced.

For Berger, after so many years, this was vindication at last. In 1937 he presided with Adrian at a symposium on electrical activity held by the Congress in Psychology. Professor P. Baudouin hailed him as the most distinguished visitor to his laboratory. Berger, in tears, said that he was not famous in Germany. He then planned to visit the United States, where his findings were even more highly regarded, but was unable to travel because of the outbreak of World War II.

In 1938, Berger was made Professor Emeritus. In his acceptance speech, he said that he had devoted himself to what he referred to as the central problem of psychiatry: the physical basis of psychic function. Shortly after this accolade, Berger's working life came to an end when he was informed by telephone that he would not be reappointed to the position of Director. It was thought that he could not adapt to the style of the Nazi Party. This seems unlikely. Berger was a loyal public official, and more likely the Nazis favoured someone with better political connections.

Shattered, Berger was unable to continue his research and got a token position running a nursing home. He became deeply depressed and, incorrectly, convinced that he had an incurable heart condition, he hanged himself in 1941.

Berger died unaware that he had been nominated for the Nobel Prize the year before, but because of the war, the awards were suspended. This added to the tragic loss. In Germany, Berger's death evoked little notice; this was due as much to his personality as to an underestimation of the importance of the EEG. The leading German periodicals published lengthy articles commenting on the neurologist Otfrid Foerster's work which occurred at about the same time. There was only one obituary of Berger, written by his former assistant.

By contrast, in the United States Berger's death was marked in the medical journals and the press. *The New York Times* carried an editorial on his achievements, notwithstanding the fact that he died on 1 June 1941, just months from the outbreak of war between Germany and the United States.

In the decades that followed his death, Berger finally received the acclaim that he deserved. Conferences were held in his honour and articles were written about him. In the United States, Berger was proclaimed a genius. He was described by epileptologist Frederick Gibbs as the Father of the EGG and the founder of modern psychophysiology.

From its inauspicious beginning in the seclusion of Berger's laboratory, the applications of the EEG recording have diversified. After World War II, with the release of technical developments in electronics, reliable multichannel EEG equipment became available, as did cathode ray recorders and cameras. The EEG is now so routine in neurology, intensive care, neurosurgery, sleep medicine, psychiatry and experimental psychology, as well as other disciplines, that a current generation of practitioners operate under the assumption that it has been there forever, completely unaware of the unusual circumstances in which this reticent and tenacious man made such a discovery.

The discovery of the EEG was the culmination of nineteenth-century neurophysiology, which among other endeavours, aimed at a method of measuring the activity of the brain while engaged in its various tasks—in metaphysical terms, trying to read the mind or penetrate the soul. The belief that electricity was the vital medium in the nervous system failed to progress in the twentieth century and Berger was a marked exception in continuing to do his lonely research, working in complete isolation over several decades until he obtained the brain tracings.

Why did Berger succeed and what does the way in which he did it say about science? Firstly, Berger's handicap may have been an advantage. With the poor technology of the time, so great were the obstacles of tracing the electricity of the whole brain regarded at the time that anyone trained in the field saw the quest as futile. Without any training in electrophysiology, Berger was not in a position to know or (probably) be deterred by this. He had to work it out as he went along, a phenomenal achievement of will, determination and struggle.

Berger's nineteenth-century education, with its belief in chemistry and physics as the basis of biological processes, drove him towards the search for electricity in the brain. Berger believed more strongly than other physiologists that brain tissue produces electricity and there is electrical activity of the cortex.

If nothing else, the manner in which Berger discovered the EEG shows that the development of science, far from being an objective matter practised by groups of like-minded individuals, is often thrown forward dramatically by isolated, marginal and quite dysfunctional individuals nursing ideas, which on scrutiny, may not be scientific at all, but quite subjective and romantic. This would apply to Berger, who seemed to have been driven by the determination to explore his early telepathic experience, although to his credit, he did not mention this in any of his papers.

While retrospective diagnosis of historical character is always a risky business, there is widespread agreement that Berger was excessively shy, generally avoided social contact and found it difficult to communicate with staff and patients alike. Consequently, he adopted a rather brusque and authoritarian manner despite the fact that his relationship with his family was warm and close and he appears to have had a humanitarian outlook.

There seems to be a paradox in Berger's case that what may have been social phobic and avoidant traits were the motivating factors for him to retreat to work in his laboratory, rather than be more engaged with his clinical work and colleagues. On the same basis, there is no evidence that he had any social life away from his immediate family.

Associated with the shy and avoidant traits were intensely obsessive and compulsive features. Nothing short of this could explain Berger's capacity, working on his own, night after night in an empty laboratory save for the occasional human subject, to keep on working in the face of failure until so many years later when he saw that magical first tracing.

If Berger had been a more socially engaged individual, participating in the local scientific community and producing work which was well regarded, there is little doubt that his experiments would have received acclaim much sooner. However, the question is would Berger have produced these results at all, in the face of such obstacles — bearing in mind that no one else even considered this work even likely to be productive — if he had another type of personality which made him more engaged with the world? Sadly, it is all too likely that his obsessive anxiety also made him prone to depression and this, tragically, led to his premature ending. It has been stated on several times by a number of authorities, that had he survived the war years he would have been a certainty to be awarded the Nobel Prize. This was Berger's loss, but his findings are our gain and we should celebrate the shy, unusual and detached man who in the end stuck to his plan to discover how to read the mind.

FRIDA KAHLO

*A little while ago, not much more than
a few days ago, I was a child who went
about in a world of colors, of hard and
tangible forms. Everything was mysterious
and something was hidden, guessing what
it was a game for me. If you knew how
terrible it is to know suddenly, as if a bolt
of lightning elucidated the earth. Now
I live in a painful planet, transparent as ice;
but it is as if I had learned everything at
once in seconds.*

FRIDA KAHLO

The Mexican painter Frida Kahlo ranks among the world's most renowned twentieth-century female artists. Kahlo's work is remembered for its intense and unique depiction of her body and its ailments with stark portrayals of pain. Her painting and drawings have been described as being like medical case reports. Kahlo's works were intensely personal, drawing on her marriage, miscarriages and operations. Her unique form of self-expression defies categorisation as either Expressionist or Surrealist.

One of the few artists to have dared to show their naked, sick body, Kahlo practised an art suffused with her experience of pain and suffering. Of her one hundred and forty-three paintings, fifty-five are self-portraits which often incorporate symbolic portrayals of physical and psychological wounds. Kahlo stated,

'I paint myself because I am so often alone and because I am the subject I know best.'

During her short life—she died aged forty-seven—Kahlo had a tempestuous marriage with the prominent Mexican artist Diego Rivera, numerous love affairs, several miscarriages, years of being bedridden or wheelchair-bound, intractable pain and multiple operations.

She was born in Coyoacán, a suburb of Mexico City, on 6 July 1907. Her father Wilhelm, who claimed to be of Hungarian-Jewish ancestry, came from Baden-Baden, Germany, to Mexico in 1891, changing his first name to Guillermo. He had two daughters from an earlier marriage who were raised in a convent. Kahlo's mother, Matilde Calderon, was of indigenous and Spanish descent. During the Mexican Revolution, which started in 1910, she would prepare meals for the revolutionary fighters who came to their home.

Kahlo was close to her father. Guillermo taught her to assist him in his work as a photographer and encouraged her to learn to draw and paint, as well as to be athletic. Matilde, a devout Catholic, ran the household. Although the marriage was unhappy, the couple had four daughters, Frida being the third.

Kahlo was born with spina bifida, non-fusion of the laminae of the spinal arches, the likely cause of her lifelong spine and leg problems. Depending on the severity of the defect, spina bifida may be symptom-free or present with skeletal, urogenital and neurological manifestations, including deformation and shrinking problems, such as club foot and paralysis.

Kahlo caught polio in 1913, aged six, and spent several months in bed. As a result, her right leg was slightly deformed and shorter than her left leg, so she had to wear built-up shoes. Kahlo disguised her legs by wearing long, colourful skirts. Nevertheless, she was able to participate in boxing and other sports.

In 1922 she entered the Escuela Nacional Preparatoria in Mexico City as one of thirty-five girls in a student body of two thousand boys. Kahlo joined a group of student rebels called 'Las Cachuchas' who discussed politics and culture, read books and carried out pranks; she had her first love affair with their leader, Alejandro Gomez Arias. Noted for her playfulness, rebellious attitude and uninhibited sexuality, she went on to cause a scandal by having an affair with an older woman. She intended to study medicine.

On 1 September 1925 Kahlo and Alejandro were riding in a bus when the vehicle collided with a trolley car. Kahlo was seriously injured, breaking her spinal column, collarbone, ribs and pelvis, with eleven fractures in her right leg, a crushed and dislocated right foot and a dislocated shoulder. A metal handrail pierced her abdomen, vagina and uterus, seriously damaging her ability to bear children. Despite the vertebral fractures, the spinal cord was undamaged.

Kahlo had to be in a full body cast for three months. Her father, who painted landscapes, lent her his paints and brushes and her mother had a special easel made so she could paint lying down in bed. She wrote, 'I felt I still had enough energy to do something other than studying to become a doctor. Without giving it any particular thought, I started painting.'

Although she recovered from her worst injuries and regained her ability to walk, Kahlo was plagued by pain for the rest of her life. A year after the accident, she was readmitted to hospital and had to wear plaster corsets for several months. After this, she had numerous admissions to hospital and was bedridden for months at a time. She underwent as many as thirty-five operations on her back, her right leg and her right foot.

The accident deeply affected Kahlo's life. She gave up medical studies and began painting her experiences using the small sizes and miniaturist detailing of Mexican *retablos*. These devotional pictures show the tiny figures of saints performing miracles or the Virgin Mary answering a prayer, together with a written commentary that describes what is happening in the scene.

In 1928 Kahlo joined the Communist Party and approached Diego Rivera, the famed muralist painter whom she had admired from her schooldays—telling her schoolmates that she intended to marry him someday—asking him for advice about art. Rivera immediately recognised her talent and encouraged her to continue. They began a relationship and married in August 1929 in the face of her mother's disapproval.

The couple were comically mismatched. Rivera, over twenty years older, was over 1.8 metres (six feet) tall and distinctly rounded; Kahlo was tiny and petite by comparison.

The marriage was turbulent. She writes in her diary about him as 'Diego: the beginning, builder, my child, my boyfriend, painter, my lover, my husband, my friend, my mother, me, the universe.'

Frida could not escape the trap she had built for herself: 'There have been two great accidents in my life. One was the trolley, and the other was Diego. Diego was by far the worst.'

Both Kahlo and Rivera had fiery temperaments and had numerous affairs. Kahlo's self-portrait *Diego in my Thoughts* has Rivera's face on her forehead, illustrating their obsessive and destructive relationship. Kahlo also had many affairs with women, including Josephine Baker; some of her women lovers had slept with Rivera. Her male lovers included Japanese artist Isamu Noguchi and the art dealer Heinz Berggruen. Rivera could tolerate the relationships with women, but her relationships with men made him jealous.

The couple were celebrities, much sought after by the rich and famous, especially artists and leftish politicians. Their guests included Russian revolutionary Leon Trotsky and his wife during their Mexican exile; surrealist André Breton and his wife, Jacqueline Lamba; Soviet filmmaker Sergei Eisenstein; and industrialist Nelson Rockefeller.

After Trotsky sought political asylum in Mexico in 1937, he and his wife lived for a time at their home, where he had an affair with Kahlo. (He later moved to another house where he was assassinated in 1940.) Describing Trotsky as a boring old man, Kahlo soon tired of the affair. Nevertheless, she painted a picture of him which Trotsky's wife refused to allow into their new home. Leaving no doubt of her political fealty, she kept a painting of Joseph Stalin hanging over her bed.

Frida painted, entertained, and was endlessly photographed at home or in public. She put considerable effort into her image, wearing traditional Mexican peasant clothes, pre-Columbian jewellery and indigenous hairstyles.

Kahlo's art was highly personal. The portraits emphasised her unbroken single eyebrow and fine moustache, described as a statement of her defiance of social mores and her provocative androgyny. Those distracted by the splendid natural apparatus of actress Salma Hayek, who played Frida in the 2002 movie, may reflect that beauty takes many forms, especially when determined by Hollywood.

Most of her paintings were about her experiences or made as gifts for people. In her searing self-portraits she depicted herself as a bedridden patient or victim. In a 1940 portrait, she wears a thorn necklace which has punctured her skin and drawn blood. *The Suicide of Dorothy Hale* (1939), by contrast, shows a formally and elegantly dressed woman killing herself in a New York City setting.

In 1930 she and Rivera travelled to the United States, where Rivera had commissions to paint murals in San Francisco, Detroit and New York. Frida continued to paint, including graphic depictions of a miscarriage in 1932 and of her disenchantment with the United States.

Learning of Rivera's affair with her younger sister, Cristina, Kahlo was devastated. The couple divorced in November 1939, but remarried in December 1940. This time, their living quarters were separate, and they continued to argue.

Kahlo continued to paint, struggle with Rivera and pursue love affairs, but her health deteriorated and the pain worsened.

From 1934 she had a series of unnecessary operations on her foot and leg. A 1943 painting, predictive of what lay ahead, shows a little boy with the face of Diego Rivera examining a doll with a detached right leg. In 1944 Kahlo was encased in a steel corset to support her spine, and was unable to sit upright without being tied to the back of a chair. In response, she painted a self-portrait depicting her spinal column as an ancient pillar broken in several places, with nails sticking into her naked body in the setting of a fissured, dry landscape.

From 1946 to 1951, Kahlo underwent eight spinal operations. After this, she was confined to a wheelchair. 'I tried to drown my sorrows,' she wrote, 'but the bastards learned how to swim, and now I am overwhelmed by this decent and good feeling.'

With the pain worsening in the last years of her life, Kahlo became depressed and dependent on pethidine and morphine. She lost interest in life and was suicidal. In 1953 her right leg developed gangrene and had to be amputated at the knee. She wrote: 'They amputated my leg six months ago, they have given me centuries of torture and at moments I almost lost my reason. I keep on waiting to kill myself . . . Never in my life have I suffered more.'

On 13 July 1954 Kahlo died. A few days before, she wrote her last entry in the diary: 'I hope the exit is joyful and I hope never to return Frida.'

The official cause of death was listed as a pulmonary embolism, although it is believed that she died from a non-accidental overdose of her medication. No autopsy was performed and she received a state funeral.

Frida Kahlo's Brain

If a condition can have a patron saint, why not a patron painter? In which case, Frida Kahlo would be far and away the best candidate for patron painter of pain, the condition that dominated her life but was never allowed to prevent her from living it to the maximum extent possible.

But what is pain? Is it a state, a symptom, a feeling, an emotion, an illness, a penitence, a delusion, an imaginary state or simply a means of communicating? Despite numerous attempts, the best definition is 'An unpleasant experience that we primarily associate with tissue damage or describe in terms of tissue damage or both.'

The universal physical affliction of mankind, pain has a special place in human history. For traditional peoples, such as hunter-gatherers, it was perceived in terms of the world of magic and spirits. Visible pain could be seen as an injury; internal pain was perceived as a form of punishment or devil invasion. Consequently, attempts would be made to scare the devils out of the person's body with rattles or gongs, pipes could be held against the skin to suck it out and, in some cases, holes drilled in the head (trepanation).

The word pain is derived from classical Greek. The Greek goddess of revenge, Poine, was sent to punish mortal fools who angered the gods. It is no surprise that people who suffer from pain feel like it is divine vengeance. In antiquity, pain referred to anything that could cause distress: physical, emotional or spiritual. This was due to the fact that all illnesses or altered emotional states were attributed to external influence. In the Old Testament, for example, people suffering pain are cured by a range of experiences, such as in the trials of Job. Pain is the central metaphor of Christian thought, the sacrificial redemption of the crucifixion. Ancient cultures believed that pain and disease were punishments for human folly by the gods who needed to be appeased by sacrifices or redemption. During the Middle Ages, pain relief came from herbs and minerals. Many ingredients were purely placebo — based on the so-called magical properties of gold, ivory and what was claimed to be unicorn horn. Not all attempts to relieve pain were misguided. The Egyptians put electric eels over wounds, a practice anticipating the use of the transcutaneous electrical nerve stimulation (TENS) machine, in which pulsed electrical currents are run into nerves to block pain impulses. Hippocrates wrote about the pain-relieving benefits of willow bark, which contains acetylsalicylate, the active ingredient of aspirin.

René Descartes, the Jean-Paul Sartre of his day, argued that the body worked like a machine and could be studied by experimental methods. The medical profession, moving at its usual pace, was slow to take this up. It was the meaning, rather than the fact or the nature, of pain that mattered. Doctors valued pain as a symptom of vitality. Consider a statement made as late as 1826: 'The greater the pain, the greater must be our confidence in the power and energy of life.'

By the nineteenth century, the accepted view was that all pain was due to physical injury. Tissue damage at a nerve ending led to signals transmitted to the brain. Pain signals were transmitted by two different types of fibres to the posterior columns of the spine, and from there to the brain. Up to that point, pain relief was not done on an organised or formal basis by doctors and pharmacists, but through herbalists, quacks and the proverbial snake oil salesmen. The preparations they marketed could include just about anything (and often did), including opiates, alcohol and cocaine. Coca-Cola, for example, was originally manufactured by John Pemberton as a cocaine-based pharmaceutical remedy, not as a soft drink of the stars. To relieve pain, doctors used opium or laudanum, a mixture of opium and sherry.

The skilled surgeon was one who operated as quickly as they could. One of the all-time speed merchants was the Scottish-born surgeon Robert Liston, known as the fastest knife in the West End. Lister could amputate a leg in two and a half minutes, with a personal record time of 28 seconds. In one celebrated case, he amputated a leg in just over a minute, removing several of his assistant's fingers in the process. No wonder he took the lead in introducing anaesthesia.

Attitudes did eventually change and by 1850, it was accepted that relief of pain was critical to medical practice; particularly acute pain, palliation in those who are dying in intractable pain, and recurrent pain such as migraines. The change of attitude was no accident. Technological developments led to the development of high-potency concentrated analgesics that could be easily administered. Wilhelm Sertürmer synthesised the critical elements of crude opium in 1804 and within two decades morphine was being produced industrially in Germany, in the United States a decade later. In 1855 Alexander Wood devised a syringe with a hollow needle for the administration of drugs. For the first time, it was possible to rapidly administer high-potency drugs.

The world as we know it changed forever with the discovery of surgical anaesthesia. Ether was first used in 1846, chloroform in 1847, and cocaine, the first local anaesthetic, in 1884 by Sigmund Freud's colleague and competitor, Karl Koller, leaving Freud no option but to invent psychoanalysis. In Edinburgh, James Simpson developed the use of anaesthesia in labour, revolutionising childbirth, which often led to the death of the mother and the baby. One of the first people to have an anaesthetic for childbirth was Queen Victoria, thereby ensuring its widespread acceptance.

The introduction of anaesthesia led to an extended debate about the possibility that relieving pain could retard the natural process of healing. Pain relief was also questioned by religious authorities, who believed that it violated God's law to inflict pain to strengthen faith and teach the need for self-sacrifice. The overwhelming response of doctors and patients made these arguments nugatory, but left a legacy which persists to this day. There is the doctor who undermedicates on the rationalisation that medication may mask crucial symptoms or cause addiction. And then there is the doctor who overmedicates patients to the point of causing oversedation or worse.

The horror of operating on fully conscious patients was over—although surgeons, working in battlefield situations with limited medical supplies as recently as the Bosnian War, have always known how to operate without analgesia. At the Battle of Stalingrad, for example, the German surgeons were reduced to packing the injured limb in snow to make it completely numb before surgery.

But it did not stop there. In 1899 Bayer produced aspirin, a remarkably safe and well-tolerated drug with analgesic and anti-fever properties as well. Within two decades, it was sold around the world and used as an alternative to opiates for treatment of mild to moderate pain. However, morphine and its derivatives remained essential for the treatment of severe pain, in particular conditions such as cancer. Problems that arose with opiate abuse led to a strong counter-reaction, with doctors expressing concern about morphine addiction, which they referred to by the poignant name of narcomania.

Curing morphine addiction was on the minds of the chemical companies and in 1898, Bayer introduced diacetylated morphine under the trade name of heroin for the treatment of cough. In what can only be described as a spectacular example of the law of unfor-seen consequences, heroin was proclaimed as an effective way of curing addiction, but this delusion did not last for long—by 1910, heroin was a street drug of abuse in the United States.

Research in the first half of the twentieth century was marked by a search for specific pain fibres and pathways and a pain centre in the brain. This resulted in a concept of pain as a sensory projec-tion system, which in turn led to attempts to treat severe pain by severing the relevant nerves. The rise of psychoanalysis meant that pain, among other physical symptoms, was seen as purely symbolic, a guide to an unconscious conflict. Intellectually appealing as this rationalisation was, it proved utterly useless as a means of treat-ment, alienating both doctors and patients alike. This tendency reached its apogee in 1957 with a description of 'the pain-prone patient' by George Engel, a psychiatrist specialising in the treatment of medical conditions but heavily influenced by psychoanalysis. The pain-prone patient was essentially a masochistic person, more often than not female, who continued to complain of problems due to unconscious difficulties that they projected onto the physician, whom they blamed for their failure to recover.

These speculative explanations were not to last and a significant breakthrough came after 1963 when Ronald Melzack and Patrick Wall discovered what became known as the pain gate. Fibres transmitted pain to the spine at differing speeds and if the one nerve could be stimulated, it would block the more intense signals from the other. This led to the development of physical treatments for pain such as the TENS machine, an understanding of how chronic pain changes the nerves in the spine, and the development of the pain clinic.

As a result we have an enhanced understanding of how pain occurs, operates and affects people and a vastly improved repertoire of treatments, physical, surgical, chemical and behavioural. While patients with cancer and their doctors faced a terrible dilemma, conditions where pain cannot be localised to a specific area—'pain without a lesion'—is a different, but equally agonising ordeal. The problem with chronic pain arose from its long duration: the belief that the initial injury would no longer cause such symptoms. This was epitomised by phantom limb and causalgia syndromes in which patients reported pain at the slightest touch and the symptoms could persist for fully thirty years. The first to make a serious attempt to explain the phenomena was the US Civil War neurologist Weir Mitchell. Despite their unexplained pain and odd behaviour, Weir believed his patients, describing causalgia as the 'most terrible of tortures'. All attempts to treat such patients were futile. The term reflex sympathetic dystrophy (RSD) was used to describe the condition, more recently replaced by complex regional pain syndrome (CRPS).

CRPS is poorly understood. Though more common in midlife it occurs at all ages and women account for about seventy per cent of cases. A predisposition to RSD also plays a role. It can strike at any age. The symptoms start at the site of an injury, which can be quite minor. With burning and electrical sensations, described as shooting pains, the patient may also experience muscle spasms, local swelling, abnormally increased sweating, changes in skin temperature and colour, softening and thinning of bones, joint tenderness or stiffness, and restricted or painful movement. Moving or touching the limb is often intolerable. Continuous pain is worsened by emotional or physical stress.

RSD has variable components of burning, aching, shooting pain, dysfunction of sweating and temperature regulation, oedema, dystrophy and atrophy of the mostly distal part (hand, foot) of the affected extremity, and restricted movement. The pain spreads diffusely from the site of the injury, often involving both or even all four extremities and is commonly associated with hyperalgesia (over-sensitivity), allodynia (exquisite sensitivity to touch or pressure), and hyperpathia (an abnormal reaction with excessive pain or numbness). These patients are almost invariably depressed and anxious. Despite treatment, the pain often is intractable; different kinds of conservative and surgical treatment usually have only partial and short-lived effects.

A related condition is phantom limb: the sensation that an amputated or missing limb or organ, such as the breast or penis, is still attached to the body, moving with other body parts and is mostly painful. Some people find that the phantom limb begins to take on a life of its own, and does not obey their commands. Sixty to eighty per cent of individuals experience phantom sensations in an amputated limb. Phantom sensations may also occur after the removal of body parts other than the limbs, for example after amputation of the breast, extraction of a tooth (phantom tooth pain) or removal of an eye. Phantom pains can also occur in people who are born without a limb and in people who are paralysed. The missing limb often feels shorter and, over time, tends to telescope, that is, pull back into itself.

Nerves that would normally detect sensation in the missing limb cause pain. The sensation varies widely among individuals.

In addition to pain, induced sensations include warmth, cold, itching, squeezing, tightness and tingling.

In the fortunate, the phantom limb will 'retract' into the site of the amputation and then disappear. However, when it persists, it can cause extraordinary discomfort and distress. In many patients the phantom limb is fixed in a cramped position that is excruciatingly painful. Every time the patient attempts to move the paralysed limb, they get an image and sense that the limb did not move. This is described as a learned paralysis.

Over the years, all kinds of treatments were tried to relieve phantom limb pain with mixed results. One of the commonest treatments was to sever the ends of the nerves in a stump in the belief that the stump had overgrown (known as a neuroma), a process that produced little benefit and could make the situation worse. Drugs and psychological treatment had, at best, only mixed benefits.

More recently, there has been a breakthrough. Melzack and his workers postulated the existence of the neuromatrix: a map of the body on the brain that can be disrupted by physical trauma such as surgery. The next step came from neurologist V. S. Ramachandran, who discovered that phantom limb sensations arose from crosswiring in the part of the brain cortex that receives input from the limbs and body — input from the left goes to the right hemisphere and vice versa. The map of the input in the somatosensory cortex is referred to as the somatosensory homunculus. Brain maps are highly malleable, and not fixed at birth as was previously believed. When the arm is amputated, the vacated cortical territory corresponding to the missing arm is 'invaded' by neurons from the face, remapping the region that no longer has input.

To overcome the problem, Ramachandran created a mirror box so that the reflection of the normal arm creates the visual illusion that the phantom had been resurrected. When the patient moves his normal hand while looking at the reflection, he not only sees the phantom move (as expected) but *feels* it to move as well. In some patients this will abolish the pain in the phantom, in others the phantom disappeared entirely—along with the pain. Amazing stuff.

The implications of Ramachandaran's work are huge. It confirms the existence of a neuromatrix. It can be used to treat a rare condition known as somatoparaphrenia (delusional misidentification of one's own body part) and, intriguingly, what is known as apotemnophilia—the desire to have a limb removed because it feels so foreign to the owner. There may even be a spin-off in explaining body dysmorphic disorder (aka transsexualism) in the future.

What caused Frida Kahlo's excruciating pain? The primary cause was spina bifida. American surgeon Leo Eloesser, who became a good friend of Kahlo's, did X-rays showing its presence, stating that 'the decreased sensitivity in the lower part of her body was characteristically compatible with this disorder. Her disability grew and various operations to her right foot and leg made matters worse.'

The 1925 bus accident led to post-traumatic causalgia, which is otherwise known as complex regional pain syndrome type II. CRPS usually develops within days or months after even minor traumatic tissue injury, bone fracture, surgical intervention or prolonged immobilisation, and Kahlo had experienced all of this.

The effect of spina bifida and polio infection left Kahlo with a crippled leg and toe deformity. These in turn were the source of recurrent foot skin sores, infections, ulceration and pain. Her congenitally abnormal spinal column, leg deformity, the displacement of several vertebrae after the traffic accident and spinal muscle atrophy due to prolonged use of orthopaedic corsets led to spinal column instability, chronic asymmetrical overstretching of the spinal muscles and back pain.

CRPS was the main cause of Kahlo's intractable pain. Distressing life events (years of being bedridden or wheelchair-bound, her husband's continuous infidelity and her devastating miscarriages) undoubtedly lowered her pain threshold and was an important psychological pain component. Her intractable pain provoked numerous unsuccessful and unnecessary operations. The many operations on her foot, leg and spine increased her neuropathic pain (pain arising from the nervous system), becoming extremely severe and devastating in her later years.

As she got older, tropical ulcers, together with deformity, were a source of constant discomfort and pain. A 1931 drawing shows a bandaged, ulcerated right leg. In her painting *What I Saw in the Water*, a pair of feet stick out of the bathwater. There is a bleeding sore between the deformed big and second toes of the right foot, a typical feature of spina bifida. After the leg amputation in 1953, Kahlo developed phantom limb pain. A sketch from the same year in Kahlo's diary shows how, severed at the right knee, the leg radiates stabbing, shooting pain.

Novelist Carlos Fuentes described an encounter with Kahlo at the Palacio de Bellas Artes in Mexico City as like meeting 'an Aztec goddess'. In 1938 the surrealist artist André Breton described her as a 'ribbon around a bomb'. The ticking bomb exploded finally after forty-seven years, into which Kahlo had packed an eventful life and produced a large body of significant art.

Frida Kahlo is an artist whose creativity was profoundly influenced by chronic, severe illness, and her work is the best illustration of her life, thoughts and illnesses. She is an inspiring example of an artist who, despite enormous suffering and setbacks, never allowed pain to overcome her.

WOODY GUTHRIE

Woody was born in one of the most desolate places in America, just in time to come of age in the worst period in our history ... He became the living embodiment of everything a people's revolution is supposed to be about: that working people have dignity, intelligence and value above and beyond the market's demand for their labour ... For me personally, Woody is my hero of heroes and the only person on earth that I will go to my grave regretting that I never met.

STEVE EARLE

The American singer-songwriter folk musician and activist Woody Guthrie is one of the seminal figures in defining the modern American music. Most famed for his riposte to Irving Berlin's 'White Christmas', 'This Land Is Your Land', an alternative anthem to many Americans, Guthrie left a lasting legacy of songs. Guthrie played traditional folk and blues songs, many of his own songs were about his experiences in the Dust Bowl during the Great Depression when he travelled with migrant workers from Oklahoma to California. Politically outspoken, supporting socialism and communism, Guthrie incorporated these themes in his writing as well. Already a legend by the time he died in 1963, his work had a huge influence on folk music and musicians, notably

Bob Dylan, Tom Paxton and Bruce Springsteen, to mention but a few. Alan Konigsberg, aka Woody Allen, chose Guthrie as a role model when he changed his name. His son, Arlo Guthrie, also became a folk musician.

Almost everyone will know at least one Woody Guthrie song, although they may not be aware who wrote it. Guthrie's output was prodigious. Songs seemed to pour out of him and it is said he forgot far more songs than he ever wrote down. Many were never performed in his lifetime. But it did not stop there; Guthrie wrote poems and books, even a study of psychology when he was very young.

Guthrie had a turbulent personal life with perennial wanderlust; he could never stay in one place and would invariably move on. This was in part due to his tendency to self-destruct. As soon as he was starting to make progress in his career, he would create problems and leave.

Guthrie's creativity and, ultimately, his life was robbed by a neurological disorder that haunted him from an early age: Huntington's disease. This is a genetic disorder that runs in affected families. In addition to Guthrie's mother and probably his grandfather, two daughters to his second marriage died of the condition. Incurable, it is an awful family curse, seldom skipping a generation and often striking the next generation a decade earlier. However, it can now be genetically diagnosed and with new developments in stem cells and gene therapy the hope of curing potentially afflicted patients is no longer a shimmering illusion.

Huntington's disease and another condition, Parkinson's disease, are movement disorders. The most visible indicator of brain dysfunction, movement disorders have been observed from time immemorial. Because they are evident to outsiders, sufferers have been accused of heresy, witchcraft and demonism, subjected to stigma, persecution and even death. The often dramatic disturbances of coordination, gait and the abnormal movements were of great interest to medicine, but it took until neurology was established as a discipline in its own right for movement disorders to achieve diagnostic respectability.

Neither of these conditions came to prominence through the studies of physicians working in hospitals or universities, but from the observation of doctors using medical acumen, intuition and an ability not to be swayed by the ruling medical dicta of their time. These doctors were George Parkinson and James Huntington, who had the ultimate honour richly deserved of having the illnesses they described named after them.

Woodrow Wilson 'Woody' Guthrie, the third of five children, was born in Okemah, a small Oklahoma town on 14 July 1912. His father was a Democratic candidate for office in the county. His mother Nora sang ballads to her children as they were growing up. Fire pursued Guthrie 'like a fury'. His early life was affected by several fires—including one that burned down the family home—a pattern that continued in his adult life. In 1919 Clara, Woody's older sister, then fourteen years old, was fatally burned during an argument with her mother. Given what we know of Nora's subsequent life, there is some suspicion that these fires were caused by her.

Nora Guthrie, at her best a loving mother who doted on Woody, was prone to periods when she would wander and was forgetful, neglecting duties such as the laundry. She became increasingly moody with outbursts of anger and broke her arm. She could not control her arms or her legs, had spasms and fell on the floor, wallowed around the house and ruined her clothes, yelling until people up the street could hear her.

In his autobiography, *Bound for Glory*, Guthrie described his mother's behaviour:

> *She would be all right for a time and treat us as good*
> *as any other mother, and, all at once, it would start*
> *in—something bad and awful—something would come*
> *over her, and it came by slow degrees. Her face would*

twitch and her lips would snarl and her teeth would show
... and she would double over into a terrible-looking
hunch and turn into another person.

In 1926 Nora became convinced her husband was cheating on her; the following year, she set him on fire. He went to live with his family in Pampa, Texas, and Nora was admitted to the Oklahoma Hospital for the Insane. By 1928, she was unable to recognise Woody. She was diagnosed with Huntington's disease and died in hospital in 1930. It is likely that her father, George Sherman, who drowned while horseback riding, had the same condition.

With his mother institutionalised and his father living in Pampa, Guthrie and his siblings were largely left to their own ends. A bright student and an avid reader, he had to drop out of school. With a natural affinity for music, largely self-taught, Guthrie played songs for a sandwich or coins. When he was eighteen, Guthrie's father got him to come to Pampa, where he spent his time busking and reading in the library. He wrote a manuscript summarising everything he knew about the basics of psychology. He read widely on alternative Eastern religions.

Guthrie lived in Pampa until 1937. He worked in a brothel, painted signs and played music. He could have earned a living as a sign painter as he was always in high demand by clients when he applied himself to this. Any money he earned, he would spend or give away as fast as he got it. At one stage, he set up as lay analyst and faith healer, using the philosophy of Kahlil Gibran for those he called troubled spirits who came to him on superstitious feet.

Guthrie married his first wife, Mary, in 1933. They had two children before he went on the road, joining thousands of Okies migrating to California for work. This was the start of his lifelong wanderlust. By the late 1930s, Guthrie was doing well enough performing hillbilly and traditional folk music in Los Angeles to

Storm Shelter Cave (image courtesy of Rock Art Research Institute, University of Witwatersrand)

Bertha Pappenheim (Getty Images)

Joseph Lis, aka Joe Silver (image courtesy Professor Charles van Onselen)

Vaslav Nijinsky (Getty Images)

Hans Berger (Getty Images)

Frida Kahlo (Getty Images)

Woody Guthrie (Getty Images)

Trebitsch Lincoln (Getty Images)   Constantin von Economo (Getty Images)

Theodor Morell (Getty Images)

send for his family. He began to write and perform the protest songs that would eventually appear on his first album, *Dust Bowl Ballads*. He mixed with socialists and communists, and wrote a Communist Party column for *The Daily Worker* from May 1939 to January 1940, but he was never a party member.

In 1938, when Guthrie was twenty-six, his personality seemed to change. He became withdrawn and indifferent towards his wife. A cousin observed him 'go berserk when a dog bit a child, running around the house trying to find a gun to shoot the dog'.

With the outbreak of World War II, employment prospects diminished, his family returned to Pampa and Guthrie headed to New York City. He mixed with the folk music community and recorded several hours of conversation and songs with musical archivist and folklorist Alan Lomax for the Library of Congress, as well as the album, *Dust Bowl Ballads*. He penned his most famous song, 'This Land Is Your Land' in February 1940. By September 1940 Guthrie had enough money to bring Mary and the children to live in a Central Park West apartment.

As soon as his family arrived, Guthrie felt disgruntled with New York, heading west to Washington State where he was employed to write songs about the Columbia River and the building of the federal dams. In a phenomenal burst of creativity, in one month Guthrie wrote twenty-six songs, including 'Roll On Columbia', 'Pastures of Plenty', and 'Grand Coulee Dam'. When he wanted to return to New York, Mary refused and it was the end of their marriage.

Guthrie worked with fellow folk singer Pete Seeger in Greenwich Village. He went on tour with the Almanac Singers, writing a song commemorating the sinking of the ship *Reuben James* in which he endeavoured to name each of the hundred crewmen who died—an early indication of his penchant for excessive writing (hypergraphia). He penned thousands of pages of unpublished poems and prose, and took up a suggestion by Alan Lomax to write his autobiography. He met dancer Marjorie Mazia who helped him complete the book, *Bound For Glory*, published in 1943. Cathy Ann Guthrie, the first of their four children, was born in February 1943.

A reviewer wrote:

> *Some day people are going to wake up to the fact that Woody Guthrie and the ten thousand songs that leap and tumble off the strings of his music box are a national possession like Yellowstone and Yosemite, and part of the best stuff this country has to show the world.*

When his attempts to become a United Services Organisation performer failed, Guthrie joined the US Merchant Marine as a mess man and dishwasher. He served on different ships on transatlantic voyages, frequently singing for the crew and troops. During one crossing, Guthrie went into the hold of an overcrowded troop ship to boost the soldiers' morale by playing music. One ship was torpedoed in the Mediterranean and another struck a mine off the coast of France.

During service on the *William B. Travis* he was noted to be easily distracted. Instead of setting the tables, he might draw a menu on the blackboard, garnished with ribbons and bows, twittering birds, children playing, a mermaid, and sumptuous impossible descriptions of the meal. He was quoted as saying, 'I'm pretty sure I've got the same thing my mother had [I] just feel queer sometimes.'

In 1944, during Army basic training in Texas, the drill instructor noticed how he would itch or pull 'some kind of wormy web' off his face. He performed poorly at the obstacle course and in marksmanship—both activities requiring good motor coordination. He was stationed in Las Vegas and then discharged in 1946.

Guthrie's behaviour deteriorated. At a fund-raising event, he grabbed the collection plate and poured the money down his shirt. He became sexually disinhibited, making unwelcome *rys and legs of lights and shapely shadows of old hopes too ...lden gone for any earthyling to have to even to try to tell or ...o describe to any other worldster.*

...sequent years heralded a further decline in his functioning. ...ng tired of his rages and unpredictable behaviour, Marjorie ...aged his travels. Guthrie wandered the country, frequently ...elcome guest because of his hygiene and manners. Most of ...ative work was done, he would struggle for the rest of his ...h recurrent bouts of psychiatric episodes and alcoholism, ...ng the last fourteen years in hospital.

...1952, during one of his stays in Coney Island, he beat up ...ie on at least one occasion. He was hospitalised for three ...on a detoxification ward, then at Bellevue Hospital after ...ng suicidal. He was diagnosed with schizophrenia and ...rred to Brooklyn State Hospital, where they wrote: 'He ...emely fidgety and does not seem to be able to sit still for ...ent'. Then follows a description of chorea and emotional ...g. The doctor mentioned Huntington's disease but did not ...is any further.

...sulin coma therapy, the fashionable treatment for psycho-...ore phenoziathines became the standard treatment, was ...nended. As a precaution, the hospital recommended a ...gical examination. The neurologist immediately diagnosed ...gton's disease, the disorder inherited from his mother, and ...e was discharged. It took some time before he was told ...doctors. Believing him to be a danger to their children, ...ie divorced him and Woody continued his wanderings. ...v, he had a severe tremor with jerky movements.

...e met his third wife, Anneke Van Kirk, aged twenty-one, ...alibu commune. During a stay in Florida, Guthrie's arm ...rt in a camp fire accident, probably under the influence ...hol, when a gas cylinder exploded. He was never able to ...e guitar again. In 1954 the couple returned to New York,

sexual advances to his first wife. He frequ
to Marjorie with explicit discussion of
sex. He continued to play with folk singer
tation for unpredictable and inappropri
trying to write books, but only complete
much editing.

Alan Lomax described 'the exaggera
around and his fingers came down to scr
head like a steam shovel; the way he p
stroked his chin when he was thinking'.

After a tumultuous courtship, Guth
married in 1945 and moved into a house
in Coney Island. This served as a base for
music on street corners. The years on Me
most productive period as a writer. As it t
ominous sign. The fire curse struck again
Ann died in an electrical fire in Februar
on Woody was savage, leaving him badly
more and fought with his family. He lung
knife and put sand into son Arlo's mout
stop crying. His behaviour became more er
dress deteriorated. In 1948, his erotic lett
to jail for a few weeks. Typically, on bein
to go back to prison to put on a Christ
inmates.

Signs of mental disturbance became evi
losing his grasp. His songs, although still p
had a more simple lyrical structure. Repetiti
(use of words chosen on the basis of rhymin
and obscenities often made his songs unpub

> *Since you come here and swum here the*
> *been seeing what you might spiritually a*
> *describe as little shafty, shifty drafty dri*

where Anneke gave birth to a girl, Lorina Lynn, but she soon filed for divorce.

Woody wandered the country for a while but unable to control his movements, he was placed in Brooklyn State Hospital in 1954, then hospitalised at several institutions. He spent the rest of his life slowly declining. He was no longer able to play the guitar but continued to write, frequently about the other patients. His disabilities notwithstanding, he managed to retain a puckish sense of humour. He told a visitor, 'Ya see that guy over there? He eats books. Said *Bound for Glory* was one of the best he ever tasted.'

Marjorie came back into his life, taking over his affairs and visiting him regularly in hospital until his death. He was visited by the young Bob Dylan, who worshipped his music and observed his decline. At his last visit, Guthrie did not recognise Dylan. A laceration on his arm became infected, making him bedridden. He became mute in 1965 and died on 3 October 1967 at the age of fifty-five.

Two of Guthrie's children to Mary Guthrie died from Huntington's disease. None of the three remaining children with Marjorie developed the disease.

In 1998 English folk singer Billy Bragg released ten songs for which Woody had written the words but was unable to put to music. 'Another Man's Done Gone' is most apposite:

> *Sometimes I think I'm gonna lose my mind*
> *but it don't look like I ever do*
> *I loved so many people everywhere I went*
> *Some too much, others not enough*
> *I don't know, I may go down or up or anywhere*
> *But I feel like this scribbling might stay*
> *Maybe if I hadn't of seen so much hard feelings*
> *I might not could have felt other people's*
> *So when you think of me, if and when you do,*

Just say, well, another man's done gone
Well, another man's done gone.

Woody Guthrie's Brain

The first medical reference to the condition known as Hunting-ton's chorea (later Huntington's disease) is in a letter from 1842. It described a group of residents in the south-east corner of New York State who had a rare hereditary disorder. In adulthood arose a syndrome of involuntary movements and unclear speech, advancing over the years to a state of dementia. In an 1848 medical textbook, reference was made to similar cases around Philadelphia, recorded by Charles Gorman, and known locally as the 'magrums'. John Christian Lund reported the same disorder affecting two families in Saetersdalen, Norway, in one instance involving four generations. The locals used the terms *rykka* (or 'jerks') or else the *arvesygen* ('hereditary disease').

In 1633 Simon Huntington, a grocer from Norwich, England, settled in Norwich, Connecticut. The generations followed. Hunt-ington's great-great-great grandson Abel qualified as a doctor and moved to East Hampton, Long Island. His son, George Lee, born in 1811, joined his father's practice. His grandson George quali-fied at New York in 1872 and joined his father and grandfather in Long Island. This is as good an example as you are likely to get of the hereditary nature of the medical craft.

George Huntington chose the topic of Sydenham's chorea—otherwise known as St Vitus' Dance: a series of jerky, twitchy movements of the legs, arms and face—for his MD thesis. The final paragraph referred to a number of East Hampton families whose members had a syndrome of jerking movements and mental disorder. The locals referred to 'that disorder' as a stigma, attrib-uted to a curse which had befallen a remote ancestor who had mocked the suffering of Christ upon the cross. The Long Island cases were the offspring of a man named Mulfoot or Mulford, who had been born and brought up in the Massachusetts–Connecticut area. All three of the Huntington doctors were familiar with the cases and, indeed, the thesis manuscript has marginal notes pencilled in by the father and grandfather.

With the discovery of other affected families in North America and the world, there was great interest raised in the genealogy of what had become known by then as Huntington's. In the sixteenth and seventeenth centuries, Essex and Suffolk in England were key areas for the persecution of witches. It is clear that among the persecuted victims were the insane, the syphilitic and those with Huntington's disease, the convulsive twitching and jerking regarded as irrefutable proof of demoniac possession.

In 1630 Herbert Pelham, the lord of the manor at the village of Bures, Essex, was a wealthy puritan who decided to emigrate to the American colonies, paying the passage of the villagers who accompanied him. The party included three young men and their wives from the adjoining village of Bures St Mary, on the border between Suffolk and Essex. The three men, and possibly their wives, were all related. It appears that a Mary Haste was the parent of at least two of these men and almost certainly of all three.

On the voyage the three couples were in constant trouble on account of their behaviour, in marked contrast to the other Puritans. After three months the Puritans landed in Salem, Massachusetts. Once settled in the colony, this pattern continued; the men were regularly jailed; intermarriage, illegitimacy and incest were common; seven of the women were indicted and punished, some burned at the stake on the grounds of practising witchcraft. The transcripts of their trials has frequent references to 'wild, uninhibited grimacing and contortions' which was assumed to confirm demoniacal possession but was, in reality, the expression of their neurological disorder.

The descendants of Mary Haste were responsible for the largest cluster of cases of Huntington's in America. Another cluster of cases in New England arose in the Welles family, the descendants of Nathaniel Welles, a prosperous tradesman who also migrated to America in 1630. Welles came from Colchester, sixteen kilometres (ten miles) from Bures St Mary, the home of Mary Haste. Cases moved to the mid-West, others as far away as Oregon, California and Hawaii.

Once Huntington's disease achieved recognition, it was found in almost every country; the only group who appear to rarely have it are Jews. In Great Britain affected family groups have been identified in Avoch (in Ross-shire), Cornwall and Northamptonshire. The majority of cases in Australia arose from a Miss Cundick, who left Somerset in 1848 to live in Tasmania. Twice widowed, she had had children to both husbands, passing the gene on to them and their descendants, some of whom later settled in New South Wales.

In 1685 a French Huguenot family from Monbeliard fled persecution to South Carolina, later settling in the village of Tatamagouche, Nova Scotia, Canada. Many family members developed Huntington's disease. In Ontario, several groups of cases can be traced to a migrant who left England in the early eighteenth century. A serial killer in Toronto had eleven close relatives with Huntington's chorea.

In the second decade of the twentieth century, when eugenics was flourishing in the United States, an economist who investigated the 4600 descendants of Mary Haste went so far as to point out that had one parent of the three brothers who came in the seventeenth century from England been excluded (or sterilised) 'the United States would have been spared nine hundred cases of one of the most dreadful diseases that man is liable to', at a cost to the taxpayer of four hundred dollars a year, going on to point out that this would not have occurred had the rules prohibiting the entry of cattle been applied to humans. This may be a fine, if somewhat rebarbative example of the worst kind of vulgar social Darwinism, but it ignores the fact that not every member of an at-risk family gets the disease, and the United States benefited from the talents of several leading educators, surgeons, State senators, Congressmen, and ministers of religion—all with Huntington's. But the most important example is Woody Guthrie.

The great neurologist Macdonald Critchley said that Huntington's disease was 'the true American tragedy'. Its genetic qualities made it a disease which was naturally liable to increase in numbers, rather than decrease. The prevalence of the disease is approximately five cases per one hundred thousand people. It is seen less commonly among those of non-European ancestry, and is rare in Jews. Typically, onset is in the thirties or forties, although onset as early as age two and well into the eighties has been reported.

Huntington's is a degenerative brain disorder characterised primarily by neuronal death in the part of the brain known as the basal ganglia, which regulate movement and position. Patients develop a dementia where the tissue below the grey matter shrinks away.

Neurological abnormalities include involuntary movements (chorea and dystonia) and disorders of voluntary movement (gait disorders, impairment of eye movements, speech and swallowing). These symptoms worsen gradually over ten to fifteen years, leading to severe disability. The rapid and involuntary movements known as chorea, the hallmark of the disease, tend to worsen in the middle stages of the illness and then decrease as the patient becomes more debilitated. Dystonia, contraction of large muscle groups, worsens as the disease progresses. Later symptoms include progressive slowness and rigidity of posture.

Juvenile-onset cases (before the age of twenty) have little chorea, making diagnosis difficult without knowing the family history. The progression of the disease is very rapid, in contrast to patients with late-onset Huntington's who have a slowly progressive illness with cognition relatively spared.

Psychiatric symptoms may occur in early, middle or late stages of Huntington's disease; they can thus predate the onset of motor impairment. Psychiatric symptoms add greatly to the burden of caregivers and distress suffered by patients, often the chief factor in the decision to institutionalise patients. Psychotic symptoms are seen in three to twelve per cent of patients. Depression can occur at any point in the illness and there are much higher suicide rates than in the rest of the population.

Woody Guthrie died from complications of Huntington's. While his life may have been relatively short, it was extremely full in the personal and artistic realms. He was obsessively driven in his personal life, having three wives, nine children, and travelling nearly continuously from age fifteen until his hospitalisation in 1954.

How much did Huntington's disease contribute to his creativity? The impulsive and uninhibited personality associated with Huntington's was integral to Guthrie's creative output. In addition to writing countless songs, Guthrie spent a lot of time at the typewriter manically committing to paper everything from children's songs to obscene letters. His penchant for reworking songs and improvising made him a brilliant entertainer. His daughter Nora commented that he never played the same song the same way twice. His free-flowing lyrical style shifted so gradually into the obscene ramblings of his later writing that the change was nearly imperceptible. Loose associations and neologisms were always present in his work, increasing over time.

Though it is difficult to know when or where Guthrie first wrote, heard, recorded or plagiarised many of his songs, in the five years preceding the emergence of his symptoms, his memorable artistic output was greatest.

As the condition took greater hold of him, the piece 'Hoodoo Voodoo' shows how his writing was affected, with a predominance of clang associations, loss of meaning and possible intrusion of odd preoccupations:

> Jinga jangler, tingalingle,
> Picture on a bricky wall

Hot and scamper, foamy lather, huggle me close
Hot breeze, old cheese,
Slicky slacky fishy tails
Brush my hair and kissle me some more.

It is therefore tempting to attribute his seemingly pressured writing to incipient Huntington's—but, as with any other brain disorder, it can be difficult to separate a person's personality from manifestations of the illness.

If there is ever an example of anatomy being destiny, it is the turbulent life of Woody Guthrie. He did not ask for the condition, fighting off the persistent fear that he had inherited his mother's curse. Despite this, his innate talent, which many regard as near-genius, was a sustaining force in his life. In its early years, Huntington's interacted with his natural talent to facilitate the expression of his music and writing, ramping up his output, but slowly becoming dominant until it swamped his capacity to create. What we are left with is a priceless musical legacy that we have not yet fully explored. This is all Woody, and nothing less.

TREBITSCH LINCOLN

> He smiled understandingly—much more
> than understandingly. It was one of
> those rare smiles with a quality of eternal
> reassurance in it, that you may come across
> four or five times in life. It faced —or
> seemed to face—the whole external world
> for an instant, and then concentrated on
> you with an irresistible prejudice in your
> favour. It understood you just as far as you
> wanted to be understood, believed in you
> as you would like to believe in yourself,
> and assured you that it had precisely the
> impression of you that, at your best,
> you hoped to convey.

F. SCOTT FITZGERALD, *THE GREAT GATSBY*

Among his large oeuvre, Woody Allen's 1983 movie *Zelig* is possibly the most charming. Filmed in black and white, it is the story of Leonard Zelig, known as the Chameleon Man for his ability to take on the personality of people around him and even change his appearance. Zelig comes under the care of a dedicated psychiatrist, Dr Eudora Fletcher, at Bellevue Hospital. She eventually succeeds in bringing him out of himself through hypnosis, they become close and form a relationship. In Depression-era America, Zelig is a celebrity but, subjected to a cascade of claims for paternity, fraud and deception, he disappears. Eudora is devastated but sees a newsreel of Zelig at a Nazi rally. She goes to Germany. Zelig, sitting on the platform behind Hitler, recognises her, they reunite and make a dramatic escape, flying a biplane across the Atlantic, and return to America to live happily ever after.

The movie took many years to be completed, in part because of the technical difficulties of incorporating historical news footage into the contemporary scenes. The end result is a triumph of the auteur. The movie is redolent with Allen touches. There are many overtones of his early film *Take the Money and Run*, portraying the hapless life of a schmendrick with a series of witty jokes and double entendres, cameo interviews of New York intellectuals and direct-to-camera monologues.

The Zelig character had a disturbance of identity. In clinical situations, this is found in personality disorders, depersonalisation states, fugue state, temporal lobe epilepsy and the psychoses. Part of the personality attaches itself to another person, making the person believe he is going through the actions of another person. Psychoanalysts saw this as the self allowing 'pseudo-personalities' to emerge from which a patient could continually wander from one to another. The 'as-if personality' involved a completely passive attitude to the environment with a highly plastic readiness to pick up signals from the outer world and to mould behaviour accordingly. Their identification with what other people are thinking and feeling rendered the person capable of the greatest fidelity and the basest perfidy.

The problem with psychological explanations is that these concepts cannot be proven, regardless of how intellectually appealing the hypothesis. Disorders of the brain, on the other hand, have the advantage of providing a link between behaviour and pathology. People with frontal lobe damage have a poor understanding of environmental, social and physical stimuli associated with loss of inhibition. They can imitate forms of behaviour in the social context of the situation without the intention (or purpose) to do so, and seem incapable of inhibiting this response. What is known as *utilisation* behaviour occurs when the patient automatically searches for and utilises objects or other stimuli in the environment. Anterograde amnesia (loss of memory before the event, such as a head injury) as a result of frontal lobe damage allows the person to 'forget' the appropriated character and adopt a new identity as soon as the external conditions change.

Zelig would have been regarded as no more than an interesting social phenomenon until 2007 when Italian neurologists Giovannina Conghiglia, Gennarg Della Rocca and Dario Corossi encountered a patient demonstrating what they called the Zelig phenomenon. A university graduate, politician and amateur actor, age sixty-five, was admitted with signs of fronto-temporal dementia. His symptoms included severe memory problems, irritability, repetitiveness and disinhibition. His doctors described 'a peculiar form of behaviour' manifesting in an amazing capacity to imitate the behaviour of people around him. The patient stated a number of times that he practised the same profession as his doctors. In discussion with the psychologists, he claimed that he too was a psychologist. Asked precise questions about the competence of a medical doctor, he would respond without hesitation, although using vague arguments.

Claiming to be a cardiologist, he announced:

> *I've lots of patients, and my fees aren't excessive ... some of my patients do not pay because they're poor. I've been working for such a long time ... when I have any doubt regarding a difficult case I refer to my superior. I graduated a long time ago ... my salary is comparable with that of my colleagues.*

The patient's behaviour arose from impairment of the frontal lobe resulting in the loss of inhibition. This led to loss of control of his usual identity and consequent 'attraction' towards a social role in his immediate environment. He became 'captured' by the interaction with the medical doctor, psychologist or other staff, then assuming their character.

The mythical character Zelig, the authors wrote, affected a psychological (and even physical) transformation from the context in which he found himself. In recognition of the analogy, the disturbance of behaviour was described as a 'Zelig-like syndrome'.

But who was Leonard Zelig, or rather, who was he based on? Allen, often reticent about his movies, said that Zelig was not based on a known character, but an imaginary concept of someone trying to assimilate in a hostile world.

Several years later came the publication of Bernard Wasserstein's book, *The Secret Lives of Trebitsch Lincoln*, about a man who would seem to be the perfect model for Leonard Zelig. The story Wasserstein disinterred is a masterful historical effort. Ignácz Trebitsch, alias Ignatius Trebitsch Lincoln, was among many other things sometime author, fraudster, Anglican curate, Hungarian Jew, German revolutionary, spy, journalist, international outlaw, Chinese cult leader, the Abbot Chao Kung of Shanghai, and British MP for the constituency of Darlington. His heroes were Abraham Lincoln—whose surname he would assume—Disraeli and Napoleon.

Described as a short, swarthy, heavy-accented fantasist and exhibitionist, he radiated an astounding self-confidence, charm and fluency and possessed a nimble mind and near-perfect ability to first find, then convince, the influential and the powerful. Never shy of publicising his cause, Trebitsch wrote articles for *The New York Times* and published a dubious biography. The diplomatic archives of the time are packed with documents detailing the official frustrations and difficulties of the police, intelligence and government officials in their attempts to nail Trebitsch. His activities caused such consternation that at different times they drew in such diverse individuals as Lloyd George, J. Edgar Hoover and Heinrich Himmler.

Ignácz Trebitsch, as he started off, was the son of a Jewish businessman, born in 1879 in Paks, a small town in the south of Hungary. When he was young, his father moved to Budapest, lost a fortune on stock market speculation and plunged his family into poverty. Whether this indicates that his father was just a bad businessman or prone to reckless behaviour is not known.

His son, however, had no such restraints. All his life, Trebitsch was unscrupulous in the acquisition of money and profligate in its spending. A trail of stolen watches marked his early career. Leaving home at eighteen, after a brief taste of journalism in Budapest, Trebitsch enrolled in the Royal Hungarian Academy of Dramatic Art but dropped out twice and was investigated by the police over a series of petty thefts. Lured by the prospect of Queen Victoria's Jubilee (he claimed), but pursued for a gold watch and chain he purloined, Trebitsch emerged in Whitechapel, London, where historian Charles van Onselen suggests that he may have rubbed elbows with Joseph Lis, the notorious sex slaver.

Following a different path to most of the Whitechapel Jews, Trebitsch converted to Christianity. He joined a society for the conversion of Jews to Christians, but soon displayed the fallibility that required considerable Christian forgiveness. He stole jewellery from the wife of the man who converted him, prompting this apt assessment: 'He is thoroughly bad, a genius, and very attractive, but taking the crooked way always for choice.'

Finding life in religious hostels in London and Bristol not greatly to his taste, and purloining another gold watch, Trebitsch went back to Hungary. From there, he moved to Germany to marry the daughter of a Lutheran former sea captain in Hamburg who had an illegitimate child. Trebitsch, who read prayers in the family, graciously accepted her as his wife for the sake of her dowry. His wife was to spend most of her life trailing her husband from one country to the next, somehow managing to remain loyal.

Becoming a minister, Trebitsch was sent by the Presbyterians to Canada to do mission work among immigrant Jews in

Montreal. However, the Presbyterians were poor so he organised a takeover by the richer Anglicans. The Archbishop of Montreal, as gullible as his flock, prophesied that Trebitsch would one day be his successor. This illusion vanished when the directors monitored his use of the mission finances too closely. Without having converted a single Jew, the death of his father-in-law provided an excuse for Trebitsch to return to Europe to collect the inheritance, along the way adding another gold watch to his assets.

On his return to the United Kingdom, Trebitsch made the acquaintance of the Archbishop of Canterbury, who appointed him as a curate in Appledore, Kent, his last ecclesiastical post. Then he had his first stroke of luck. He met Quaker Benjamin Seebohm Rowntree, the chocolate and cocoa millionaire and prominent Liberal Party member. Rowntree offered him a position as his private secretary. For Trebitsch, this was the equivalent of hitting the golden lode. The Rowntrees, like other Victorian Quaker families, had a commitment to doing good works among the poor and reading the word of God. Completely taken in by Trebitsch, Rowntree lent him £10,000 (the equivalent of more than $900,000 today). From 1906 to 1909, Trebitsch had a handsome salary and unquestioned expenses, staying in the luxury he thought he deserved.

Then followed what Wasserstein described as 'one of the oddest aberrations in British political history'. Three Quaker families—Pease, Backhouse and Rowntree—dominated Darlington; the Rowntrees owned the influential paper, *The Northern Echo*. Liberalism was in the ascendant and, with Rowntree's support, Trebitsch, not yet thirty, was nominated in 1909 as Liberal candidate for the parliamentary constituency of Darlington in County Durham. To qualify as a candidate, Trebitsch had to falsify his naturalisation date, a small matter for him. From this point, he was known as Trebitsch-Lincoln or simply Lincoln. 'His most intimate friends have the strongest faith in his future as a statesman', Rowntree wrote in *The Northern Echo*.

Endorsed by Winston Churchill and David Lloyd George, Lincoln campaigned essentially on a xenophobic and animal rights basis, alleging that German tariff laws, of the kind his Unionist opponents advocated, were starving the Germans into eating their dogs.

In the election of January 1910, Trebitsch won Darlington by twenty-nine votes, beating the sitting Unionist Pike Pease, whose family had held the seat for decades. Trebitsch, not one to restrain his gloating, said, 'They have brought out a poster in Darlington—The foreigner's got my job. Well, he has got it. I am the foreigner; I have got Pike Pease's job.'

Trebitsch's parliamentary career was destined to be short. His maiden speech was delivered to an empty Chamber. His fellow members, it is reported, regarded him as an object of mirth, mocking his foreign accent. Lincoln used Rowntree's funds to invest in the Austrian Petroleum Syndicate. Showing something of his father's ability to pick a good share, the syndicate collapsed and the Austrians informed Earl Grey, the Foreign Secretary, of Lincoln's record as a petty thief.

Having blown all his money, Trebitsch was facing bankruptcy. The response around him was inevitable; the Liberals and Quakers washed their hands of him. Rowntree sued him for forging his signature to raise money. Insolvent and under pressure, Trebitsch resigned the Liberal nomination weeks before the second general election of 1910; Darlington returned to its old allegiance. Never one to let setbacks get him down, Trebitsch later wrote in his autobiography *Revelations of an International Spy*, 'I was a great success.' He established his family at Watford with a nurse, butler, cook, housemaid, charwoman and gardener. A year later, fortunate to escape criminal charges, he settled his debts for five shillings in the pound.

Trebitsch had hardly started. To make money, he established a scheme to lure investment into the oil wells of Galicia in Poland and Romania. His new string of oil companies having failed, he became the Post Office's censor of Hungarian mail at the Mount Pleasant Sorting Office in London. They fired him after he wrote comments on the letters. He altered letters stolen from the National Liberal Club to authorise payments to his account, leading to an investigation by Scotland Yard. He covered the Balkan Wars of 1912–13 as a foreign correspondent, becoming a spy for Bulgaria. Realising he could double his income, he offered his espionage services to Turkey, Bulgaria's enemy. The Bulgarian secret service soon discovered his treachery, throwing him into a Sofia prison. His release was brought about by the chief of German military intelligence, possibly because he was already a spy for the Germans or agreed to spy for them once he returned to England.

From this point, Trebitsch's life became peripatetic, his trajectory erratic and he latched on to politicians, financiers and prominent people as circumstances dictated.

In the years leading up to the outbreak of World War I he was involved in a variety of failed commercial endeavours, living for a time in Bucharest, hoping to make money in the oil industry. Back in London with no money, he offered his services to the British government as a spy. Turned down, he went to the Netherlands to make the same proposition to the Germans, who responded like their British counterparts. Both intelligence services correctly held the same view: Lincoln was only interested in the money and would sell to the highest bidder.

By 1914, he was penniless and wanted on fraud charges in London and Bucharest. The onset of the war brought the opportunity to establish himself in the role in which he became world-famous: international spy. He returned to London to persuade 'Blinker' Hall, the Director of Naval Intelligence, to offer a copy of the German code that he had obtained, offering to lure their fleet to destruction. It was immediately evident that he had made up the code himself and was acting as a double agent. After stalling a few weeks, Hall told him that 'the sooner you turn your back on England, the better it will be for you'.

Hall demanded his arrest, and gave orders that the ports be blocked to prevent his escape. Trebitsch, whose self-image was of a man with a character as unblemished as the purest snow, was deeply shocked that someone failed to trust him. The next day, he sailed for the United States on board the *Philadelphia*, arriving in New York on 9 February 1915.

He lived off several German women before inflicting himself on his brother, who promptly volunteered for the US Army. Obsessed with gaining revenge on Britain, Trebitsch offered his services to the German military attaché, Franz von Papen. Papen was instructed by Berlin to have nothing to do with him, whereupon Trebitsch sold his 'story' to *The New York World Magazine*, which published under the banner headline 'Revelation of I. T. T. Lincoln, Former Member of Parliament Who Became a Spy'. A reviewer described his piece as 'a spitball of wastepaper and spleen at his former European employers'.

He next tried his luck with the FBI, but unsurprisingly failed to convince them that he could decrypt German codes. To stifle Lincoln's propaganda, the British government demanded his extradition to face the criminal charge of forgery. The Americans proceeded to facilitate his extradition to Britain. Arrested on 4 August 1915, he escaped, holding a press conference on the run, engaging hundreds of New York policemen in the operation to recapture him. He was extradited, charged with forgery and served three years in prison, and was held in a cell next to the Irish spy Sir Roger Casement, who was awaiting a less happy fate.

Released in 1919, Trebitsch was deprived of his British nationality and deported to Hungary where the communist leader Béla Kun was conducting a reign of terror. He promptly left for Germany, declared himself an ardent monarchist and gave public speeches urging the restoration of the Kaiser. The postwar chaos provided a fertile ground for Trebitsch to be involved in espionage and plotting subversion, particularly in Germany. Despite the handicap of being Jewish, he managed to inveigle himself into extreme right-wing—and highly anti-Semitic—groups. He attached himself to Colonel Max Bauer, the political agent of the German wartime military leader, General Erich Ludendorff. Bauer had close ties to Adolf Hitler.

Trebitsch sought interviews with the ex-Kaiser and the ex-Crown Prince, but was rebuffed. On 13 March 1920 Trebitsch, with Wolfgang Kapp, General Ludendorff and General Walther von Lüttwitz were instigators of the Kapp Putsch (more accurately the Kapp–Lüttwitz Putsch) in Berlin aimed at overthrowing the Weimar Republic. 'Power is in our hands', he said, taking office as head of Press and Propaganda.

The *putsch* collapsed within days. Then occurred one of the most bizarre intersections in history. Trebitsch, the last to leave the Chancellery building, met two men who had flown up from Munich too late to be involved: Dietrich Eckart (an early Nazi supporter) and Adolf Hitler—the two greatest deceivers of their time coming face to face.

In 1922 Trebitsch went to China. Undeterred by the minor issue of not speaking the language, Trebitsch was soon offering advice to Szechwan warlords. Disguised as a Buddhist monk, he boasted he would get Central Asian Buddhists and Muslims to overthrow British rule: 'When you hear of a great religious revival there, think of I.T.T.Lincoln.'

Barred from Germany, Trebitsch returned to Europe, using Budapest as his base. He stayed in the spying game, winning the confidence of intelligence agencies, then stealing their documents and offering to sell them to other governments, always one step ahead of their outrage or interdiction. With Bauer and General Ludendorff, he organised a 'White International' to recreate a Greater Germany, a Greater Hungary and a Bolshevik-free Russia. This soon collapsed. He was arrested in Vienna, sentenced to four months in jail and deported from Austria.

Going to Italy in 1924, he joined Mussolini's Black Shirts and was reported to be involved in the abduction and murder of the Socialist Deputy Giacomo Matteotti, a politician opposing Mussolini. The Italian police charged Trebitsch with complicity in Matteotti's murder but, leading a charmed life as usual, he fled the country, going first to Chile, then to China again, where he served as an intelligence agent, working under the direction of Chiang Kai-Shek's spymaster, Morris 'Two-Gun' Cohen.

On 27 October 1925, still in China, Trebitsch had a mystical vision in the Astor House Hotel in Tientsin: 'I made the great renunciation, I quitted the world, I forced the doors of the lunatic asylum open and—walked out'. In the face of seemingly impossible obstacles, Trebitsch reinvented himself as, of all things, a Buddhist. He was ordained a Monk, and on his return to China, raised to the rank of Bodhisattva. He shaved his head, enduring painful branding of symbols on his scalp, wore robes, and declared himself the Abbot Chao Kung. He announced that he was preparing to spend his last days in pious contemplation in China. He later promoted himself to 'The Venerable'.

In a tragic interlude, Trebitsch's son, John Lincoln, was charged in England with murdering a travelling salesman whose house he was robbing. Found guilty, he was sentenced to hang. In March 1926 a petition was mounted that the execution be delayed for a few days to allow the condemned man's father to arrive from Ceylon, where he had surfaced. When Trebitsch reached the Netherlands, he was informed by the British Legation at The Hague that he would under no circumstances be allowed to enter England and the judicial execution proceeded without him.

Obsessed by Tibet, the capital of Buddhism, Trebitsch intended to mobilise all Asia to overthrow the British Empire—unless the British Empire made amends to him. He went with ten disciples from Canada to England, was locked up in Liverpool for five days and sent back to Canada. The disciples followed him back to China, where they were reduced to living in conditions of monastic slavery. After numerous unsuccessful attempts to travel to Tibet, Trebitsch established his own monastery in Shanghai. He set himself up as a guru to gullible Westerners who wanted to explore the mystic Eastern religions. All initiates were required to hand over their possessions to Abbot Chao Kung. Trebitsch being Trebitsch, there are reports of him sexually accosting the female acolytes and nuns.

When Shanghai fell to Japan, he played off the Chinese Nationalists against the Japanese. In 1937, with his unerring instinct for sniffing out where the power was held, he committed himself to the Japanese, advising the Chinese to surrender to the Japanese as 'a chivalrous, well-intentioned and spiritually superior race'.

Following the outbreak of war in Europe in 1939, Trebitsch, with characteristic humility, issued a statement that the British, French, German and Russian governments should resign or 'the Tibetan Buddhist Supreme Masters . . . will unchain forces and powers whose very existence are unknown to you and against whose operations you are consequently helpless'. When the four leading governments of Europe failed to comply with his orders, he sought help from the German intelligence service to go to Tibet. He explained that he was authorised to speak for 'the Sages of Tibet' who formed 'a sort of unofficial world government'. He intended to broadcast from Tibet to get the Buddhists of the East to rise against British influence in the area. Colonel Josef Meisinger, the Gestapo chief in the Far East, supported this millenary madness. Meisinger, later known as the 'Butcher of Warsaw', boasted that he trusted no one: 'Sometimes I even have doubts about myself!' He was executed in 1947 for war crimes.

Always keen to push his luck as far as he could, Trebitsch suggested that he be sent to Berlin to meet the Führer, 'The pseudo-messiah of the Third Reich'. When they got together, 'Three of the wise men of Tibet would appear out of the wall'. The matter was referred to at the highest levels in Berlin, where both Heinrich Himmler and Rudolf Hess were enthusiastic, but after the latter fled to Scotland in May 1941, Hitler put an end to the scheme and Trebitsch's involvement with the Nazis ceased.

Although he abandoned Judaism in his youth, Trebitsch's last interview was conducted with *Unzer Lebn*, the Yiddish-Russian-English newspaper published by Jewish refugees in Shanghai in July 1943, a few months before his death. The reporter describes him residing in the Shanghai YMCA, serene in his monk's robes. Trebitsch, always keen to solve the world's problems, explained his stand on Jewish issues. He had devised a plan to solve Jewish homelessness by settling Jewish refugees on Buddhist-owned territory near Shanghai, 'proposing to build there a Model Settlement, a Tel-Aviv in miniature'.

On 7 October 1943 Radio Tokyo announced that the revered Abbot Chao Kung had died after an unsuccessful operation. Another view is that the Japanese learned Trebitsch had concluded that Japan would lose the war and had gone back to Chiang Kai-Shek to spy for China. There were rumours that he lived for a few more years in Japan—but that is the end of the tale.

Trebitsch Lincoln's Brain

Who was Ignácz Timothy Trebitsch-Lincoln, the perpetual vaudeville act on three continents? Did he even know this himself? His identity concealed behind veil after veil of obfuscation and fantasy, Trebitsch's completely pliant personality immediately overpowered everyone he directed himself at, enabling him to insert himself into the highest levels of three separate national élites: the British, the German and the Chinese. Constantly changing his name, his nationality, his religion, nearly always on the run, Trebitsch made no attempt to keep a low profile. Carrying dozens of passports in different names, he slipped through the nets, cast off his pursuers, escaped from prisons, and reappeared in another country in the eye of the next international storm. The diplomats, the press, the police forces of the world kept believing that they could close his file—but constantly failed.

Trebitsch was utterly self-obsessed, without inhibition in the steps he would take to achieve his goals, unconcerned by any laws, regulations, prohibitions or sanctions to bring him to account, indifferent to the consequences of his actions and, above all else, grandiose to the point of delusional in believing that there were no restraints in what he could aspire to.

Trebitsch began his career of perpetual deception as a Christian missionary, but it seemed this was pure opportunism. In his examination for ordination as an Anglican deacon, 'he disgraced himself in nearly every paper' and was turned down. The ascent to Buddhism seems to have been different, more likely driven by his mania, not opportunism, and the only example of genuine sincerity on his part. His Buddhist theology was decidedly shaky, but it was convincing enough to lure unsophisticated Westerners to his cause, if not assure some of those within the spiritual community.

Was Trebitsch mad? Bernard Wasserstein says Trebitsch's religiosity was an expression of his messianic drive, akin to other Jewish pseudo-messiahs, such as Sabbatai Zvi or Jacob Frank. Wasserstein states that the latter part of Trebitsch's life was driven by a severe manic-depressive psychosis that produced gloom, pessimism and paranoia on the one hand, and omnipotence, euphoria, gregariousness and elation on the other. The mood cycle found expression in periods of withdrawal and despair, followed by manic phases of hyperactivity, prophetic claims and grandiose political delusions.

Despite the mood swings, Trebitsch was still able to succeed as a confidence trickster of extraordinary capability. The idea that a Jew of humble Hungarian origins, at the time in which he lived, should be variously a member of the British Parliament, a member of the German Government (albeit an extremely short-lived coup) and a figure of note in the Buddhist hierarchy in China is fantastic beyond belief—but true. This says as much about the world in which he lived as it does about his remarkable gift for sensing what people wanted to believe.

The most extraordinary aspect of the Trebitsch story is his symmetry with Adolf Hitler, with whom he had intersected in Berlin in 1920 and sought to meet in 1941. The two men came from the same world: Habsburg Empire provincials, each heading to their respective metropoles (Budapest and Vienna) to fail their examinations (Trebitsch in drama, Hitler in art), then seeking fortune further afield before exploiting the disarray that followed the German collapse of 1918. Hitler believed that he was a great thinker and a great statesman, dominating and overpowering all men by his personality. Trebitsch had the personality, but not the politics, to be a dictator in the age of monsters.

Will we see another Trebitsch again? Aside from the wretched fate of his immediate family, those who were taken in by Trebitsch were scarcely victims. Whether it was power, money, proselytising, spying or spiritual salvation they were seeking, everyone he dealt with was seeking to take something and he gave them all exactly what they deserved. There are worse kinds of madness to have and, from Hitler down, many of them had it.

ARTHUR INMAN

Another damned fat book, Mr Gibbon?
Scribble, scribble, scribble, eh Mr Gibbon?

ATTRIBUTED TO KING GEORGE III, UPON RECEIVING A VOLUME OF
EDWARD GIBBON'S BOOK

Arthur Inman may well be the most prolific writer in history. His seventeen-million word, one hundred and fifty-five-volume diaries, all written by hand from 1919 to 1963, provide an extraordinarily detailed record of events and activities of the reclusive and eccentric US poet over four decades. By way of comparison, it is worth noting that Marcel Proust's magnum opus *Á la recherche du temps perdu* (*In Search of Lost Time*) is one and a half million words, a mere eleven per cent of Inman's output.

Arthur Crew Inman, born in 1895, came from an affluent Atlanta family. His grandfather, Samuel Inman, was the largest cotton merchant in the world. His neurasthenic mother, beset by fatigue and the conviction of serious illness, kept a diary and, like her son, was prone to advise and counsel others. Inman had an unhappy childhood, did not relate to his parents and was bullied at boarding school. His father's injunctions against masturbation haunted him for the rest of his life. He went to college but only lasted two years before having a breakdown in 1916. The thirty-four eminent doctors who examined him were unable to find any physical ailment.

A hypochondriac of extreme versatility, Inman was preoccupied with a range of complaints for which there was no evident cause. Among them was a sensitivity to light, so he restricted himself to a heavily draped bedroom, often spending whole days in the bathroom. If he was not photosensitive when he started, he certainly would have been so before long. His nemesis, however, was noise, to which he was abnormally sensitive. He suffered from nosebleeds, hay fever, arthritis, influenza, a slipping rib cage, migraine headaches, neck, collarbone, shoulder and testicular pain, chills, sweats, sores, rashes, stomach upsets requiring frequent pumping, throat infections and trouble with his coccyx.

Inman's search for relief led him to Boston. From 1915 he lived in five rented apartments at Garrison Hall, a somewhat seedy seven-storey residential hotel in St Botolph Street. Garrison Hall was scarcely salubrious accommodation for a young man from a wealthy southern family. It was described as the sort of place where you hired a woman in a room by the hour, instead of having lunch with her. Inman hired two servants and insisted on renting the flats above and below to shield himself from noise. An attempt to move to the country to escape the city's noise resulted in him taking pot shots at songbirds, and a rapid return to Garrison Hall.

His father supported him financially, and after his death in 1951 Inman inherited substantial assets. Inman paid a succession of staff to assist him as he lived out his life in darkened, soundproofed rooms as best he could. They cooked for him, massaged him, read to him, and told him about their lives. Some let him cuddle or caress them as well.

Ever seeking a solution for his ailments, Inman saw Ida Frome, an osteopath of unusual benevolence who attributed his symptoms to the misalignment of his bones. To ensure that he had a full understanding of how bones could be aligned, she obligingly undressed to explain female anatomy and 'many things . . . concerning procreation, allowing his hands "the freedom of her body"'. Inman, unsurprisingly, became a lifelong convert to osteopathy—a treatment based on the idea that diseases and disorders result from minuscule derangements of certain bones, derangements, incidentally, which only the osteopath can detect.

For the rest of his life Inman was treated by a team of osteopaths who realigned his bones and organs, pumped his stomach, administered enemas, and prescribed quack medications. Among these were massive amounts of bromide, which ensured that Inman continued to have problems from side effects including blurred vision, sleep disturbance, headaches, constipation, rashes and irritability. Recurrent enemas and stomach pumping caused a whole range of problems on their own. To these top- and bottom- end cocktails, Inman added barbiturates and alcohol, a potent combination that caused disturbed sleep, mood swings and hallucinations, if not delusions.

For as many as sixteen hours of a normal day he would stay in bed, when not sitting or reading in the bathroom. On his rare excursions outdoors, he would ride in a black 1919 Cadillac, the paint sanded down to prevent any light reflection. The analogy with the life of an urban vampire, albeit literary, is unavoidable.

Despite his reclusive lifestyle, Inman still managed to marry Evelyn Yates in 1923. Naturally, she was a constant subject in his entries, described as a 'treasured girl with a heart of gold', 'a pathetic little wren' and, less felicitously, 'as homely as a stump fence built in the dark, but she doesn't giggle all the time'.

As a poet, Inman was a failure. He published several volumes of his work, which sank like a stone. This example will show why poetasters need not lose sleep at night.

> *Ho, for the road once more!*
> *Ho, for the winged dawn!*
> *Ho, for the larks' clear flight,*
> *Carolling the day reborn!*
> *Ho, for the road once more!*
> *Ho, for the drifted skies!*
> *Ho, for the distant hills,*
> *Purple where sun set dies!*

From this point, Inman devoted himself to writing a diary, starting on 27 December 1918 with the words 'Am I now very much interested in Genghis Khan?' He had kept a line-a-day diary during his Haverford College days, but what began as 'a sort of safety valve' was to be the central obsession of his life above all else. He wrote in the diary daily. Into it he fed a stream of recollections, anecdotes, storylines, judgments, letters, reports, threats, newspaper clippings, dreams, jokes, apologies, history, speculation and despair; he, literally, fed his life into it, until only the diary remained.

Inman later came to regard his daily reports as 'a morning laxative, to get me started'—without which the diary could not exist. He frequently concedes that the enterprise is the 'laughable product of self-love and vanity', but cannot halt the interminable 'self-exploration and self-analysis'. His preoccupation with the matter is indicated by the statement that 'a diary expurgated and deleted is a eunuch of a diary'. Later he edited each volume, and had much of it typed and microfilmed. He constantly reviewed it and over the years would comment on his comments.

Inman would advertise in the newspapers for 'talkers', offering to pay one dollar an hour for people to discuss their lives with him. In an age before Oprah, *The Jerry Springer Show* and Facebook, many responded. In addition to hearing their stories, which went straight into his diary, Inman gave them advice. In this regard, he was emulating his mother. In no position to be critical or condescending, his recommendations were straightforward and sensible.

And he wrote. During the forty-four years in Garrison Hall, Inman's obsession was the diary. Every excursion outside his apartment, every tiff with his father, wife or staff, every stock and real-estate manipulation, the lives of people who worked for him or visited him, personalities and public events from the Great Crash of 1929 to World War II to the election of John Kennedy, the wreck of the Hindenburg, the only known 'petrified ham', the rise of Hitler, the stock market crash, the Depression, Mr Farnsworth's Flea Circus, his domestics' sex life, the Lindberg kidnapping, the Coconut Grove fire, Joe Louis' defeat of Max Baer, stockpiling during the war, the perils of a small-time dancer in Hollywood, the deaths of Joe McCarthy and Franklin Roosevelt, the Jackson Day benefit dinner for the Democrats. Everything found its way into his diary, but more than anything, his own life.

Inman was suicidal all of his life; there are fifty or so entries on death and suicide from 1912 until his death in 1963. He often slept with a pistol under his bed and berated himself for not using it on himself. For his first attempt, he lost his nerve at the last moment, a wavering which he regarded with contempt. While he longed for death, the diary kept him going; this was the most important role writing played in his life.

The tone of the diaries is deeply acerbic, if not misanthropic. Inman's lengthy shit-list included Jews, African Americans, Italians, English, Slavs, Irish, Franklin Roosevelt ('Roosie the Rat') and blue-eyed people. Not surprisingly, he became a fan of General MacArthur and Senator Joseph McCarthy, Mussolini and the Japanese war effort. He both detested and admired Adolf Hitler, but admired Mahatma Gandhi, the Chinese and the Japanese people.

At times he recognised where his misanthropy arose: 'I hate Jews, English, Roosevelt, life, myself.'

His xenophobia often did not survive direct contact. When he met someone from such a background, he had a good relationship with them, which changed his views for the better.

The diaries are a detailed account of Inman's sexual behaviour extending from World War I into the 1960s. Bedding a woman did not exempt her from being pilloried in his pages. Inman first had sexual intercourse in 1922 with a woman hired to read books to him. A late starter in exploring sex, his role model (improbably) was Casanova and he favoured 'younglings', probably an indication of regression from his upbringing. He disliked sexual intercourse, and sex with his wife (despite her instructions) was always unsatisfactory; he complained in his diary about impotence. The thing that seemed to most activate him was cuddling and caressing young women.

Of the women who came as talkers, he liked to lie naked in bed and have them describe their sexual feelings. He fondled a number of them and had sex with those who allowed it. He made no secret of this, Evelyn allowed him to do so and even offered to buy contraceptives. What is surprising is how many women were quite agreeable to this — possibly he played up his invalidity as a ploy.

As he got older, the women got younger. At the end of his life, sixteen-year-old Kathy Connor moved into his building. Inman described Kathy as his bewitching daughter and she responded in kind. He did fondle her, but they never had intercourse and she always spoke of him in glowing terms. When she went to work as a saleswoman, Inman would have her driven to work in his car. She was deeply distressed when he died.

Inman, endlessly manipulative and voyeuristic, encouraged his wife to socialise and experiment sexually with his osteopath Dr Pike. He only learned after Pike's death that they had had a prolonged affair, becoming so enraged that he and Evelyn separated for a while.

By 1963 Inman was getting older, he was drinking heavily and then had to deal with something he had avoided all his life: change. Construction commenced on the fifty-two storey Prudential Center, very close to Garrison Hall. For Inman, this was catastrophic. 'The Prudential Tower,' he wrote, 'is 28 stories into the sky, soon will be goosing God'. He moved to an apartment hotel in Brookline, Boston, but was bombarded by a series of new noises. He took an overdose in March 1963 and ended up in Massachusetts General Hospital. He was a wreck and could not go on much longer.

His last, virtually indecipherable, entry reads:

This is horrible beyond credible. Twelve divisions of migraines. Idetic images until I am harried and frightened into desperation. Can't see any more than is adequate to get around. Everything overgrown with hands and the imaginary element of substance visible.

Then, on 5 December 1963, he went into his toilet with a Colt revolver and shot himself.

Throughout the diaries, Inman cajoles, pleads and instructs his future editor as to how he would like the work published. Inman's overweening desire was for literary immortality. More than anything else, he had wanted his diary published.

The task of publishing the diaries was left to the long-suffering Evelyn. It took her and two other trustees of his estate until 1977 to secure Harvard University as a publisher. Professor Daniel Aaron, in what can only be described as a Herculean task, waded through all 155 volumes, taking over seven years to do so. Realising that few (probably, no) readers could deal with such a marathon task, Aaron distilled the collected works down to a mere 850,000 word, 1599 page two-volume abridged edition, weighing in at well over two kilograms, published in 1985 as *The Inman Diary: A Public and Private Confession.*

Aaron described the diaries as an account of Inman's day-to-day thoughts and activities, as well as a history of his early life in Atlanta, his family, his life in Boston, contemporary events, and his many eccentricities, opinions and prejudices. According to Aaron, Inman provided a unique record of the cultural, social, political, economic and sexual mores of his time:

'Of the 1000-plus talkers, Inman gave a distinctive outlet only sporadically touched upon in contemporary fiction.'

The only way Aaron could keep his own sanity during the marathon enterprise, was to write complaining, angry letters to his mega-verbose muse:

Arthur, you are a comic figure finally, and you are disgusting and sick, an embarrassment; you make your readers at times want to avert their gaze from your public writhing; and you are 'great' too in your persistence, which you call 'pertinacity.' You go on like some petty pharaoh building your pyramid, no matter what the cost in human felling. So hail, Arthur Inman (I say this more than merely facetiously), the Genghis Khan of Boston.

And, later, becoming a little frustrated: 'Oh, for God's sake, Arthur, SHUT UP!'

Displaying considerable restraint, Aaron called Inman a repulsive weakling, a voyeur and a sadist whose work was repellent. Despite this, Aaron conceded that Inman was capable of generosity and could be, over time, quite endearing. Even his wife only separated from him for one brief period until his death and seemed to have loved him. 'You have to read the whole diary through,' writes Aaron. 'You begin by despising him and end up sympathizing, even admiring him—while not embracing his attitudes.'

Pulitzer-prizewinning historian David Herbert Donald called it 'the most remarkable diary ever published by an American.' Other critics were less generous, describing Inman as repugnant, repellent, warped, selfishly indulgent and corrupt. Other compliments were that he was one of the most bizarre Americans in the history of the Republic and a psychological voyeur whose diaries were this 'monstrous fungoid growth'.

Despite this litany of disdain, to everyone's surprise the book went into at least three printings. A play followed and there was talk of a film. Today the 155 volumes of the diary are kept in the Houghton Library at Harvard. At long last, Inman had achieved his goal of literary fame, albeit not the type he may have had in mind.

Or perhaps so:

> *Do you find me repellent, sordid, amusing in a reverse sort of way? I shall never know. But reader, I do not want to lose your affection or your respect ... Do not esteem me less now that I have written truth in black and white'.*

Arthur Inman persisted in his goal to write a response to the times in which he lived, and he succeeded.

Arthur Inman's Brain

Writing is controlled by different parts of the brain. The organising and editing of ideas is controlled by the frontal lobes; the understanding and meaning of words is controlled by the temporal lobes; instincts and inspiration — the drive to write — arises deep in the brain from the limbic system. The physical motion of the hand is controlled by the cerebral cortex, which comprises part of the outer layer of the brain. Any injury or malfunction of these areas will affect the production or comprehension of writing. Medical disorders that can lead to temporary or permanent interference with writing include stroke, Parkinson's disease, liver failure and renal failure.

However, it is hypergraphia — the excessive production of writing — that attracts our interest, rather than meaningless doodles or repetitive phrases. One of the most well-known examples is Lewis Carroll, the author of *Alice in Wonderland*. In his lifetime he wrote over 98,000 letters in different formats, backwards and in curlique patterns such as the 'mouse tail'. Fyodor Dostoevski, who had temporal lobe epilepsy, wrote in a hypergraphic frenzy between seizures, often attempting to reconcile the fact that the periods when he experienced his ecstatic or religious aura in which the world around him was flooded with meaning was the result of his seizures. Robert Louis Stevenson's *The Strange Case of Dr Jekyll and Mr Hyde* was reportedly produced during a six-day, 6000-word cocaine spree. Stimulant drugs like cocaine and amphetamine stimulate the production of dopamine in the brain, exciting nerve activity in many centres.

A thirty-seven-year-old woman with Tourette syndrome who had wires surgically implanted into her frontal lobes to control the tics associated with the disorder, reported experiencing increased creativity and productivity in her work and personal activities when the electrical stimuli it produced were too frequent, a side effect that showed the extent to which creativity arose from the activity of the brain.

Virginia Ridley remained secluded in her home for twenty-seven years in Ringgold, Georgia, in the United States. When she died in bed of suffocation in 1997, her husband Alvin Ridley was charged with her imprisonment and murder. At the trial, her journal of ten thousand pages was submitted as evidence, showing that she had epilepsy and had remained housebound of her own will. It is likely she died as a result of a seizure and the hypergraphia indicated that she had temporal lobe epilepsy. The written evidence, from beyond the grave, resulted in her husband's acquittal.

The Reverend Robert Shields maintained a diary chronicling every five minutes of his life from 1972 until a stroke disabled him in 1997. The hypergraphic work filled eighty-one boxes and contained approximately thirty-eight million words.

What is believed to be the longest novel in existence, *The Story of the Vivian Girls,* was written by Henry Darger, who would (and should) have remained an otherwise obscure writer.

One of the most prolific composers of the twentieth century was American Alan Hovhaness. He always carried paper and pen on him and would compose daily in shopping malls, restaurants, even on buses. While he was young, he threw over 1000 of his compositions into the fireplace and at the time of his death in 2000, had penned around 500, most of which are published.

United States Senator Bob Graham kept meticulous records of his daily life. Between 1977 and 2003, Graham filled almost

4000 notebooks, recording such trivia as his weight, the clothes he wore, what and where he ate, the movie he and his daughter rented on the eve of his grandchild's birth, details of strangers he'd met at airports, and later serious matters of state. Each notebook, colour-coded by season, covered two to three days. When the company that made the notebooks closed, Graham bought up hundreds of the remaining stock. During the 2000 presidential race, Vice President Al Gore considered Graham as a running mate, but it was decided that Graham's constant jotting would be perceived by voters as eccentric, and the idea was dropped.

Graham maintained his notebooks were not diaries, but an efficient management system: 'I would rather have more detail than less,' he told *Time* magazine. The article quoted a source who suspected the suicide of Graham's half-brother spurred Graham to seek control and discipline through the notebooks.

Hypergraphia has been observed in eight per cent of patients with temporal lobe epilepsy, bipolar disorder (manic-depression), schizophrenia, fronto-temporal dementia and Asperger's syndrome. Seventy-three per cent of cases of hypergraphia have temporal lobe epilepsy.

What are we to make of Arthur Inman? That he had hypergraphia is not doubted, but could he have had temporal lobe epilepsy? This disorder can have bizarre seizures triggered by light and sound. Describing his breakdown in 1916, Inman wrote:

> *My whole nervous system went on strike. Specks of light zigzagged in front of me. My ears whistled ... The room began to circle with a curious rotary motion, very bewildering. I heard them talking, asking questions, but my ears were full of noise, and I could not understand. Suddenly ... I began to cry, long, racking sobs, without any end.*

The attacks continued, with Inman writing in 1919: 'I feel as though I were undergoing a change such as occurs in a violin string when the pitch is raised. This condition has occurred to me time after time.'

He later wrote:

> I live in a box where the camera shutter is out of order and the filter doesn't work and the film is oversensitive, and whatever that is beautiful or lovely by rights registers painfully or askew ... The simplest factors of existence, sunlight and sound, uneven surfaces, moderate distances, transgress my ineffective barriers and raid the very inner keep of my broken fortifications, so that there exists no sanctuary or fastness to which I can withdraw my sensitivity, neither awake nor asleep.

Inman had hypergraphia, pedantry, socially inappropriate behaviour, mental stickiness, obsessiveness, extreme views and reduced sexual drive associated with perverse outlets. These features are more than sufficient to confirm that he had the Geschwind syndrome.

An example of his stickiness is recounted by one of his osteopaths:

> I would be sailing off Cape Cod. The Coast Guard cutter would come up, They'd say they had just had a flash that Arthur Inman wanted to see me immediately. I'd have to call him, ship-to-shore, and tell him I couldn't come right away. He'd say, 'You have to come.' I'd tell him it would cost him a lot of money. He'd say, 'I don't care, just come.'

Neurologist David Bear and Libby Smith, an editor of the diaries, filled out the Bear-Fedio questionnaire (a diagnostic test for the Geschwind syndrome) for Inman. They were aware that Inman was addicted to two drugs originally used as anticonvulsants—

potassium bromide and barbiturates. Both gave Inman high marks for nearly all of the eighteen traits listed on the questionnaire. 'Compulsive attention to detail' described Inman's need to make lists and keep rigid schedules. His child-like behaviour and tendency to fly into rages translated into high scores in several categories: 'dependence', 'deepening of all emotions', 'humourlessness' and 'paranoia'. And his effort to chronicle his era demonstrated his 'grandiosity' and 'sense of personal destiny'. Their assumption was that this could only have been caused by temporal lobe epilepsy.

But can this diagnosis be justified? For the last four decades of his life, Inman was surrounded by his wife, his staff and his talkers. There are no reports of fits, blackouts, unusual behaviour or automatic behaviour found with epilepsy. He certainly had hypergraphia but there is no way of showing that it was due to epilepsy or any other medical condition.

Seen from a strictly psychiatric point of view, the description of Inman's condition would be what is now portentously listed as a somatoform disorder, the group of conditions dominated by a preoccupation with physical symptoms for which there is little or no explanation. Inman's life revolved around the conviction that he was seriously ill. Yet his symptoms were hardly life-threatening, but rather chronic, disabling and frustrating, shading over into anxiety, depression and sleep disturbance. If his symptoms had any distinguishing feature, they were largely neurological: photosensitivity, hyperacusis (excessive sensitivity to noise), lethargy, fatigue.

Added to this were his unusual, if not pathological, relationships with his immediate circle, his obsession with his health and symptoms and dependence on those he turned to for treatment, who had no hesitation in applying a range of quack treatments to reinforce his need for them, as much as his illness behaviour. In addition, the drugs he took caused far more problems than they ever cured.

Dr David Musto, in the appendix to the second volume of the diaries, states that Inman's constant treatment-seeking had a destructive effect on his emotional stability, judgment and physical health. Despite this, the illness allowed him to create a secure environment in which he was able to be productive along the lines he chose. This solved (or effectively deflected) so many of his emotional problems that he had little incentive to change his lifestyle.

Inman's condition was scarcely unique. It was recognised in biblical times and by the Greeks, but came into its own in the nineteenth century with the description by George Weir of neurasthenia. This was hardly a disorder of the working classes but a feature of the new affluence where people from middle- or upper-class backgrounds developed a range of such symptoms, often as an expression of the extreme social restrictions in their life, which is why women were so often affected, and led directly to the flourishing of hysterical disorders and the development of psychoanalysis.

It took root in Paris where the neurologist Jean-Martin Charcot paid considerable attention to the study of hysteria. It was one of his protégés, Paul Briquet, who took a novel path in classifying the condition. Whereas the usual approach was to look at the characteristic symptoms, such as fitting, paralysis or altered states of consciousness, Briquet counted the number and type of symptoms. He found a group who had well over twenty-five symptoms clustered in the neurological, gynaecological and abdominal areas. Most of these patients were women, they tended to have pathological relationships with their families and were usually addicted to prescription drugs, if not alcohol. They spent their lives seeking treatment and could often be recognised in the waiting room by their flamboyant appearance and melo-dramatic behaviour.

The disorder became known as Briquet's syndrome, and it would be difficult to find a primary care physician who has not encountered such a patient, even if they were not aware of the classification. It goes without saying that these patients were impossible to treat and died far more often of suicide, complications of treatment or drugs than their actual complaints.

When the psychiatric apparatchiks produced the DSM-III, the classification manual, Briquet's syndrome was unceremoniously dumped in the used-eponyms bin and replaced with the ghastly term of somatisation disorder, one of the somatoform disorders. Briquet's syndrome or somatisation disorder regardless, such cases have a considerable fascination. The individuals, mostly women, are often charming, intriguing and creative, if not accomplished. They have a condition that can be said to have as many cultural and social as biological and psychological features.

And it took a Russian writer, Ivan Goncharov, to bring to fictional life the state that Arthur Inman adopted all his adult life. In 1859 Goncharov published his novel *Oblomov*. Oblomov, the central character, represents the decadent state of the Russian upper class. Oblomov has an indulged childhood in which he is never required to do anything, and frequently has holidays from school. He fails to leave his bed for the first 150 pages of the novel and, after that, rarely leaves his room or bed. These limitations notwithstanding, he manages to meet Olga, they fall in love and plan to marry. However, she calls off the engagement after he endlessly delays the wedding to avoid putting his affairs in order.

Oblomov's slothful attitude dominates his lifestyle; he would conduct whatever business he could not avoid from his bed. His morning is described:

> *Therefore he did as he had decided; and when the tea had been consumed he raised himself upon his elbow and arrived within an ace of getting out of bed. In fact, glancing at his slippers, he even began to extend a foot in their direction, but presently withdrew it.*

Half-past ten struck, and Oblomov gave himself a shake. 'What is the matter?' he said vexedly. 'In all conscience 'tis time that I were doing something! Would I could make up my mind to — to —' He broke off with a shout of 'Zakhar!' whereupon there entered an elderly man in a grey suit and brass buttons ...

For a few moments Oblomov remained too plunged in thought to notice Zakhar's presence; but at length the valet coughed.

'What do you want?' Oblomov inquired. 'You called me just now, master?' 'I called you, you say? Well, I cannot remember why I did so. Return to your room until I have remembered.'

Later Oblomov has a child with his landlady, but they never marry and for the rest of his life he is taken care of by Agafia Pshenitsina. After many sad events, Oblomov dies of cerebral haemorrhage. Oblomov was philosophical about his situation, blaming 'Oblomovitis' as the cause of his demise.

'Oblomovism' was added to the Russian lexicon, became a byword in Russia for someone who withdrew from the world due to inertia, apathy, sloth or indecision, generalising to a sort of fatalistic laziness as an integral part of Russian character. To Polish physician Wladyslaw Wermut goes the credit for naming Oblomov syndrome in 1975 for the refusal to get out of bed.

This was no passing fashion, reaching as far as Vladimir Lenin who said, with characteristic restraint, in a speech in 1922: 'Russia has made three revolutions, and still the Oblomovs have remained . . . and he must be washed, cleaned, pulled about, and flogged.'

Arthur Inman chose a lifestyle that few of us could tolerate, let alone have the funding to support. We shall never know the cause of his hypergraphia, which in all likelihood may have just been, as Norman Geschwind said, the intellectual expression of heightened emotional affect that resulted from an overcharged temporo-limbic system. In the end, we are left with the image of Inman sitting in his bedclothes in a semi-darkened room, writing, writing, writing, year in and year out, decade after decade, an Oblomov to the end until he found he could no longer write out the outside world and took his own life.

> *I have tried to please no public of uncertain taste, for, Fate willing, my public will be the mysterious and uncertain one of the future. I have written down to no clique, no mob, no nation. I have held as my inspiration in inexorable judgement of an ideal posterity, the elite among them.*

HOWARD HUGHES

*I intend to be the greatest golfer in
the world, the finest film producer in
Hollywood, the greatest pilot in the world,
and the richest man in the world.*

*I'm not a paranoid deranged millionaire.
Goddamit, I'm a billionaire.*

HOWARD HUGHES

Engineer, industrial tycoon, aviator, philanthropist, film producer and director, Las Vegas entrepreneur, CIA partner and mysterious celebrity, Howard Hughes was one of the wealthiest men in the world. He set air-speed records, built the H-1 Racer and H-4 'Hercules' (the 'Spruce Goose') planes and developed Trans World Airlines. A maverick film producer, he made *Hell's Angels*, *Scarface* and *The Outlaw*.

Time magazine described Hughes as one of the world's richest, most imperious, capricious, outrageous, eccentric and powerful men, who spun a web that ensnared the state of Nevada, reached into the highest levels of the US Government and entwined with the Central Intelligence Agency. Arguably the most glamorous American of the twentieth century, Howard Hughes led what can only be termed a fabulous life until the compulsions that drove him became his downfall. But, as much as his motivation to achieve these goals revealed a phenomenal drive, his inner demons destroyed him and he spent much of his later life as an eccentric recluse leading a bizarre lifestyle that inexorably ground itself away into a haze of addiction and psychosis.

There is a marked resemblance between Howard Hughes and Jay Gatsby, F. Scott Fitzgerald's fictional character. Both men were driven to follow a dream such as few of us could know, in the process becoming completely undone. Unlike Jay Gatsby, Howard Robard Hughes did not come from humble origins. His father invented a novel oil-drilling bit, founding the Hughes Tool Company in 1909. His mother Allene Gano came from a wealthy family considered the 'monarchs of Dallas society'.

Born in 1905, Hughes attended private school in Boston before moving to the Thacher School in California. Described as 'the brightest student in physics the school had in years', despite this, Hughes overall was a poor student and never graduated. A loner, he only had one friend. By donating a large sum, his father got him into Rice University in Houston, but he dropped out in any event. From an early age, however, Hughes showed a remarkable mechanical aptitude. When he was eleven, he built a radio transmitter; the next year, he made Houston's first motorised bicycle with parts taken from his father's steam engine. Since childhood he had impaired hearing and ringing in his ears (tinnitus), refused to wear a hearing aid and started flying lessons at fourteen. Only in the cockpit of a plane, did the ringing cease. He was also a talented golf player, but he never took this further.

By the time he was nineteen, Hughes was an orphan, but one of considerable wealth. Inheriting a controlling share in the Hughes Tool Company, Howard Hughes bought out his relatives by 1924 using a dubious legal manoeuvre to become the sole owner of the company. Possibly in reaction to his parents' deaths, Hughes wrote a will bequeathing a medical research laboratory. He never got around to completing the later wills he wrote—like so many other things he started—so this will was ultimately to lead to the creation of the world's most lavishly funded medical establishment, the Howard Hughes Medical Institute.

Hughes then married Ella Rice and moved to Los Angeles to make movies. His first films were successes, several were nominated for Academy Awards. He then took complete control of the movie-making process, searching for a perfection which could never be attained regardless of the cost (or censorship difficulties). *Hell's Angels* (1930), starring Jean Harlow, cost $3.8 million to make. Hughes used eighty-seven World War I aircraft and hired the world's best pilots to make the film. *Scarface* (1932) was delayed by the censors' concern about its violence. *The Outlaw,* starring Jane Russell, was released 1943. Hughes had no illusions about the appeal of the movie but was obsessed with Jane Russell, going to the extent of getting his engineers to construct a special bra to reveal her splendid breasts. He said, 'There are two good reasons why men go to see Jane Russell. Those are enough . . .'

Divorced, Hughes had serial affairs with the most beautiful and famous women of Hollywood, including Billie Dove, Bette Davis, Ava Gardner, Olivia de Havilland, Claudette Colbert, Lana Turner, Marlene Dietrich, Joan Fontaine, Bessie Love, Carole Lombard, Ida Lupino, Corinne Griffith, Olivia de Havilland, Lilian Bond, Fay Wray, Ginger Rogers, Linda Darnell, Rita Hayworth, Yvonne De Carlo, Barbara Payton, Jean Peters, Terry Moore and Zizi Jeanmaire. And if Hughes' biographer Charles Higham is to be believed (Higham's unsourced gossip is questioned by many), added to the list are Tyrone Power, Robert Ryan, Randolph Scott, Errol Flynn, Gene Tierney, Russell Gleason, Richard Cromwell and Cary Grant, Hughes' bisexual activities having commenced when he was seduced by his uncle as a teenager. Not all the women Hughes pursued reciprocated and some, like Jean Harlow, were only paraded for professional reasons.

In 1938 Hughes began living with Katharine Hepburn, like Hughes a good golfer, but continued to dally with Cary Grant, Fay Wray, Ginger Rogers and Olivia de Havilland. Hepburn discovered his infidelity and moved out, writing in her auto-biography that her love for him had turned to water.

In 1932 Hughes turned his obsession with aviation into another arm of his corporate power, establishing the Hughes

Aircraft Company. His intention was to build the world's fastest plane. His first step was to buy as many of the best airplanes, engineers and designers he could get. As the company released new models, he would use them to set new speed records. In 1934 he personally test-piloted the H-1, the world's most advanced plane, using it to set a new speed record on 13 September 1935. Three years later Hughes took a Lockheed 14 with a crew of four around the world, breaking Charles Lindbergh's New York to Paris record.

During World War II, by dint of relentless lobbying and bribery, he won contracts to create and build two revolutionary aircraft: a giant plywood seaplane to carry thirty-five tonnes of men and weapons, and the F-11 photo-reconnaissance aircraft. The 'Spruce Goose' was the largest plane ever built, but also the ultimate aviation white elephant. In 1947, determined to show that it was feasible—despite the fact that there had been several plane generations since its inception and the war was long over—he took it for a brief test flight. It has never flown again and is now on exhibit at an aviation museum in Oregon.

In July 1946, while piloting the XF-11 experimental aircraft, Hughes was involved in a near-fatal accident. The plane crashed in Beverly Hills, hitting three houses; the fuel tanks exploded, setting fire to the aircraft and a nearby home. Hughes had a fractured collar bone and ribs, crushed chest and collapsed lung, shifting his heart to the right side of the chest, and third-degree burns. Lucky to survive, his lengthy convalescence marked the start of his opiate addiction.

Although he returned to flying, this was a turning point in his behaviour. As early as the 1930s, Hughes had displayed signs of obsessive-compulsive disorder. His eating habits were unchanging: dinner was always steak and peas, followed by vanilla ice-cream and cookies. He was obsessed with the size of peas, insisting on having precisely twelve peas on his dinner plate every evening. He threaded the peas in a row on a special fork. If one of the peas was too big to fit on the prong with the rest, it was returned to the chef to be replaced by a pea of standard size. He drank only Poland Springs mineral water bottled at the source in Maine in quarts—he refused to drink water from pint bottles.

While directing *The Outlaw*, Hughes became fixated with Jane Russell's blouse, claiming that the fabric gave the appearance of two nipples on each breast and writing a detailed memorandum on how to fix the problem—a pointer to the behaviour that characterised his life as a recluse. Hughes insisted on using tissues to pick up objects to protect himself from germs. He demanded that people take care of dust, stains or other imperfections he spotted on their clothes.

His obsessional concerns and fear of contamination were evident to his many women. In 1947 Hughes had his first breakdown. Moving into the Goldwyn studio's screening room, he sat naked in a chair for four months, masturbating to movies he had RKO make for the purpose, living on chocolate bars and milk, relieving himself in empty bottles. When he emerged, he had not bathed or cut his hair and nails for weeks. Later, when producer Otto Preminger screened a cut of *Porgy and Bess* in the room, Hughes, a bigot of the highest order, refused to go there again. Moving into the Beverly Hills Hotel, he would sit naked in his bedroom with a pink napkin over his genitals, watching movies.

In 1947 a highly publicised romance with Jean Peters did not last, possibly because he had his security officers follow her. Hughes, never deterred in these matters, continued to pursue her and they married in 1957. The couple lived in a large bungalow in Palm Springs. By then, his bizarre lifestyle dominated his waking hours. He hired three Mormons, the only people he trusted, to work in eight-hour shifts at the bungalow to keep away the insects, a remarkable demonstration of how affluence influences paranoia, considering he would have been far better advised to simply hire a pest removal company. However, there was a spin-off for contemporary culture when one of them wrote a memoir entitled *I Caught Flies for Howard Hughes*.

He would send messages at all hours to his employees, a habit that did not disturb his wife as much as his constant clicking of toenails, by then of Mandarin length, so she put tissues between the toes to muffle the sound. To no great surprise, they did not stay together long, although it was years before the divorce was finalised.

In 1966 Hughes sold Trans World Airlines for $546 million and moved to Las Vegas, where he bought four hotels and six casinos. Extending the compulsion, Hughes tried to buy all the restaurant chains and four-star hotels in Texas. Concerned about underground nuclear testing in Nevada, Hughes instructed his minions to bribe Presidents Lyndon Johnson and Richard Nixon, to whom he had made large political donations over the years.

With a media profile somewhere between that of Bill Clinton and Paris Hilton, Hughes vanished from public view becoming, like Elvis, a subject of endless tabloid speculation, his mythological status growing in the process, despite reports of being terminally ill, mad or dead. One of the richest men in the world, Hughes spent the last twenty years of his life living in seclusion in settings so bleak they could only have been bettered by a nursing home in Soviet Russia. In this time, he lived in Las Vegas, Nassau, Freeport, Vancouver, London, Managua and Acapulco.

With his enormous wealth and power, Hughes was able to delegate his compulsive behaviour to his employees. The only people he trusted were his Mormon attendants (even though he was not a member of their church), who had no medical training. All staff were under instructions not to look at or speak to him, but only respond when spoken to.

Hughes always stayed in the top-floor penthouse, sitting naked in the air-conditioned suites, touching nothing—doorknobs, telephones, unless his hands were protected by a Kleenex tissue from boxes which he continuously stacked and rearranged—and constantly writing detailed memos to his aides. Tightly closed curtains were never opened. The room was only furnished with a hospital bed, reclining chair and a television set. The bed was surrounded by piles of newspapers and *TV Guide* magazines; the syringes and drugs were in a metal box alongside the bed. The sheets were never changed; instead, aides would put down layers of paper towels for him to lie on. Magazines were brought in on a trolley by other aides who had to move one step at a time to Hughes' signal so that no dust was disturbed in the room. There had to be three copies of each magazine, and when within arm's reach, Hughes' Kleenex-wrapped hand picked out the middle copy. Eventually, Hughes only had his hair cut and nails trimmed once a year.

Constantly plagued by constipation, at one time, he sat on the toilet for seventy-two hours, occasionally propping himself on a chair set next to him to support himself while dozing. The cause, of course, was his addiction to codeine-based analgesics, emulating the late great King (Elvis), who went to the great juke box in the sky during a marathon session on his custom-made commode.

After going to the bathroom, Hughes sat in a chair watching selected movies. Favourites were *The Sting, Butch Cassidy and the Sundance Kid, The Clansman* and *The High Commissioner*. He only looked at the James Bond pictures starring Sean Connery and liked films about flying (except *The Great Waldo Pepper*). Obsessed with *Ice Station Zebra* (1968), he ran it on a continuous loop, watching it 150 times. As he no longer watched television, he no longer knew the day, month or season. When his soiling became impossible to ignore, he signalled one of his staff to clean him, lying there without stirring or paying attention as he was mopped up like an incontinent dementia patient.

Before handing a spoon or fork to Hughes, his servants would have to wrap the handle in tissue paper, seal it with cellophane tape, then wrap a second piece of tissue over the first protective wrapping. Once he took the spoon, Hughes would use it with the handle still covered. To remove his hearing-aid cord from the bathroom cabinet, they had to use six to eight tissues to turn the knob on the bathroom door; six to eight tissues to open the bathroom cabinet, remove an unused bar of soap and clean their hands with the soap; up to fifteen tissues to open the door to the cabinet containing the hearing aid; two hands to remove the sealed envelope containing the hearing aid, each hand covered by another fifteen tissues . . .

Suffering with anaemia, arthritis and any number of ailments, his 1.9 metre frame shrunk by seven centimetres and his weight went down to forty kilos. Several doctors were kept on very large retainers, as Hughes seldom saw them, their sole purpose to write his prescriptions. It is estimated that from 1966 to 1970, Hughes consumed 33,000 codeine pills, in addition to 'blue bombers', Valium ten milligrams, up to seven a day—twenty-eight times the recommended daily dose. This ensured that he slept through until 5.30 p.m. One of Hughes' doctors was Dr Verne Mason, the Hollywood doctor who treated him after the 1946 plane crash. Mason was given a highly paid position at the Hughes Medical Institute, where no work was required of him.

Hughes died on 5 April 1976, sliding into a coma on a plane flying from Freeport, Bahamas, to Houston, Texas. Taken to hospital for the autopsy, he was unrecognisable; his hair, beard, fingernails and toenails were long. He was so emaciated that observers likened him to a captive from a Japanese prisoner of war camp. The FBI had to use fingerprints to identify the body. The autopsy found kidney failure and severe malnutrition as the cause of death. X-rays showed broken-off hypodermic needles embedded in his arms. He left an estate estimated at $2 billion. Four hundred prospective heirs, some of whom were actually relatives, tried to establish their right to a share, but Hughes' fortune eventually went to twenty-two cousins on both sides of his family.

Thus ended the life of a man of enormous wealth, influence, ability and talent in circumstances scarcely different from that of any street addict. How had it all come to this?

Howard Hughes' Brain

An anxiety disorder with a difference, obsessive-compulsive disorder has a long history and is documented as far back as the Old Testament in the form of scrupulosity—the intense preoccupation with religious observance that rabbis, priests and ministers of all creeds recognised as excessive and abnormal. The primary features are obsessions and compulsions; the latter are the best known and tend to attract the most attention. However, obsessional symptoms dominate the mental horizon of the sufferer and drive the subsequent compulsions (although the sufferer may often ignore or deny the underlying thoughts). In addition to obsessions, phobias for dirt, germs, cleanliness and contamination are common.

While other forms of anxiety often overlap, obsessive-compulsive disorder has a distinct identity and is the only anxiety that can, in some cases, lead to a psychosis. It remains a matter of debate whether there is such a thing as a distinct obsessional psychosis or whether it is a version of a schizophrenic disorder. A slight male predominance further distinguishes it from most anxiety disorders.

The most common symptoms in obsessive-compulsive disorder, washing and concern with contamination and dirt are seen as evolutionarily meaningful behaviours inappropriately released in this disorder. Other behaviours associated with obsessive-compulsive disorder, such as trichotillomania (compulsive hair plucking), onychophagia (severe nail biting) and face picking. These are what is known as grooming behaviours, a characteristic feature of the social behaviour of the higher primates, such as gorillas, chimps and baboons. Grooming behaviour played an important part in human socialisation and, ultimately, in the origin of language. When they become compulsive, they can be regarded as grooming behaviours out of control.

Repeated obsessions and compulsions can be frightening, embarrassing and even painful, and interfere markedly with work and social life. Compulsions involve activities to 'undo' the perceived fears. This may include cleaning, checking, tidying, washing, writing and counting. There are many ritualistic or superstitious behaviours involved, such as following a repetitive pattern when leaving the home by touching and counting the windows or walking over cracks in the pavements. The rituals and behaviours are usually related to security and the need to make things safe. For example, compulsive hand washing is usually associated with a fear of germs, while ritual checking behaviours before leaving home are generally driven by worries that the home would otherwise burn down or be broken into.

Among the plethora of associated features are perfectionism, pedantry, tic disorders such as Tourette syndrome, compulsive gambling, hair plucking (trichotillomania), nail biting (onychophagia) and skin excoriation (picking). The compulsions can include several features which are often regarded as independent conditions in their own right: hoarding and pathological jealousy, the latter having a very persistent quality and sometimes going on to overt paranoia. It can also can present with abulia — obsessional slowness and inability to reach a decision. This may affect routine activities, for example, when to leave home (or alternate with hyper-punctuality), but causes severe difficulties with decision-making.

Several neurological disorders show us the likely location in the brain of obsessive-compulsive disorders. In 1885 French neurologist Gilles de la Tourette reported a relationship between recurrent tics and obsessive-compulsive behaviour. Sydenham's chorea, a disorder of children and adolescents, is characterised by sudden, aimless irregular movements of the limbs associated with emotional instability and muscle weakness. Patients with Sydenham's chorea have a higher incidence of obsessional symptoms and illness. The disorder occurs after rheumatic fever, a reaction to streptococcal infection affecting the basal ganglia.

The condition known as encephalitis lethargica, which will be discussed in a later chapter, is associated with a sense of compulsion, a range of peculiar tics associated with difficulty opening or closing the eyelids (blepharospasm), hissing and clicking vocal tics, torticollis (neck spasm), twitching or tics of the arms and legs, as well as fits of yelling and yawning. These motor disturbances strongly resemble compulsive movements. Encephalitis lethargica was shown to arise from the basal ganglia. Finally, Parkinson's disease, another condition found in the basal ganglia, can also lead to obsessive-compulsive symptoms.

The basal ganglia are collections of nerves on both sides of the thalamus and above the limbic system on the underside of the brain. They are best understood as a series of nerve junctions with an involvement in movement. They work by inhibiting different movements; a release of this inhibition permits a motor system to become active. Receiving signals from many parts of the brain, notably the frontal areas, they are involved in action selection, deciding which behaviour to execute at a given time. This is the likely site in the brain from where obsessive-compulsive disorders arise.

In addition to motor functions, the basal ganglia have a complex perceptual and cognitive role. Their dysfunction underlies obsessive-compulsive disorder. Obsessive-compulsive disorder can arise from the inappropriate triggering of genetically stored and learned behaviours in these nerves.

Within the basal ganglia is the striatum (consisting of the caudate nucleus and putamen), involved in the processing of messages with sensory information from other parts of the brain and translating the information into body movements (like rubbing one's hands together). Normally the translation of sensory inputs into motor outputs (moving parts of the body through the nervous stimulation of particular muscles) is a smooth and finite activity: a speck of dirt is seen, the hands wipe it away. In obsessive-compulsive disorder the caudate nucleus does not function properly. The defective mechanism results in recurrent obsessive movements, like rubbing hands together or repeating phrases.

Obsessive-compulsive disorder is one of the few psychiatric disorders for which psychosurgery may be indicated. A tiny lesion, no more than several millimetres in size, is made in the connection between the thalamus (one of the basal ganglia) and the frontal lobe, leading to good results in patients with intractable disorders who would probably die otherwise.

Despite his privileged background, Hughes did not have a helpful childhood. His emotionally distant father was always working. His difficult mother was prone to depression, a hypochondriac with a germ phobia, indicating the genetic basis of his own condition. The gene pool that led to this state was not encouraging. His germ-phobic hypochondriacal mother died during surgery, an alcoholic aunt hanged herself and his father died of an apoplectic stroke.

Hughes went on to pursue aviation, filmmaking, star-chasing and corporate imperialism with an intensity that has never been seen before or since. For armchair analysts, this would be explained as a desire to outdo the father with whom he could never compete after he died. But the only person Hughes was competing with was himself, his übercompulsions reflecting a drive for perfection that was not only unattainable but frequently sabotaged by himself. This was the personality that Hughes took into life.

Obsessive-compulsive disorder drove Hughes until his death. That he had a severe, if not extreme, condition is beyond doubt. His great wealth allowed him to wallow in this state in a way that few other sufferers would have been able to. Although this spared others around him (except for the paid Mormons) from having to live around his fixations, it effectively ensured there was no chance he would be forced to seek treatment.

If we look at Hughes, we can see all these features of obsessive-compulsive disorder are present. Despite his own promiscuity, he was deeply suspicious, to the point of pathologically jealous, of his female companions and would have his squad of private detectives follow them. His inability to complete a will, an item where he would have to declare his emotional affiliations, became ultimately impossible, leaving a mess after he died to be sorted out by litigation.

There can be little doubt that the later Howard Hughes, sitting naked in a seat in a darkened hotel penthouse, greasy, lank hair down to his shoulders, a bleeding encrusted tumour growing out of his scalp, bedsores and ulcers proliferating on his body, his limbs covered with needle track marks, grotesquely long and splintered nails, rank and squalid bodily hygiene amid a pool of his own faeces and urine, endlessly watching reruns of old movies, was out of touch with reality and psychotic.

No one summed it up better than writer Joan Didion:

> *It is impossible to think of Howard Hughes without seeing the apparently bottomless gulf between what we say we want and what we do want, between what we officially admire and secretly desire, between, in the largest sense, the people we marry and the people we love. In a nation which increasingly appears to prize social virtues, Howard Hughes remains not merely anti-social but grandly, brilliantly, surpassingly, asocial. He is the last private man, the dream we no longer admit.*

CONSTANTIN VON ECONOMO

*God, or nature, or whatever else you wish
to call the mysterious creative force of this
world . . . has, of all living beings,
endowed only the human species with the
capacity to create new things. Creation
has impressed a part of its own creative
craft upon the brain of humans. This same
force of nature, which in the course of
aeons gave the eagle its flight, has in the
last decades enabled humans to construct
wings and overcome the ties of gravity that
bind us to the earth.*

CONSTANTIN VON ECONOMO

In 1917 doctors in several European countries were baffled by an illness with bizarre symptoms, unlike any illness known; in an earlier age, it would have been blamed on demonology or witchcraft. The new condition affected children and young adults. Patients went into a deep sleep; they could slump into somnolence any time of the day. Others developed a range of neurological and psychiatric symptoms, outbursts of frenzied behaviour or extreme flailing, twitching and jumping movements. One of the characteristic signs was a sudden uncontrollable upward movement of the eyes that could appear quite bizarre to the observer. About a third of the victims would die in the acute phase; many survivors dwelt in a strange twilight zone, locked in their bodies by loss of movement or perennial sleep, sometimes alternating with hyperactive agitation. Some patients, although aware of what went on around them, could not communicate; others demonstrated disorders of speech or thought, either echoing what was said to them (echolalia), repeating words or phrases (palilalia) or spewing out streams of speeded-up sentences. In addition, there was a range of behaviour changes. The patients could become sexually disinhibited, with lewd or perverted activities. They became criminally destructive, unable to see any need to restrain an impulse or consider the damage they could do to another person.

For all of its shocking and strange manifestations, the new disorder was misconstrued by many because it overlapped with the most lethal epidemic in history, the 1918–19 influenza pandemic, which killed more people than the preceding four years of World War I. The apparent crossover led to confusion in nomenclature, with names such as *Hirngrippe, Kopfgrippe* and influenza encephalitis.

To say the new disease caused consternation would be an understatement, but in the prevailing circumstances in Central Europe, there were other priorities. World War I was in its third year, millions had died in the trenches and the end of the conflict could not be known yet.

Almost as suddenly as it had begun, the illness started to wane in 1926 and the epidemic was effectively over by 1930. It is an indication of the concern aroused by the condition that 9000 papers and books were written on the topic by 1936. Between 1917 and 1930, it killed about five million people. The figures showed that one-third of the victims died, one-third made a recovery and one-third were chronically or incurably ill.

The epidemic had antecedents. From the fifteenth to the eighteenth century, there were reports of outbreaks in Europe and it appeared to have been documented at intervals as far back as two millennia. A 'lethargus' accompanied by fever was described by Hippocrates. It was 'mendosa' in Lisbon in 1521, 'pestilence soporeuse' in Italy in 1561, 'lethargy with ocular palsies' in 1605 Germany, the 1673–75 'febris comatosa' epidemic outbreak in London, the 'Tubingen sleeping sickness' of 1712 and the 'coma somnolentum' of 1763 in Rouen. Other names included *Schlafkrankheit* (sleep sickness, Germany), *nona* (Italy, during an epidemic in southern Europe in 1899–1900, named after the prevailing wind).

As it had been first observed in soldiers, it was attributed to gassing. However, this was shown to be untenable. Doctors wondered whether it was a variant of rabies, schizophrenia, epidemic delirium or multiple sclerosis, but none of these theories lasted. African sleeping sickness, or trypanosomiasis, was well known, but these patients were lethargic and it seemed unlikely that an illness only found in the tropics could suddenly appear in the temperate zones of Europe.

Although the pathological changes were intensely studied, and helped delineate how the brain regulates the sleep, there is still no agreement on what caused it and the agent of the disease remained elusive. To this day, the cause of encephalitis lethargica has never been confirmed, although it is widely believed to be an auto-immune phenomenon related to infection.

As the knowledge base accumulated, the prominent features were classified into the lethargic-somnolent form, the hyper-kinetic form (acute agitation with psychotic manifestations) and the amyostatic form (early Parkinsonism). The initial attack was no guide to the development of later problems, which could occur up to forty years later. Parkinsonism would occur in at least forty per cent of cases, an exceptionally high incidence, especially in an age group much younger than those who usually contracted the illness.

Other post-encephalitic features included altered sleep cycle, a cold fish-like stare, intestinal difficulties (notably constipation and flatulence), excessive sweating with a great need for fluid, wanderlust, micrographia (shrinking and constricting of the handwriting), weight loss and hyposexuality. Mania and depression were common, and there was a very high suicide rate. There was an increase in schizophrenic disorders as well as confusional states.

But it was the behaviour of sufferers over time, merging imperceptibly into lifelong personality traits, that was the most intriguing. Lying, swindling and reckless behaviour were typical. Such individuals could commit crimes without restraint but remained intellectually intact, a significant difference to all other neurological infectious diseases. Ominously, as later seen in serial killers, they were prone to cruelty to animals, torture and acts of wanton destructiveness. Most were described as being absolutely devoid of all moral or altruistic feelings.

Noted first in children and adolescents, these changes fitted perfectly with the psychiatric concept of moral insanity. Years, even decades, after a known episode, the individual would present with social or legal problems. In at least some cases, if carefully examined, the original history could be obtained. The disruptive behaviour would seem otherwise out of context, if not inexplicable, if their social, familial and personal situations were considered.

Some people who had suffered from the illness had a deceptive charisma that would be interpreted as a capacity for leadership. Victims could become constant talkers with a supercilious attitude to social situations. They could be brilliant conversationalists, stimulating company, enticing companions and utterly plausible, but they also had no hesitation in exploiting people in a manner that was described as vengeful, vicious and coldly egotistical. Such people had an extraordinary capacity for not just convincing others, but governing, controlling and dominating them.

The condition was first described and named by a remarkable doctor rightfully regarded as a true twentieth-century Renaissance Man: Constantin von Economo.

If Leonardo da Vinci was the definitive Renaissance Man, in modern times his successors have evaporated. If one wanted to succeed in science or medicine or engineering, a prolonged period of training was required, to say nothing of being force-fed a mass of knowledge to acquire the basics of the discipline. All of this tended to attract men (women were only reluctantly allowed to squeeze past the defenders of the gates) who had little time, let alone inclination, to engage in activities that were often seen as frivolous, intellectually soft or simply irrelevant: art, exploration, culture. It was mostly the primary benefit of an aristocratic or noble class, who had the financial security to engage in a range of pastimes, often leisurely, frequently indulgent, and pursue more important activities. Those of the upper classes who survived World War I, the redistribution of wealth and communist confiscation brought an end to the era of the gifted amateur. However, one individual who stood out against the tide of mediocrity was the hugely talented and brilliant Constantin von Economo.

Born Constantin Alexander Economo von San Serff on 21 August 1876 on the family estate in Braila, Romania, near the Black Sea, he was the sixth of seven children (one died when very young) from a distinguished family of Greek origin. His parents had married in Budapest in 1866. The two families had their roots in names such as Karajan, Ypsilanti, Dumbas and Christomano in Edessa and Serres in the Hellenic region of Macedonia. Members of the Economo family had held high ranks in the Greek Orthodox Church; Johannes Economo's uncle was the last bishop in the family. His father Johannes was from a family of bishops in Edessa (or Aegeia), the old capital of Macedonia, the birthplace of Alexander the Great. He fought with distinction against the Ottoman Turks, becoming a wealthy industrialist, and was made Imperial Baron in 1904, acquiring large estates in Thessasalonika and Romania. Known to his family as Costaki, he was devoted to his younger brother Leonidas, who had a similar demeanour: dashing, courteous, elegant and accomplished. They had an idyllic upbringing, leading a lifestyle that has vanished: raised on sumptuous estates with servants and a

French governess and summering in the Austrian Alps. When he was seven, the family moved to Trieste—now a backwater, but then one of those sparkling southern European cosmopolitan melting pots that attracted such noteworthies as James Joyce, who lived there (Trieste is called 'Tarry-East' in *Finnegans Wake*) from 1903–1919, with a break during World War I. It is likely that Joyce and von Economo crossed paths, although there is no mention of them ever making contact.

It was a measure of his cosmopolitan background that von Economo spoke Greek with his father, German with his mother, French with sister Sophia and brother Demetrius, and Triestine (an Italian dialect) with his brother Leo. This exquisite multilingual Triestine culture would come to an end with the Nazis.

Always energetic, Constantin revelled in mountain hikes and horse riding. At school, his outstanding intellect was soon recognised and his classmates would call him 'Your Eminence'. However, he happily stood down two years so he could be in the same class as brother Leo. From an early age, he was entranced with the idea of flying. A voracious seeker of information, he read Cesare Lombrozo on criminology and eugenics. He found himself inexorably drawn to the idea of studying how the variations of upbringing could affect the subsequent working of the brain.

Their affluent lifestyle notwithstanding, the von Economo family led a life that was far from sybaritic. Johannes chose the field in which each son would train and planned out their careers to the last detail. Constantin was to study engineering; he commenced the course at Vienna Technical School at the age of seventeen. For a young man with a distinguished background, good looks, excellent connections and an engaging manner, Vienna had much to offer, not forgetting that it was one of the most corrupt cities on earth, with prostitutes to meet every need in abundance. These details are added to provide colour only.

Von Economo was now to develop interests in art, literature and women (in descending order of preference?) and turn them into lifelong accomplishments. It is a measure of the man that these endeavours did not deter him from his intellectual pursuits, which were shading into biology and medicine. He lived at an inn, giving up meals to continue his voracious reading. It became increasingly difficult for him to continue in engineering and, with Leo's support, his father agreed to allow him to change to medical studies at Vienna Medical School in 1895.

Here he excelled, and was soon given a position as a student demonstrator. Unlike other students, he did not have the financial pressures to graduate as soon as possible and was happy to take off six months for a cruise with his brother. In 1897 von Economo published his first paper, which described the pars infundibula (a stalk-like connection) on the pituitary gland of birds for the first time, no mean achievement for a medical student.

Graduating the following year, von Economo went on the medical equivalent of the Grand Tour, working for six to twelve months at a time at the leading neurological and psychiatric centres in Europe, moving on when he felt he had learned as much as he needed to. He went from Paris to Nancy to Strasburg to Munich. In 1905 he published a book on the nerve ganglion that became the standard text on the subject. He was a leading figure in the Munich social set. Here he came under the aegis of Emil Kraepelin, already a significant authority and destined to be the most influential figure in twentieth-century psychiatry. Always seeking new talent, Kraepelin was impressed by von Economo and offered him the post of Chief of Divisions—an unheard of honour in the rigid hierarchical world of German medicine for a young man under thirty. Von Economo was torn by the offer. Nevertheless, he decided to honour a commitment to work in Berlin, which (unsurprisingly) he found dreary and soulless, before going back to Trieste and then Vienna in the autumn of 1906. Here he happily immersed himself in his collection of books and paintings in his flat at Rathausstrasse 13—the location later commemorated with a plaque stating 'Constantin von Economo the great brain researcher and friend of mankind lived in this house from 1905–1931'. Von Economo continued his explorations of the brain. But a new interest began to intrude, or rather, the return of a dormant passion: flying, now a reality following the Wright brothers' first flight in 1903. He learned how to fly a static balloon, then a free balloon which he called *Sonja*, before going to Mourmelon-sur-Marne, France, to get a pilot's licence and buy one of the first models of the Voisin aeroplane. This was scarcely more than two wings held together with poles, but he was not deterred and soon set a record for being able to keep it in the air for fifty-five minutes. His next plane was an Etrich Taube, which he flew before the Austro-Hungarian Emperor in 1911. The first Austrian to obtain an international pilot's diploma, von Economo was given Field-Pilot's Certificate No. 1 by the Austro-Hungarian military aviation authorities in 1912, served a sixteen-year term as President of the Austrian Aero Club, and was chairman of the Aviation Board at the Austrian Ministry of Commerce and Transport.

Von Economo happily ran his obsessions in tandem. He would get up early for a flight, work at the clinic until five, then race off to the airfield and have a further few hours' flying. He traded in the Voisin for better and faster models, setting air speed records and winning international air races. His flying activities led to considerable publicity and he gained an image as the dashing young aviator clad in leather, silk and goggles.

Soaring in the heavens did not interfere with scientific work and he produced papers on the role of the pons (a section of the midbrain) and scientific aspects of paranoia. All this came to a halt with the outbreak of war in 1914. Desperate for action, von Economo immediately volunteered. Because of his aviation experience and reputation, however, he was required to establish the Austrian Air Force, far from the action. Intensely frustrated, he managed to finagle a position—by offering to drive his own car—on the Eastern front against the then-resurgent Russians, certainly no sinecure. He later said that he could deal with front-line combat, but found the long periods of boredom far harder to stomach. In 1915 he was finally given permission to fly and posted to the Tirol. He took to this with vigour, using his off-time during bad weather to drive an ambulance or work at the local hospital.

In 1916 Von Economo's brother Janko was killed fighting in Italy. His devastated parents prevailed on him to accept a position he had been repeatedly offered but refused: assistant to Professor Julius Wagner-Juarreg in Vienna. This was the end of von Economo's flying career, but once he put it behind him, he had no regrets. The Austrian forces, deployed against the Russians, the Italians and various Balkan countries, were facing defeat and the Habsburg Empire would be over by the end of 1918. But if war does one thing, it provides plenty of clinical material: young men with injuries. And many of these ended up in the Vienna Psychiatric Hospital unit run by Wagner-Juarreg. These patients had problems ranging from malaria and syphilis to brain damage and psychosis. It was from this pool of casualties that Wagner-Juarreg got the malaria strain that he successfully used in 1917 in the world's first treatment of neurosyphilis (see Antoine Laurent Jessé Bayle chapter).

And it was in January 1917 that von Economo encountered seven patients with bizarre symptoms, all with one common feature: severe somnolence, or hypersomnia. Other doctors in several European countries were seeing cases with the same symptoms, but it was von Economo who had the critical faculty to focus on the most prominent and unusual symptom, the peculiar form of stupor.

The cases nudged von Economo's memory of a holiday in Italy when he was young. He described the new cases to his mother, who told him that the *nona* epidemics were associated with somnolence.

On 17 April 1917 he presented the new entity to the Viennese Psychiatric and Neurological Society, naming it encephalitis lethargica, noting the somnolence and autopsy findings of changes in the pons, consistent with inflammation.

He accumulated more cases and did more autopsies. He also injected brain tissue from a deceased patient into a monkey, which died, confirming his belief that it was an infectious disorder.

Von Economo's most important finding was that the pathological changes were at the base of the brain. This led to a major change in understanding of brain function. Until then, it was held that sleep was controlled by the forebrain, where thinking occurred. The new concept led to a far more sophisticated understanding of consciousness, sleep, movement and related activities.

Von Economo wrote his first book on the subject in 1929. In recognition of his mother's assistance, he dedicated it to her, stating that 'this conversation perhaps turned my researches into the right path'. Here is an excerpt from his classic description:

> We are dealing with a kind of sleeping sickness, having an unusually prolonged course. The first symptoms are usually acute, with headaches and malaise. Then a state of somnolence appears, often associated with active delirium from which the patient can be awakened easily. This delirious somnolence can lead to death, rapidly, or over the course of a few weeks. On the other hand it can persist unchanged for weeks or even months with periods lasting hours or days or even longer, of fluctuation of the depth of unconsciousness extending from simple sleepiness to deepest stupor or coma ...

By the end of the war, von Economo was going through something of a lag time. The Austro-Hungarian Empire and the Habsburg Monarchy had crumpled into history, leaving the rump state of Austria with dubious prospects. The encephalitis lethargica epidemic, although continuing, was swamped by the influenza pandemic. It was at this time he met Princess Wilhelmine Windischgratz, the daughter of Austrian Prince Alois von Schonburg-Hartenstein, and the couple married on 10 June 1919, his removal from the list of eligible bachelors causing lasting regret in many circles. Von Economo was happy to spend time with his new bride reading in his library, or buying an old castle for those weekend breaks outside Vienna (as one does!). In constant demand for consultations, he continued working at the Clinic.

By 1920, encephalitis lethargica could not be ignored and was recognised to be a serious pandemic. Widely regarded as the leading authority on the condition, he was given that ultimate medical compliment, the eponymous disease. Von Economo, however, strongly resisted this encomium and always referred to it as encephalitis lethargica.

Von Economo put out more papers and constantly gave lectures to conferences. In 1923 a huge conference in his honour was held in Vienna. He was offered professorships in Athens, Frankfurt, Munich and Zurich, declining all. When Wagner-Juarreg retired in 1928, he was the first choice for the vacant chair of psychiatry and neurology, but refused so that he could continue his brain research without the imposition of administrative duties. He constantly rejected offers of lucrative appointments elsewhere, content to remain in Vienna, where he and the Princess, despite his own work schedule, were a constant presence at operas, theatre, concerts, social events, receptions, galleries and dinners.

In 1922 he returned to a decade-long project, a major atlas of the cerebral cortex. This was published in 1925, becoming a widely sought-after publication with multiple editions. The atlas, at 810 pages, had detailed photographic illustrations and was published in different languages. In 1927 he published a series of ten lectures summarising the book to make it available to those who could not afford the full edition.

All his life, von Economo wanted to go to Greece to explore his family roots. A golden opportunity arose when he was awarded a gold medal in Athens, but he postponed acceptance, saying he would rather collect it later when he had time for a longer visit.

He continued to work on the biological basis of sleep, seeking the sleep centre in the brain, and doing detailed hereditary studies to clarify the role of genetic factors in the evolution of the brain. However, his health was beginning to suffer. In 1924 he experienced chest pain, which was attributed to stress or overwork, and he continued writing, travelling and lecturing. In 1929 he sailed to the United States for a tour with his wife, becoming a media star when *The New York Times* ran the headline, 'Scientist Visions Mental Supermen'.

Von Economo assumed that the progress of mankind shows itself most significantly in the brains of gifted and talented individuals which he wanted to study to gain insight into the future evolution of the human brain. On the gifted and talented he wrote:

> *The study of the brains of the gifted forms one of the most important problems which we have. No one can ignore the important role which is played in the life of a people by those gifted beyond the average. To such individuals are principally owed the periods of ascendancy in history.*

In a speech in March 1931, von Economo (like Leonardo before him) foresaw human space flight:

> *Calculation shows that to lift a body to regions in space beyond the gravitational pull of our earth, it would require a wholly terrific amount of explosive material, several thousand times the mass of the body in question. Those who then as worthy sons of the Titans make these first journeys will be of the same stuff as their predecessors who conquered the air, and from the ranks of the conquerors of the air will advance these stormers of the heavens.*

By May 1931 it was evident that he was unwell, his wife and brother commenting on his fatigue. In the grand tradition, he went to the fashionable resort at Ragasz for a spa cure, but to no avail. He died, after going rapidly downhill over four weeks, on 31 October 1931 at the age of fifty-five. On the human lifespan von Economo had commented: 'Only a few decades are allotted to us, of which a part has to be spent acquiring the necessary knowledge, then comes the short span of productive activity, and then it is all over!'

Von Economo was nominated three times for the Nobel Prize in physiology or medicine for his work on encephalitis lethargica, but his premature death robbed him of the opportunity to collect this recognition. On his death, the tributes flowed, as they still do. He was called the greatest Austrian neuroscientist, 'passing like a meteor in the firmament of neurology'. Michel Jouvet described him as a neurologist of genius, who, confronted with a random experiment of nature (an epidemic), drew attention for the first time to the role of the brainstem and the hypothalamus in controlling sleep and wakefulness. American neurologist Smith Ely Jeliffe said that if the changes in a specialist discipline were like medical towers flourishing unnoticed, then von Economo's work on encephalitis lethargica was like the Rockefeller Center to neurology. Wagner-Juarreg, not a man prone to idle praise, said encephalitis lethargica had the true scientist's talent for taming the visionary seductress who could take one far from the solid earth. In 1976, the Austrian Government honoured von Economo with a stamp.

Constantin von Economo was a scientist in the best sense of the word. Despite his shortened lifespan, his published work was considerable and, in marked contrast to the current academic psychiatric industry, all of his papers were significant. In thirty-three years he produced 4200 pages of published work, one-third of it on sleep, anticipating many of the current views on sleep regulation. His conjecture on the location of lesions that lead to narcolepsy was confirmed by the discovery of hypocretin neurons, loss of which causes narcolepsy.

But it did not stop there. A highly read man with a phenomenal range of interests and ideas, keeping the *Odyssey*, the New Testament, and Faust on his bedside. He was a fluent and riveting speaker. He had a pronounced artistic talent; his drawings of the nervous system were described as works of art; music and nature were his greatest delights. And, in marked contrast to many of his colleagues, he was extremely generous, kind and sympathetic to his patients. He used humour and would toss witty comments into conversations.

His wife said that he had never regretted the decision to give up flying; he had achieved all his goals and there was nothing left to conquer, the work in medicine was the next challenge. She described his personality as kind, calm and harmonious; he had an ability to separate the essential from the non-essential, getting directly to the heart of the matter. Who knows what he could have achieved if he had lived longer?

There is one challenging what-if from his Munich days. Kraepelin was desperate for him to stay and there is every indication he would have replaced him at Heidelberg after his death in 1926. The position instead went to the repulsive Ernst Rudin, who went on to run the Nazis' so-called euthanasia program and plunge medicine to the lowest point in its history. There is nothing to suggest von Economo would have had any truck with such attitudes, and had he stayed, history could have been changed for the better.

As it is, we are left with an enhanced knowledge of the brain and therefore of human nature. Even though the name never achieved official recognition, there are still many who refer to encephalitis lethargica as von Economo's disease—and rightly so. As his biographer said, von Economo had shown that it was possible to fly without leaving the ground.

JACK RUBY

*Someone had to do it. That son of a bitch
killed my President.*

The world's most public execution, watched by millions of television viewers, occurred at 11.21 a.m. on 24 November 1963 before the assembled media at the Dallas police station. Lee Harvey Oswald, the assassin of President John F. Kennedy, following his interrogation at Dallas police headquarters, was to be transferred to prison. To get to the van, he had to pass through a crowd of police, journalists and television cameras. Just before he was to leave headquarters, Oswald (all his life a chronic obfuscator) delayed several minutes to change his shirt. As he came out of the door before the press, the cameras whirled, a burly man standing in the crowd stepped forward and fired a Colt pistol into Oswald's lower belly, gruffly shouting, 'Oswald!' Looking surprised—the last expression in his life—Oswald crumpled to the ground, virtually lifeless. He died two hours later. The lynching, for there is no other word for it, was seen live by an estimated eighty million viewers around the world. The man who fired the gun at Oswald made no effort to escape. He appeared pleased with himself, expecting to be congratulated for what he did, saying to the police: 'I'm Jack Ruby, you all know who I am.'

While Oswald's impromptu execution had an atavistic appeal to many citizens in Dallas, if not the rest of the United States, what Ruby had done was to eliminate the only man who could explain the assassination of the US President, setting in train a mass conspiracy delusion that continues to cast doubt on the likely assassin to this day. As it turned out, Ruby went to his death as a small footnote to history, an otherwise forgettable nonentity who bore a remarkable resemblance to his victim, Oswald.

Who was he, and what motivated Jack Ruby to do this extraordinary lynch murder that changed history?

Jack Ruby liked to big-note himself as a high-ranking mobster running a hotshot nightclub, an associate of leading figures in the Dallas demimonde, and an intimate of police, press and politicians. All serious writers on the assassination regard the idea of Ruby having connections to organised crime as risible. It is possible that he may have been confused with a known Chicago criminal, Harry Rubenstein, but in the end it just amounts to another of the many exaggerations that Ruby spun about himself. The truth is that far from being a mob lieutenant, Ruby was dependent on not antagonising the real mobsters to ensure that his clubs stayed open.

Ruby ran two seedy clubs that barely managed to survive. An inveterate self-promoter, he constantly inflicted himself on anyone he met, pressing invitation cards in their hands. He was friendly with the police—who tolerated him as a minor snitch who gave them freebies at the club, and hung around the press—who regarded him as a 'born loser'. Another description of him was an unbalanced roughneck.

But fact, rather than fiction, never played much of a part in Ruby's life. Jacob Rubenstein was born on 25 March 1911. Ruby's father came from a Polish *shtetl* in the old Pale of Settlement of the Russian Empire. He was conscripted into the Tsarist Army, a fate that amounted to a life sentence unless one could escape. As it was, he learned to use his fists and to drink before going AWOL and marrying Ruby's mother, who came from a marginally more up-market Jewish family near Warsaw. The couple, who were quite unsuited, emigrated to Chicago and proceeded to have eight children.

Life for poor Yiddish-speaking migrants in the United States was hardly a picnic, and the rough side of Chicago was about as bad as it got. Ruby Senior drank, was violent, seldom held a job and deserted the family for most of Jack's teenage years. His mother, who would have struggled to hold together a large family, under any circumstances, was quite unsuited to the task. Described as severely neurotic, she had no ability to control her children, who grew up on the streets where they had to hold their own against the competing ethnic gangs. Her mental state gave in, she was hospitalised, the children were taken away, and Ruby spent eighteen months in foster homes. She later died in a home, having become paranoid, which was attributed to early senility.

These circumstances fostered truancy and Ruby was assessed by a psychiatrist when he was eleven. Ruby had learning problems and would misspell and mispronounce words all his life. His IQ was ninety-four—within normal levels, but he was hardly likely to progress beyond high school. He left school after fifteen, continuing his education on the streets.

From an early age, Ruby was known for his temper, with a tendency to lash out at any provocation. He lived by his wits, a hustler selling anything that could earn a quick buck, from scalping tickets to hocking cigarettes, real estate, gimmicks and gadgets. This was a common trajectory for someone in Ruby's position; as a rule, people either moved up or down the social scale as they got to adulthood. If they moved down, minor brushes with the law would escalate into more serious crimes and violence, setting them up to be a career felon and criminal, often based in an ethnic gang. Alternatively, they could follow an upward path, socially, occupationally, economically and legally, into the American melting pot. Ruby and his siblings followed the latter path, although with some fits and starts. Despite the disruptions and difficulties, the children remained close, maintained their Jewish identity—albeit in a less devout form to cope with a different lifestyle to that of Eastern Europe—and then got on with their lives.

Ruby's ascent, nevertheless, was fitful, if not erratic. He had few legal problems, mostly minor transgressions. He always had difficulty earning a living. He was voluble, to the point of being regarded by most as a loudmouth, patriotic in a wear-your-heart-on-your-sleeve way, and intensely proud of his Jewish heritage. There are many reports of him taking on people who made anti-Semitic remarks.

When he was fifteen, while trying to sneak into a ballgame, Ruby was hit on the head by a policeman. His family later said he was hospitalised with a serious head injury, having a steel plate inserted into his skull. No other information is available, but in view of his later problems, a head injury could explain his behaviour. However, if he had a steel plate inserted in his skull, this would have been detected on X-rays done later.

Ruby did national service without incident. He was described as a Sergeant Bilko character, always looking for ways to hustle the system; he beat up a sergeant who made anti-Semitic remarks. He returned to civilian life, mostly working as a travelling salesman. He was involved in setting up a union. Its president was shot, but this did not involve him. Mostly, Ruby was going nowhere.

In 1947 he moved to Dallas, Texas, where he had a sister Eva and a brother. Still called Rubinstein, he then legally changed his name to Jack Leon Ruby. Americanising a surname was not uncommon for Jews trying to assimilate in US society. Several of his siblings had also changed their names to Ruby. He may have taken this step to make himself stand out less in Dallas, a town hardly receptive to a Jewish hustler from the wrong side of Chicago.

Before long, Ruby went into the nightclub business. But the first club failed and, after five years, his situation was looking dire. Facing bankruptcy, barely managing to stay off the streets, he was depressed for several months. He returned to Chicago for a while, bounced back and returned to Dallas. He managed to get back in the business and followed along this path, just managing to keep his head above water, until 1963.

By then, he ran a rock-and-roll dance hall, The Vegas Club, and a strip club, The Carousel Club. The Vegas was run by his sister and the Carousel became the central focus of his activities, if not his identity. Ruby liked to portray it as a classy entertainment joint, but in reality, it was a strip club catering to tourists, visitors and anyone who had a taste for seedy burlesque. He was his own bouncer and would use his fists more than was necessary. This tough-guy image was reinforced by working out in the gym.

Ruby would press invitation cards into the hands of anyone he met. He liked to describe himself as a *ganzer macher*—a big man around town. Ruby, something of a cop groupie, encouraged officers to come to the club where they were always treated generously, often walking out with a bottle of whisky under their arm. There was, of course, an element of self-interest in this as it was easy to lose his liquor licence if the police issued an adverse report.

Ruby had minor legal offences from time to time. He was twice convicted for carrying concealed weapons and had several convictions for threatening violence, but most charges were for issues such as dodging taxes and rates. Ruby, who regarded himself as a mostly law-abiding citizen, did not regard these as real offences.

By the time of the presidential visit in 1963, Ruby's accomplishments had been below the waterline for years. No amount of bluster could hide the fact that he was a nonentity, constantly seeking recognition but regarded with contempt or disdain by those who counted in Dallas. He ran the Carousel Club at night, usually getting home at 3 a.m. His strippers both loved and loathed him. He worked his way through them sexually and could threaten violence when they upset him, but would go to extraordinary lengths to help them if they had trouble, especially with boyfriends. He still looked after unruly patrons, seeming to relish the opportunity to become physical, often using knuckledusters for emphasis. He had George Senator, a Korean War veteran, living at his apartment for a year—which was later thought to indicate that he was homosexual, although this was strenuously denied.

While not devout, Ruby remained intensely proud of his Jewish ancestry. This was one of the reasons for his admiration for President Kennedy, which bordered on frank worship, as Kennedy had a number of Jews in high positions in his administration. However, despite this enthusiasm for the President and his stylish wife, Ruby did not go to the parade.

When he heard of the assassination, Ruby was shattered, going round in tears, a level of distress which, despite the awfulness of the event, surprised many who knew him. The next day, preoccupied with the slaying of the President, he carried out his usual duties in a distracted fashion. At mid-morning, he drove his car, accompanied by his favourite dog, Sheba, and went into the Western Union office to mail twenty-five dollars to one of his strippers. Then, he walked across the road to the police centre where he glided easily into the crowd of police and press awaiting the passage of Oswald to the police truck. Three minutes after leaving the Western Union office, he had shot Oswald and been arrested.

Oswald's death attracted extraordinary publicity. Ruby was arraigned for trial in February 1964, barely three months after the country had been traumatised by the assassination and in the same city where it had occurred. For his defence, Ruby's family hired the flamboyant lawyer Marvin Belli, a specialist in negligence cases with little experience in criminal trials. Belli, who believed in winning his cases through the media, was desperate to get Ruby as his client. 'Get me that case,' he said, 'I want it so badly I can taste it.'

Ruby proceeded to trial. The judge, a local legal lightweight with an eye to publicity, refused to allow the trial to be moved to another location and, after much equivocation, reluctantly kept television cameras out of the court.

Considering the public circumstances of the killing, Ruby could hardly claim that he had not been the gunman, instead relying on a temporary insanity defence, based on the M'Naghten rule, which applied in Texas. In order to qualify for being found not guilty by virtue of insanity, it had to be shown that Ruby did not know the difference between right or wrong, or realise the nature or consequences of his actions. Ruby, to no great surprise, insisted that he had no recollection of what had occurred at the time, describing himself as being in a mental fog, which coincided with a fugue state, a frequent consequence of automatism. Automatism is a pattern of behaviour that appears normal to the onlooker, but over which the person has no conscious control; fugue states are prolonged automatisms associated with movement or travel, for example, the person who gets on a train and arrives somewhere without any awareness of how they got there.

Despite the brevity—it only lasted eight days—Ruby did not have a good trial. It started badly and became steadily worse. He had to sit silently through it all, listening to himself described as a mentally unstable individual who needed to be institutionalised, a latent homosexual and, worst of all, a loser. He did not give evidence—a serious error in the light of his deteriorating mental state as the trial progressed. If he was not insane by the start of the trial, he certainly was by the time it finished.

The prosecution calmly laid out its case, showing that Ruby had been obsessed by the presidential assassination, telling people that Oswald should be shot to spare Kennedy's widow any more grief. He had attended the earlier press conference with Oswald using faked credentials, but no one paid any attention. After all, that was just Ruby hanging around where the action was, trying to look important.

The impulsive nature of Ruby's act was evidenced by the fact that he left his dog Sheba in the car before going to police head-quarters. Furthermore, Oswald's transfer had been advertised for 10 a.m. and Ruby only turned up at 11.20 a.m.

Belli followed his usual tactics of histrionics and bluster to discredit unhelpful witnesses, rather than conducting a detailed forensic examination of the available evidence. The key defence evidence was Ruby's single EEG tracing taken after the shooting, which showed short bursts of six per second slow waves arising from the right temporal lobe. Frederick Gibbs, an authority on epilepsy, had described such readings in 1952 as a psychomotor variant. This rare type of epilepsy was associated with instability, loss of emotional control, convulsive and excessive behaviour. However, there was no record of Ruby having any kind of seizures or demonstrating unusual or automatic behaviour in the past.

Belli brought in an array of specialist witnesses to testify for the defence that Ruby was not in control of his actions due to a state of automatism induced by a psychomotor epileptic state. These included a psychologist, psychiatrists Manfred Guttmacher and Walter Bromberg, and a gaggle of neurologists, including Frank Forster and Martin Towler.

The defence questioned the specialists. A bizarre argument broke out over the testimony from psychologist Dr Roy Schaffer, who had administered a series of psychological tests to Ruby, including the Rorschach test, otherwise known as the Inkblot test. Few nowadays, aside from those of psychoanalytic persuasion, regard this test as having any more validity than the statement that the moon is made of blue cheese. According to Schaffer, his tests showed the presence of organic brain damage due to psychomotor epilepsy. The Rorschach findings, in particular, showed signs of confusion, fluidity of thinking, incoherence, misuse of words and breakdown of sentence structure. There was intense sparring between the counsels over admitting the evidence because Schaffer had not interviewed Ruby, insisting that this was the task of the psychiatrist. For those who have serious doubts about the validity of psychological testing—and there are many—this reinforces the belief that such tests only muddy the waters, rather than assist diagnosis. Having thoroughly discredited Schaffer

(Belli did not need their assistance in doing this), the prosecution allowed the evidence to stand.

While neurologist Dr Towler agreed that Ruby had a psychomotor variant, Dr Forster was the more impressive witness—although this did not help the defence case. The six per second theta waves in the EEG, he said, were a slight abnormality and Ruby did not have epilepsy at the time of the shooting.

Psychiatrist Dr Guttmacher agreed that Ruby was not in control of his actions. Unfortunately for the defence, he attributed this to a temporary, very short-lived psychotic episode, rather than a psychomotor variant of epilepsy. Ruby had a lifelong history of mood swings, impulsivity and a voracious need to be accepted by people in positions of authority and social prestige. He constantly attempted to assert a shaky masculinity by fighting, sexual promiscuity and body building.

The trial lasted eight days. After a brief discussion, the jury found Ruby guilty and he was sentenced to death.

The trial of Jack Ruby remains an enduring source of legal fascination. It has been meticulously described in *The Trial of Jack Ruby* by Kaplan and Waltz. The book reveals in great detail the problems of the adversary system, US state law, the problems of specialist witnesses and, most of all, Belli's appalling ineptitude as a trial advocate.

Awaiting his appeal in jail, Ruby's mental state continued to deteriorate. It was evident to all that he was grossly delusional. He believed his brother had been tortured, castrated and burned to death in the street outside his cell, and the Jews in America were being killed in a pogrom because the Kennedy assassination was blamed on him. He became suicidal, on one occasion ramming his head against a wall, another time trying to electrocute himself. He was examined by prison psychiatrist who found he was psychotic. Ruby's delusions about the conspiracies he saw around him continued to escalate. He made persistent appeals to the Warren Commission investigating the assassination to give testimony, but was rebuffed until his family went to the media. He made a request to be interviewed in Washington as he claimed his prison was unsafe. This was refused and he was interviewed in jail by members of the Commission, who were unimpressed with his paranoid rodomontade.

An illustration of Ruby's state of mind can seen in the transcripts of his interview by the Warren Commission:

> *I am as innocent regarding any conspiracy as any of you gentlemen in the room. I have been used for a purpose, and there will be a certain tragic occurrence happening if you don't take my testimony and somehow vindicate me so my people don't suffer because of what I have done.*
>
> *Well, you won't see me again. I tell you that a whole new form of government is going to take over the country, and I know I won't live to see you another time.*
>
> *All I know is maybe something can be saved. Because right now, I want to tell you this, I am used as a scapegoat, and there is no greater weapon that you can use to create some falsehood about some of the Jewish faith, especially at the terrible heinous crime such as the killing of President Kennedy.*
>
> *Now maybe something can be saved. It may not be too late, whatever happens, if our President, Lyndon Johnson, knew the truth from me. But if I am eliminated, there won't be any way of knowing.*
>
> *Right now, when I leave your presence now, I am the only one that can bring out the truth to our President, who believes in righteousness and justice.*
>
> *But he has been told, I am certain, that I was part of a plot to assassinate the President.*
>
> *I know your hands are tied; you are helpless. All I want is a lie detector test, and you refuse to give it to me. Because as it stands now—and the truth serum, and any*

other—Pentothal—how do you pronounce it, whatever it is. And they will not give it to me, because I want to tell the truth.

And then I want to leave this world. But I don't want my people to be blamed for something that is untrue, that they claim has happened.

Ruby's appeal (this time not handled by Belli) went through and he was granted a retrial on the grounds of unfair pre-trial publicity. However, he never faced his accusers again. By then his physical condition was deteriorating. He had constant stomach pain. Ruby collapsed; in hospital he was found to have lung cancer with brain secondaries and soon died. The official cause of death was listed as pulmonary emboli (blood clots) in the lungs from his legs.

Jack Ruby's Brain

Was Ruby insane or in the grip of an epileptic automatism at the time he shot Oswald? If not, what did explain his behaviour? What other factors played a part in his behaviour?

Ruby's timeline can be divided into four periods:

1 His life up to the arrival of President Kennedy in Dallas.

2 The period until the assassination.

3 The period until Oswald's shooting.

4 The period from Oswald's shooting until Ruby's death.

Ruby was a product of his environment and his genes. He had more difficulties with his mood, behaviour and learning than his siblings, who were exposed to the same environment. With his mother's psychiatric history and the episode of depression in 1952, he would be predisposed to psychiatric illness, but nothing more can be deduced, bearing in mind that his mother's paranoia was most likely the presenting feature of a dementia, rather than a disorder like schizophrenia.

Ruby's intelligence was in the normal range, but no more. By all accounts, he got by with cunning, bluster and sheer chutzpah. That he always had difficulty with words could be a subtle sign of brain damage, but was more likely a persisting feature of childhood learning difficulties.

The most intriguing feature of Ruby's history prior to the shooting is the reported head injury, but without other evidence, no conclusions can be drawn. If such an injury occurred, there are several possibilities. Firstly, frontal lobe damage would explain many of Ruby's personality characteristics: impulsivity, prone to violence, blustering, superficial and alternating between periods of hyperactivity and apathy. Secondly, such an injury would increase the likelihood of epilepsy.

Ruby's attitude and demeanour revealed marked traits. He was gratuitous, crude, insinuating, intrusive, annoying and extremely gauche. Subtlety was beyond him; he dealt with everything in a crude and abrasive manner. The most vivid (and emetic) example of his insensitivity is his demonstrating to a friend how he could masturbate his dog (the friend was appalled and refused to watch).

Ruby's brashness can be seen in his work; selling gadgets, cigarettes and tickets, running nightclubs. None of this needed any skills except hustling. If a deal came off, then he used it to boost himself. However, the police only tolerated him because he was a snitch and gave them freebies; the media regarded him as a pain in the butt; the real criminals simply ignored him.

His constant need to be where the action was, in the centre of the crowd, indicates a sense of emptiness. In fact, aside from his immediate family and a few others, he was friendless. That

Ruby had a perilously fragile and low self-esteem goes without saying, but the problem, as with all psychological explanations of this type, is that it explains nothing.

There is nothing discreditable in Ruby's patriotism, only that it was over-the-top, almost belligerent and at odds with the rest of his character, which was glib, shallow, ingratiating, provocative and frequently just repulsive.

His quick temper, no doubt modelled on his father and many others he encountered during his upbringing, was a product of his sense of inferiority. But a Jewish boy raised on Chicago's mean streets would be expected to have one thing going for him: a quick mouth to talk his way out of any situation. This Ruby conspicuously lacked; his blustering was hardly a substitute. Consequently, the only option was to use his fists. He modelled himself on the boxing champions of his day and used violence to fill the gap. To this can be added his preoccupation with appearance, manifesting in exercising, weight-lifting and dieting. Exerting himself by his physical presence and aggression was the only way Ruby knew to prevent a constant sense of inferiority from surfacing in any encounter.

There is more to this, however. While going to some effort to keep within the law, if only to avoid having more hassles with his liquor licence, he did not consider problems such as late payment of fines or tax to be offences. Ruby had several convictions for assault and people commented that he would use any excuse to beat up a customer, often going well beyond what was necessary. His violence was coupled with an extraordinarily poor driving record. He was a menace on the road, constantly getting fined for speeding and running red lights. This combination of poor impulse control and low frustration tolerance is known as an impulse control disorder. Like many such behaviours, it can arise for any number of reasons, ranging from intoxication, substance abuse, organic brain injury, mania, psychosis or epilepsy.

Ruby's close relationships were as expected. His siblings were tolerant and supportive, notably his sister in Dallas. Despite the severe disruption, if not deprivation, they had all experienced during their upbringing, they maintained close links, kept their Jewish identity and went on to lead settled lives in the community.

There was much speculation about Ruby's sexuality at his trial which he found very humiliating. It is unlikely he was homosexual, although whether there was some inner deeply suppressed conflict is impossible to know. He had a ten-year relationship with an older Dallas woman, described as very dignified, until 1959, and he always tried to bed his strippers—although never more than once. The most commented on feature of his relationships involved not women, but dogs. Ruby, it was widely agreed, was crazy about his dogs and would go to extraordinary lengths to care for them, often having a pack of seven to nine dogs at any time. Why? Probably because they were uncomplicated, devoted and he needed an outlet for his affection which he could not find in an adult relationship.

This is the Jack Ruby who waited in anticipation of the arrival of his hero, President John F. Kennedy in Dallas, although he never even went to the parade. The first sign of anything amiss on that fatal day in Dallas occurred on the morning before the presidential group had arrived. Reading *The Dallas Morning News*, Ruby's attention was caught by a half-page advertisement, bordered in black, accusing the President of being a communist tool, signed by 'The American Fact-Finding Committee, Ben Weissman, Chairman'. The advertisement incensed Ruby, who thought it was disrespectful of the president, more so because it was signed by someone who appeared to be Jewish. Ruby believed that the advertisement was a right-wing conspiracy aimed at discrediting Jews. As it happened, the Ben Weissman who signed the announcement was not Jewish and there is nothing to indicate that it was an anti-Jewish conspiracy, let alone a plot.

The possibility of an anti-Jewish conspiracy weighed on Ruby's mind throughout the day. When he heard that Kennedy had been assassinated, he was devastated, breaking down in tears, unable to believe what had happened. He could not understand how anyone would want to murder his hero, a man who held the highest office in the land. But despite his distress, the political advertisement did not leave his thinking. He spoke to a journalist on the paper and went round to the Times Herald office at 4 a.m. the next morning, complaining that the advertisement in *The Dallas Morning News* was a conspiracy to make the Jews look bad. His preoccupation with the matter worsened when he saw a roadside billboard with the inscription, in large letters, 'Impeach Earl Warren', which listed the post-office box number (1754). Ruby, in his inflamed state, with his penchant for reading difficulties, immediately linked the number with that listed with the newspaper advertisement (1972). He went to the billboard at 5 a.m. with his housemate George Senator and one of his staff, to take Polaroid photos of the poster, then driving down to the post office to look at the box, annoyed to see that it contained a large volume of mail. Shortly after, when he opened the morning paper to see the Weissman advertisement again, he unleashed a long tirade to George Senator on the matter. Senator later commented that he kept rereading the advertisement with tears in his eyes and 'a strange and abnormal stare'.

This is all highly unusual behaviour. Distraught at the President's death, Ruby had contacted his rabbi and his sister, almost making a public spectacle of his grief in a city (if not the whole country) that was paralysed by the news. Yet, from the morning before the arrival of the cavalcade through the news of the shooting until well into the next morning, Ruby's activities, random or otherwise, were driven by one overriding obsession: the presumed plot by right-wingers to implicate the Jews of America.

It was in this frame of mind that he faced the rest of the fateful day. Until 11.18 a.m., Ruby's activities were mostly random, attending to matters at his club, paperwork and then going to the Western Union office to send money to one of his strippers, leaving his beloved Sheba in the car. The evidence has been repeatedly and convincingly reviewed. If Ruby had any serious plan to kill Oswald (for his own reasons or for someone else), as the conspiracy nutters still allege, then this would have been the worst possible way to go about it. Had it not been for a single last-minute and totally unpredicted decision to delay Oswald's departure, he would have missed him completely.

Another factor pushed Ruby across the line that usually kept him a nightclub bully and a serial pest. Always concerned about his weight and appearance, Ruby would work out at the gymnasium and use diet drugs, notably Benzedrine and Preludin; in short, he was on a cocktail of highly stimulant amphetamine drugs, a combination notoriously conducive to aggression, paranoia and violence.

Unfortunately, the records do not specify the quantities that he was taking at the time. Bugliosi and Posner, the two most credible writers on the assassination, state that Ruby was dieting at the time—the implication being that he would be taking more of the drugs than usual, or had just started taking them again. The result would be the same. While he would lose appetite, he also ran a greater risk of side effects including impulsivity, aggression, violence, paranoia and grandiosity. The last factor should not be underestimated. For Ruby, a serial loser with just enough intelligence to know that everyone else knew it as well, this would have been almost as lethal as the paranoia.

When Ruby's car, which also functioned as an alternative office, was searched, amid the mess was found pictures of the billboard and his diet drug prescriptions.

After the arrest, Ruby's elation did not last. As the implications of his act sunk in, coupled with the realisation that most

Americans were appalled at what he had done, he slumped further and further into a mire from which he never emerged. As he became convinced that he was now the central figure of a conspiracy to persecute all the Jews of America, he became suicidal. In a psychotic and suicidal state, he was then found to have disseminated cancer and died shortly afterwards.

To all intents and purposes, the bowel cancer would have been seen as no more than an unfortunate event, unrelated to his mental state, and leading to a rapid demise because it was so advanced when discovered. But the cancer could have played a more significant role in his earlier behaviour. Brain tumours, primary or secondary, can cause a range of psychiatric difficulties, including epilepsy, dementia, psychosis and depression. And bowel cancer can produce what is known as a silent secondary: a single tumour slowly growing undetected in the brain, only manifesting with what appears to be a psychiatric disorder before the cancer is discovered, in the brain or elsewhere. If this was the case with Ruby, then a secondary cancer in his frontal lobe would have been the crucial issue that affected his mental state.

In the past, Ruby's personality, although reckless, annoying, intrusive, aggressive but mostly shallow, was kept within the broad limits of abiding with the law. He was bullying and thuggish, but not murderous; he drove recklessly, but had never tried to shoot anyone; he was far more sycophantic than he was ever threatening. Then, without Ruby or anyone around him realising, the silent tumour altered the balance between the reality of his perceptions of the world around him and a profound feeling that no matter what he tried, he would always be a failure, a nobody. This attached itself to the only meaningful moral landmark in his life: his Jewish identity, expanding to the position of all the Jews in America.

As there is no information avaliable from the autopsy report, we can never know where the brain tumours were located—

although it is worth pointing out that psychotic changes can occur with tumours located elsewhere in the brain. It will remain speculative whether Ruby had a silent brain tumour when he shot Oswald, but the natural history of cancer, especially bowel cancer, is consistent with this possibility.

The likelihood that Ruby's behaviour was affected by high doses of amphetamines is reinforced by Posner's statement that once he was imprisoned, deprived of these medications, he went through withdrawals and his mood plummeted.

Here is the likely explanation for the events that affected Ruby from the time before the presidential assassination until his death.

All his life, Ruby was impulsive, in part because of his learning difficulty which caused subtle comprehension problems, in part because of a pervasive sense of failure which he compensated for with a range of behaviours intended to demonstrate his manliness, authority and refusal to be cowed.

By the time of the President's visit, Ruby's often shaky control of his emotions was affected by two factors of which neither he nor anyone else was aware: a silent brain tumour, possibly in his frontal lobes; and the effects of amphetamines which he was taking to excess, sufficient to cause withdrawal problems when he was jailed. The changes went way beyond his usual edgy sense of being at odds with a hostile world in which he had to continually flaunt himself to gain even token recognition. In all likelihood, his loss of control and ability to distinguish reality from fantasy had started slowly but the heightened emotional tension of first the President's impending visit, then the assassination, imploded his hold on reality to the point that he was largely a passive responder to his impulses, rather than a consciously sentient adult.

By the day after the assassination, distraught and sleep deprived, Ruby had lost all ability to know what was going on in his mind. That the President had been shot, in his home town no less, was bad enough, but it was also a blow to the aspirations of Jews in America with whom he so intensely identified. Having latched onto the right-wing plot, Ruby could only see conspiracy all around him, conspiracy which must have included the presidential assassin, Lee Harvey Oswald.

Ruby several times remarked to people around him how awful it would be for the President's widow, Jackie, to have to come back to Dallas to testify at Oswald's trial. True—but hardly the issue which most people had in their minds at the time as they struggled to come to terms with the killing. He also expressed his views on Oswald as a creep or a punk. In the first statement, he gave to the police after he shot him, he said that Oswald had a smirk on his face, which drove him to shoot him. While it is difficult to imagine anyone finding a single spark of goodness in Oswald at that time, again this is not the issue most would focus on.

As much as one can untangle the flitting and surging emotions that Ruby was operating under at the time, at the centre of the emotional cyclone was a conspiracy that threatened to swamp him and everything he valued. His presence at the Dallas police headquarters was, in all likelihood, driven as much by his habitual desire to be at the centre of everything as anything else. That he carried a gun on him in Dallas, Texas, was nothing unusual. He would have barely had time to catch his breath and size up the situation when Oswald, between two policemen, came within one metre of him. The smirk that had caught his attention transmuted into an intuition that for once in his life he could impress the people who mattered, at last he could be a hero, and seconds later it was all over.

In the first flush of the slaying, Ruby experienced a surge of hubris he had never known. He expected to be declared a national hero, convinced that he would walk free and be applauded. As the realisation began to sink in that this was far from the case, his false euphoria slowly dwindled and then collapsed completely. In this manner Jack Ruby did achieve what he had wanted all his life: fame, but obtained the wrong way. A man who but for a single act of impetuous violence, would have remained completely obscure, eminently forgettable, ended up as a footnote on the page. And still an utter nebbish.

ADOLF HITLER

> *I go the way that Providence dictates with*
> *the assurance of a sleepwalker.*

ADOLF HITLER

Ernst 'Putzi' Hänfstaengl, the flamboyant scion of a wealthy German publishing family, was a social gadfly and dilettante. Franklin D. Roosevelt was a distant family connection. In his youth he had studied at Harvard, where he mixed with William Randolph Hearst, Charlie Chaplin and was briefly engaged to the writer Djuna Barnes before returning to Weimar Germany. When he first heard Hitler speak in a Munich beerhall, he was entranced. 'What Hitler was able to do to a crowd in two and a half hours will never be repeated in 10,000 years. Because of his miraculous throat construction, he was able to create a rhapsody of hysteria. In time, he became the living unknown soldier of Germany.'

Hänfstaengl became one of Hitler's constant companions in the early days of the fledgling Nazi Party. Hitler, the godfather of Hänfstaengl's son Egon, used him as a conduit to gain access to the wealthy upper classes but, most of all, valued his piano playing, which he would listen to when he needed to relax.

As the party's fortunes rose, Hänfstaengl, who fully subscribed to the Nazi Party ethos, became head of the Foreign Press Bureau in Berlin. His access to the leader was resented by other members of the Hitler court and he was no match for the political skills of Herman Goering and Heinrich Himmler who smeared him with allegations of disloyalty. Hänfstaengl was able to flee to Switzerland in 1937 and from there to the United States.

Detained by the authorities in Canada as an enemy alien after the outbreak of war, he used his connections with FDR to be turned over to the United States in 1942 to work on the S-Project, providing information on 400 Nazi leaders, with sixty-eight pages on Hitler alone, including details of Hitler's private life. FDR read his gossipy accounts with keen interest, although the value of the intelligence was doubtful.

Released after the war, his family fortunes lost, Hänfstaengl returned to Germany where he wrote a book, claiming that had Hitler not fallen under the influence of the other party figures, he could have restrained his excesses, allowing him to be the great unifying figure in Germany that he undoubtedly was. In postwar Germany, this view was not destined to attract many followers and the book is mostly remembered for the personal account of the early life of the German dictator. An interesting vignette after the failure of the Munich Putsch was Hitler's melodramatic threat to Hänfstaengl's wife Helene to kill himself, typical of the necromantic obsession that would recur until he finally killed himself and Eva Braun in the Berlin bunker.

The information Hänfstaengl provided on Hitler's sexuality, an area on which he was well qualified to comment, was either too sensational or ambiguous to be of assistance; for example, Hitler only played 'the black keys of the piano'. Other *bon mots* included the revelation that Himmler would select good looking boys from the concentration camps for his pleasure.

But among the hagiography, self-praise, gossip and flim-flam was an intriguing description of Hitler's functioning. When he made his speeches, Hitler would carefully arrange his notes on a table by his left hand, then pass each sheet to the right table when he had finished with each one, indicating that he would have to *look to the left* to read them.

The left-sided gaze at the notes was coupled with his characteristic speechmaking. Hitler would begin in pianissimo: subdued, low key, with long pauses, often after the audience had a long wait to raise their anticipation. As he worked through the speech, the intensity would increase until the climactic ending in a spasm of intense emotion that captured all who listened. During this time, Hitler was described by observers as being in a state of detachment. It was 'as if he spoke out of his body', said his boyhood companion, Auguste Kubizek.

In the thinking process, the left hemisphere will produce verbal, rational and logical concepts, the right hemisphere has abstract perceptions that are not anchored in reality or time. EEG studies show how the right hemisphere is specialised for orientation in space, recognition of faces and musical activities, while the other side controls language and linear features of time. These affect the production or appreciation of music, dealing with numbers and spatial concepts, mysticism or occult preoccupations.

People are consistent in the direction of their gaze, for example, in responding to questions, the direction opposite to the dominant hemisphere. As Hitler was clearly right-handed, the dominant hemisphere would have been expected to be the left but the direction of his gaze rather shows that, unusually, the right hemisphere had a dominant role. This indicates a link between a range of left-sided physical symptoms and a right-sided brain.

What caused Hitler's unusual laterality? Although we can never know for certain, considering the poor preservation of the brain at the autopsy, there is now a body of evidence based on observable facts, rather than abstraction or speculation. Before examining this, we need to look at the vast and turgid cesspool that surrounds the life of Adolf Hitler.

The Family Tree

Trawl back to the early nineteenth century in the Waldviertel, an isolated rural province near the border of Austria–Hungary. The riparian dwellers of the region had a long history of intermarriage, leading to complicated and intertwined family trees with confusing boundaries. Consider the following family history. In 1837 Maria Schicklgruber, forty-two, unmarried, gives birth to a son, Alois. No father is listed on the birth certificate. Five years later Schicklgruber marries Johann Georg Hiedler. Alois is sent to live with Hiedler's brother, Johann Nepomuk Huttler, who is already married. Georg Hiedler dies. In 1847 Alois Schiklgruber returns to the church where he was baptised and has the priest change the birth certificate to list the late Georg Hiedler as his father. From then on, he is known as Hiedler, or Hitler. The names are Czech in origin; the confusion in spelling is typical of a time when many people were illiterate and birth certificate records were lax.

To add to this already confusing palimpsest of identities, parental affiliation and family alliances, Alois Hitler proceeds to lead a more than complicated life himself. While he has a steady ascent—for someone from a peasant background—to the position of a minor customs official, his relationships are—to put it mildly—not just blurred, but scrambled. Alois makes his first marriage opportunistically to Anna Glassl, a wealthy woman fourteen years his senior. He lives with Anna at an inn where incorrigibly he carries on an affair with a maid, Franziska. Before long, Klara, an attractive teenager working there, is (predictably) added to the mistress roster. Anna fortuitously dies and Alois marries Franziska, who (sensibly) has Klara ejected from the residence. Fate intervenes: Franziska (unfortunately) gets tuberculosis and goes away for treatment. Klara, now (of course) pregnant to Alois, is moved back into the home and stays there when Franziska returns, soon to tragically die.

Now living openly with Klara, Alois decides to legitimise their relationship but encounters a problem. Johann Georg Hiedler is the father of Alois and the granduncle of Klara—making her his niece. Displaying what can be described as a nice touch in genealogical jargon, the local priest describes the connection between the couple as 'bilateral affinity in the third degree touching the second'. Under pressure from Alois, he reluctantly refers the matter to the Vatican. Undeterred by such sensibilities as might trouble a parish priest, the more worldly papal officials do not see a problem, dispensation is granted, and Alois and Klara marry. Klara always refers to her husband as uncle. She proceeds to have three children who die very young, possibly from congenital defects arising from intermarriage. She is finally successful with her fourth child, a son, on whom she dotes. His name is Adolf.

Despite having a healthy childhood and adolescence, Hitler had little compunction in exaggerating health complaints to suit his ends; for example, he claimed to have serious lung disease (tuberculosis) to get out of secondary school. Hitler's indifferent course as a student, failure to get accepted to the School of Fine Art or the School of Architecture in Vienna and subsequent down-and-out life in Vienna, has been well described. Both his parents died by the time he was seventeen; he was indifferent to his father's death, but devastated by his mother's death from breast cancer. Dr Bloch, the Jewish doctor who treated Klara Hitler, said that in all his years of practice he had never seen anyone so upset at a funeral as Adolf.

By all accounts, Hitler was extremely prudish. The likelihood that he visited prostitutes in Vienna must be regarded with scepticism after being accosted by a seductive landlady. While looking for lodgings in Vienna with his friend Kubizck, an appalled Hitler accused the woman of being a Potiphar, the lascivious biblical wife.

Hitler regarded the Austro-Hungarian Empire and its military forces with contempt. Tracked down by the Austrian authorities in Munich, he wrote a bathetic letter pleading his case, was examined by a medical panel and discharged as medically unfit. There is no way of knowing why this occurred as the records were conveniently made to disappear after the Anschluss.

World War I broke out shortly after. Delirious with excitement, Hitler rushed off to enlist in a Bavarian regiment where they were not concerned about medical niceties, passing the physical without difficulty—although in the hysterical enthusiasm that greeted the start of the conflict it is doubtful whether recruits required anything more than a pair of eyes, arms and legs.

In *Mein Kampf*, Hitler described himself as a front-line fighter in the List Regiment, being wounded twice but surviving the duration of the conflict, and receiving two Iron Crosses. The Nazi propaganda machine constantly promoted the image of Hitler as a brave front-line soldier who had endured the worst conditions of battle and could identify with the lot of the common soldier. Weber has shown that the truth is somewhat less than that. Hitler was based at regimental headquarters as a dispatch runner—a position described by front-line soldiers as a 'rear area pig' for its comfort and safety. His principal duty was to take messages to the battalion headquarters, which were not on the front line. In doing so, he was exposed to artillery fire, but unlikely to be hit by machine-gun bullets, the real killers on the Western Front. While the ranks of the List Regiment were repeatedly decimated, Hitler was photographed with seven other regimental dispatch runners in 1915. All survived the war. It should be noted that the List Regiment's papers do not give any indication that its Jewish soldiers were subject to anti-Semitism. After Hitler came to power, those who could fled; at least twelve Jewish veterans of the List Regiment died in the Holocaust.

Being assigned to regimental headquarters increased his medal prospects as medals tended to be awarded to soldiers whom the officers were familiar with. Hitler won two Iron Crosses, being nominated for the Iron Cross First Class by the regiment's Jewish adjutant Hugo Gutmann. These findings explain why, despite being in action for four years, Hitler remained a corporal. To move up the ranks, he would have to serve in the trenches, giving up his better accommodation and food, hence his refusal to accept promotion.

Regarded by his comrades as the 'mad Austrian', Hitler could never give a brief answer to a question and seemed to live in his own world. He constantly annoyed his comrades by refusing to grumble or blame the generals. He was reluctant to take leave and refused to accompany his comrades to brothels, staying back at the base to draw buildings.

In the last action he was involved in during the war, Hitler's unit was gassed. Experiencing visual difficulties from exposure to mustard gas, he was transferred to a military hospital at Pasewalk near Munich where he learned of Germany's defeat. In *Mein Kampf*, he claimed that the shock of the news led to him losing his eyesight for three days. If this autobiographic snippet is true—*Mein Kampf* is rife with exaggeration and distortion—Hitler's eyesight was not harmed by the gassing. He had severe blepharitis and conjunctivitis which would have recovered over several days, rather than a hysterical blindness when he learned of the German surrender.

The Party Leader

Segue to 1929. Adolf Hitler is a rising political star in Germany. The Depression has rung the death knell of the Weimar Republic and the Nazi Party is rising above its Bavarian street-fighter origins, assuming national significance. The Hitler family romance (to quote his fellow Viennese, Sigmund Freud), redolent with incest, age discordance and power imbalance continues. Living in Munich, Hitler installs his half-sister, Paula Raubal, as housekeeper of his Obersalzburg lodge. Paula is accompanied by her voluptuous niece, Geli, eighteen. Soon enamoured of her glamorous male relative, Geli is constantly by his side. Hitler responds in kind and is completely infatuated with her. Uncle Wolf, as he likes Geli to call him, carries a whip and boasts about how long he can hold up his arm to receive party salutes. Geli, not only promiscuous but indiscreet, is reported to have said that Hitler had a highly abnormal approach to sex involving sadomasochism, undinism and coprophilic practices—as this book is written for family readers, the rest of you can look it up.

Unsurprisingly, Hitler, a control freak of Olympian dimensions, is prone to jealousy, and complains about Geli's flirting and frolicking. Geli, a free spirit and no great thinker, resents the restrictions and, in all likelihood, is bored with the relationship. Hitler catches Geli and his chauffeur in a compromising position. (For the rest of his life, the man considered himself lucky not to have been shot on the spot.) They quarrel. Geli goes to Vienna to train as an opera singer. She returns. Arguments break out. Hitler accuses her of an affair with her Jewish opera coach; she responds by claiming he is making up to Eva Braun—correctly, as it happens. Geli shoots herself in the chest in her bedroom. Hitler, once the matter was covered up to avoid a political scandal, is devastated. Geli's room is preserved as a shrine with no one allowed to enter. Hitler gives up eating meat.

The Dictator

After the Nazis came into power in 1933, Hitler maintains his bohemian habits, rising late, dismissing administrative tasks and staying up till the early hours of the morning with his sycophantic court. A proselytising health crank, he refuses to allow smoking in his presence, and seldom drinks. Constantly lecturing his acolytes on the iniquity of killing animals, he eats a bland vegetable diet, supplemented with Austrian cream cakes, guzzling down two plates at a sitting. With this combination, it is not surprising that he has flatulence, constipation and diarrhoea.

Hitler, a mass of terrifying insecurities, has to maintain an environment where his grandiose worldview could not be threatened. In most cases, he can use his blustering rhetoric to defend himself or surround himself with sycophantic or inferior characters. Pathologically secretive, he lies about his medical history, of which he discloses very little in any event. He tends to accept or reject treatment according to his whim.

Possibly the most flatulent leader in history, Hitler is obsessed with bowel function. In 1936, beset by dyspepsia and a spreading rash, Hitler agrees to see Dr Theodor Morell, the physician recommended by his photographer Heinrich Hoffman, who had successfully treated him for pyelitis. Morell promises to cure Hitler within a year. When the eczema disappears as promised, he is appointed the dictator's personal physician. With Morell as his doctor, Hitler knows that his profound fear of being discovered to have any hereditary deformities is safe, and doctor and patient can collude in treatment to maintain their respective self-beliefs.

Morell had a fashionable practice on the Kurfürstendamm, Berlin's equivalent of Harley Street. He had a rich and famous clientele, including a number of Jews, such as the singer Richard Tauber. He treated skin and urological diseases, one of the main planks of evidence in the school of thought that believes Hitler had syphilis. Morell joined the Nazi Party as a precaution but continued to treat Jews until 1938, two years after Hitler had become his patient. In this regard, he was no less opportunistic than virtually the entire (non-Jewish) German and Austrian medical profession, who joined the Nazi Party in droves after 1933 — sooner and more so than any other profession.

Morell has virtually exclusive care of Hitler from 1936 until the dictator's death. He became a fixture at the Nazi court and is constantly in Hitler's presence after the war started. Adding to the bizarre pantomime of the retinue, the obese Morell enjoys wearing a uniform, surely the largest size available aside from Goering's. His hygiene is poor, he never washes his hands and has dirt under his fingernails. Added to this his constant bowel rumbling, making for a less than appetising spectacle in public, to say nothing of the deterrent effect at the thought of having someone like that doing a medical examination.

Hitler constantly praises Morell to his followers, urging them to see him for consultations. Eva Braun finds his hygiene, or lack thereof, so repulsive she refuses to see him again. Speer goes through the motions but ignores his recommendations, regarding Morell as a screwball obsessed with making money. Goering, a professional morphomaniac, for reasons which can only be imagined, refers to him as the *Reich Jabmeister*.

Becoming the dominating figure in European politics in the thirties, Hitler is on the centre stage. In post-Depression Europe, still recovering from the devastation and subsequent chaos, he is admired as having brought back national pride and returning Germany to its rightful place on the international stage. To others, more prescient, he is darkly ominous, a figure intent on war at any cost.

What did the rest of the world make of this? Hitler's behaviour was a source of constant speculation. Two diplomatic figures give an idea of what he was like up close. Sir John Rumbold, the British ambassador to Berlin from 1928, described a meeting in 1933, three months after Hitler became Chancellor. Hitler commenced by making several claims so far-fetched that Rumbold declined to even respond. The tone remained affable until Rumbold raised the issue of the treatment of the Jews. The effect on Hitler was dramatic. He immediately began shouting, as if he were addressing an open-air meeting, with such ferocity that Rumbold could not respond with other issues.

Sir Eric Phipps, who succeeded Rumbold, had a similar experience at their first meeting in October 1933. Hardly had they started when Hitler began ranting that he was prepared to die, rather than sign away Germany's honour to foreign dictates. After this, he could not be interrupted. Taken aback by the 'shouting crescendo', Phipps left in a state of shock that such an unbalanced leader had such power in his hands.

At their meeting in November 1934, Phipps raised the issue of Germany's disarmament. Hitler, who had just supervised the killing of fifty-seven leading Nazis in the Night of the Long Knives, flew into such a rage that further discussion was impossible. In December 1935, asked about illegal rearmament and relations with the Soviet Union, he became virtually incoherent, repeatedly muttering that Germany was a great power, while the Russians were 'noxious microbes'. While doing so, he ground the floor with his heel, 'as though crushing a worm'.

The significance of these responses will be discussed below.

His hold on power consolidated, the German people completely in his thrall (and those who were racially or politically unacceptable kept out of sight, held in concentration camps or driven out of the country), Hitler went to war. Despite initial success, after the invasion of Russia the tide turned. The German advance slowed down to a crawl, their logistics stretched to the limit. It became apparent that they had no answer to the Russians' two greatest assets: 'General Winter', and their capacity to replace their soldiers and weapons. Following the reversals at Moscow and Stalingrad, it was a dogged struggle just to hold the line, and after the Battle of Kursk, a retreat all the way to Berlin. Although he knew he could no longer win, Hitler persisted with the war, directing the campaign from the Eastern military headquarters, isolated from events, totally absorbed with maps, battle despatches and radio conversations with his commanders.

After the fall of Stalingrad in early 1943, Hitler's health slumped drastically. General Guderian commented that Hitler appeared shaky and uncertain and had a vacant gaze. Albert Speer and Joseph Goebbels noted how he had aged.

Hitler's meticulous appearance and hygiene began to fray. He spilled food down the front of his uniform, walked with a stoop and struggled to sit and stand without supporting himself. In the past, he had gone to considerable lengths to hide this from his staff. Now it was impossible to hide. He found it difficult to attend the twice-daily briefing sessions and the times had to be changed to suit him. He developed an uncontrollable tremor, severe headaches and had two episodes of jaundice. His behaviour, became increasingly erratic, paranoid and driven by flights of fantasy, rather than a hard-headed appraisal of the military situation. Having appropriated every military leadership position, he got lost in the minutiae of detail, immersing himself in managing affairs at unit level while the overall situation lapsed into chaos for lack of clear decisions.

His sleep pattern was now completely inverted, so he stayed up till 5 a.m., regaling his unfortunate staff with the same anecdotes about his past and his appalling views on anything and everything, then sleeping during the day. By now, his audience could repeat the tales off by heart and a detached observer may have noted that he was increasingly prone to repeat himself during the same conversation.

Morell redoubled his efforts, giving Hitler daily glucose, multivitamin and hormone injections. Hitler also took Vitamultin (an amphetamine and vitamin preparation) tablets, praising their tonic effects. Opiates, orally and injected, were used for pain, worsening his bowel problems. Morell attributed Hitler's problems to hypertension and cardiac failure, and sent ECG tracings, under the nom-de-plume of Patient A, to a leading Berlin cardiologist. The cardiologist, who may have guessed who the patient was, diagnosed coronary sclerosis (hardening). Morell (who had heart disease himself) applied leeches, a procedure still used by doctors at the time, and administered powerful cardiac glycosides—the Strophanthin cure—on several occasions, as well as Metrazol, a cardiac stimulant. There was no need for this potentially harmful treatment but it should be noted that to this day, Germany has the world's highest prescription levels of cardiac medications based on the belief that the heart is the source of well-being.

In the assassination attempt on 20 July 1944, Hitler, who narrowly escaped death, suffered abrasions, contusions, superficial burns and torn eardrums. Other doctors were brought in to assist Morell. This put his treatment under scrutiny and led to what became known as the Doctors' Feud. Hitler's ears and sinuses were treated by ENT surgeon Erwin Giesing. He had the Dr Koester's Anti-gas Tablets that Hitler took (eight to sixteen tablets a day) analysed. When the results showed minute doses of strychnine and atropine, Hitler's surgeon Karl Brandt (later hanged by the Nuremberg medical tribunal for his role in the so-called euthanasia program) and the other doctors accused Morell of poisoning Hitler with his pills and injections. Morell emerged victorious. Hitler would not hear a word against his physician and refused to see the specialists again. However, their relationship steadily deteriorated after that.

By 1945, the Soviet forces were advancing steadily on Berlin and the Allied forces were pushing across the Rhine, a two-front attack on Germany. Hitler, by now quite out of touch with reality, moved non-existent forces around a map, still believing that in some way that he could stall Soviet forces long enough for them to fall out with the Allies and prolong the war. Despite his disintegrating grasp of reality, he played a big role in planning the doomed Ardennes Raid (*Battle of the Bulge*) and was able to argue fine points of strategy even though he was hopelessly wrong. Leading military figures, such as General von Manstein, would go to confront him, coming out yet again converted to Hitler's fantastic views about the possibility of holding back the enemy forces.

In February 1945, while checking Hitler's eyes, ophthalmologist Dr Lohlein diagnosed Parkinsonism. It still took for Morell until April to wake up to the screamingly obvious. Hitler, his diary stated, could have 'the shaking palsy' and he was given the Italo-Bulgarian cure, a belladonna extract of atropine and hyoscine. Even under ideal circumstances, this would have scarcely made much difference.

As it became impossible to ignore the military failure, Hitler reacted by blaming others. First it was individual commanders, the entire General Staff, then the subversive military clique who tried to assassinate him. As the Russians closed in, the Third Reich reduced to two blocks around the bunker in which he huddled, Hitler finally accepted the war had been lost. He blamed the German people, who had shown that they were not able to meet the requirements for an idealised Nazi society, and left them to their fate without a second thought.

His attitude is summed up in this statement to Speer:

> *If the war is lost, the nation will also perish. This fate is inevitable. There is no necessity to take into considera-tion the basis for which the people will need to continue a most primitive existence. On the contrary, it will be better to destroy these things ourselves because this nation will have proved to be the weaker one and the future will belong solely to the stronger eastern nation [Russia]. Besides, those who will remain after the battle are only the inferior ones, for the good ones have been killed.*

Hitler, a necromantic of Olympic dimensions, made his obses-sion with death a central feature of Nazi eschatology. There was more to this than mere posturing. Once he embarked on a politi-cal career, Hitler would melodramatically threaten to kill himself whenever he encountered any setbacks, such as the failure of the Munich Putsch. He was outraged when General Von Paulus surrendered to the Russians at Stalingrad, rather than kill himself. On 21 April 1945, as the Russians closed in on the bunker, and his suicide was inevitable.

Several days before his death, Hitler finally turned on Morell, accusing him of poisoning him, and dismissing him. This inadvertently saved Morell's life, allowing him to escape from Berlin. He was captured by the Allies and held for questioning.

The historian Hugh Trevor-Roper was selected to interrogate the top captured Nazis. Exposed to some of the most appalling mass murderers in history, Trevor-Roper was less than impressed by Morell, whom he described as a charlatan with the hygiene habits of a pig. Morell, who could consider himself fortunate he had not been captured by the Russians, was not charged with war crimes and was released from prison in 1947. Destitute and senile, he died in hospital in March 1948.

As Hitler's personal physician for nine years, Morell had more contact with the guarded and reclusive dictator than most people. Most of the information about his treatment of Hitler comes from Morell's medical diaries, now in the US archives, providing a unique insight into the dictator's health. The diaries need to be read with caution. Himmler would have been happy to hand Morell over to the SS if anything went wrong with Hitler; the diaries were written to provide him with an alibi. Morell knew all too well what it meant to get on the wrong side of his patient:

> *Hitler would go as white as a sheet and tightly clench his jaws, while his eyes would dilate. Everyone in his entourage would get panicky because these fits were always followed by an order to dismiss or to execute somebody.*

The view of Morell as a benign character compared to the rest of the Nazi hierarchy cannot be sustained after the revelation that he participated in the discussion about gassing 'euthanasia' patients, a process that led inexorably to the gas chambers of Auschwitz. For his work, he was richly rewarded by Hitler, getting several pharmaceutical factories confiscated from Jews in the East which he used to amass a fortune by supplying the German forces with a defective anti-lice preparation and a failed attempt at synthesising penicillin. In the end, the dictator got the only doctor he was comfortable with and, in all likelihood, deserved.

Adolf Hitler's Brain

Hitler had an extraordinarily dysfunctional personality, perhaps one that is beyond the scope of psychiatry, and for which use of the term 'psychopath' is both mundane and pointless. The personification of evil in history, Hitler was obsessed with racial hatred. It is often forgotten that he was not German, but Austrian. But it can be said with some certainty that his upbringing in a generationally confused, boundary obscuring, morally indistinct environment, interlaced with sadomasochistic themes like a Sacher torte, laid a distinctive template on which subsequent experiences were to encrust themselves in the most rebarbative fashion. In an astonishingly short period he had risen to be the greatest conqueror of Europe in history; then, entirely through his own errors in invading Russia and declaring war on America, he threw it all away.

Hitler continues to be a fixation of biographers, and new works on him pour out at an astonishing rate. Herein lies the problem; the available pool of information has been much picked over, and there is little chance of anything new emerging unless the Russian archives disgorge something unexpected in future.

The vast web of rumour, innuendo, court gossip and malicious invective that surrounds Hitler should be regarded with the greatest of scepticism. There is no consensus on what constituted Hitler's psychological make-up. The theories put up to explain his behaviour and personality cover every known form of psychopathology — and then some. The more gratuitous examples include being a victim of childhood abuse (Alice Miller) or a raging queen (*The Hidden Hitler*).

As an individual, Hitler was profoundly shallow, opaque and largely unfathomable. Only known to display affection towards Geli Raubal and his dog Blondi, his relationships were remarkably bleak; he had no friends, maintaining superficial relationships with his staff as a substitute. Unsurprisingly, his relationships with women were pathological. Of the five he was known to be involved with, three attempted suicide, two successfully.

In considering Hitler's medical history until the fall of Stalingrad the terrain is mostly empty. There is only secondary documentation before 1936; after 1936, the only source is

Morell's diaries plus a few comments from other doctors and individuals around him.

Discrepancies and discordant reports on Hitler's condition can be related to the strong impact he had on most people, as well as his constant tendency to hide his medical symptoms and avoid medical examination. Had the public known that the Führer was suffering from a neurological disorder (let alone a psychiatric condition), his public image would have slumped, his enemies in the military would have attempted the coup much earlier, and his would-be successors would not have waited until the very end to start their manoeuvring.

After he was gassed, Hitler ended up in the Pasewalk Hospital. Here, the patients learned from a priest of the German surrender. In *Mein Kampf*, Hitler stated that 'darkness' came over his vision for several days, the implication being that he lost his sight, which then recovered. The speculation on the Pasewalk incident is enough to fill several shelves. The 'Pasewalk School' holds that this was akin to a mystical experience, sufficient to turn the bohemian vagabond into a political leader who could first unite Germany, then conquer Europe and destroy the Jews. In the most sensational account, a psychiatrist, Dr Edmund Forster, hypnotised Hitler, inducing a grandiose hallucination, setting in motion the events that led to war and the genocide of the Jews. Unfortunately this intriguing scenario cannot be sustained. The idea that one soldier, suffering from what would at best be regarded as a minor affliction, would receive intense psychiatric treatment in a hospital trying to deal with huge numbers of battlefield casualties is untenable, to say nothing of the notion that anyone can be hypnotised into becoming a genocidal dictator (the *Pasewalk Candidate?*).

Hitler's front-line experiences during the war were more than sufficient to cause shell-shock, battle fatigue, or that current cynosure of victimology, post-traumatic stress disorder (PTSD). However, Hitler did not have any such condition. Given the public scrutiny of his situation as his political star ascended, it is difficult to see how this could have been hidden. The most significant pointer against it is Hitler's attitude to war. Far from abhorring it—the commonest response of PTSD victims—he glorified his front-line experiences and spoke longingly about them until the last days of his life.

A severe hypochondriac, Hitler was convinced he would die before his time. His most bizarre belief was his preoccupation with syphilis. He had the delusional idea that congenital syphilis equated to hereditary syphilis, and constantly conflated it with his other, terrible belief that Jews spread the disease.

It is a recurrent response for tyrants, dictators and the like to be accused of having syphilis. Stalin did not have syphilis. Mao did not have syphilis (although his doctor later disclosed that he had episodes of gonorrhoea). Since 1992, when Israeli doctors published a paper based on documents in the newly opened Kremlin archives, we know that Lenin died of neurosyphilis, something the USSR had tried to keep secret since 1924. And, despite the wishes of most of the civilised world, neither does Robert Mugabe.

Did Hitler have syphilis? One of the chief sources of specu-lation was the rumour that Morell had treated Hitler for this. However, the medical diaries do not mention examining, diag-nosing or treating Hitler for syphilis or any venereal disease. The likelihood that Hitler visited prostitutes in Vienna must be regarded with equal scepticism.

To date the most methodical examination of Hitler's health has been by Fritz Redlich, a psychoanalyst who had to flee Vienna to the United States, where he became a leading psychiatrist. Redlich believed that giant cell (temporal) arteritis could have explained many of Hitler's symptoms, on the basis of his coronary artery insufficiency, frontal headaches and visual difficulties. However, rheumatologists have disputed this assessment.

Since his early days as a politician, there has been an enduring debate over whether Hitler had genital abnormalities—what Alan Bullock genially described as the one-ball theory. Morell maintained that Hitler's genitals were normal, as did his childhood family doctor, Eduard Bloch. Hitler would not allow himself to be examined, particularly in the trunk area. He insisted on self-administering an enema, making Morell remain outside the toilet door. The opinions of Bloch and Morell that Hitler had normal genitalia did not end the debate. Bloch, the only Jew in Austria after the Anschluss to have a personal letter from the Führer addressed to the SS, was interviewed at the end of his life in New York where he was something of a minor celebrity as a result of his notorious patient. Morell made so many untenable claims about examinations he had performed on Hitler that he has no credibility at all.

Redlich thought that Hitler's self-consciousness, refusal to undress in front of anyone, constant hand washing and refusal to have X-rays of the abdomen indicated that he had congenital deformities and was going to some effort to ensure that no one learned about this. The tendency to dribble after urination, coupled with the repeated insinuations of penile and testicular deformities, is suggestive of spina bifida occulta which is often associated with genital abnormalities such as monorchidism (missing testicle) or hypospadias (a hole in the penis from the urethra). Spina bifida occulta is a congenital condition due to lack of closure of the lower spinal canal; 'occulta' means that it is not evident, but may be associated with various abnormalities, including the urogenital area.

It is no longer possible to accept that Morell's injections did not have a significant psychoactive effect. He regularly gave Hitler amphetamines in a special vitamin injection 'Vitamultin'. There are reports of Hitler being fretful and listless before an injection, after which he would become lively and energetic, which leaves no doubt about this. Psychiatrist Leonard Heston believed Morell had addicted Hitler to amphetamines, causing irrational behaviour, outbursts of anger and poor decision-making. While cautious about confirming addiction, Redlich did not deny that there were times when it was evident that Hitler was affected by amphetamines.

In order to understand how Hitler's brain affected his behaviour, we need to work backwards. It is now widely accepted that by the end of his life Hitler had Parkinson's syndrome (PS). A distinction needs to be made between Parkinson's disease (PD), the common age-onset condition, and (PS), which can arise from trauma, vascular insufficiency, infection or drugs. The most well-known case of PS is that of Muhammad Ali, as a result of repeated head trauma during his boxing career.

Several writers advanced the view that Hitler had severe PS causing high-grade gait, posture deficiencies, and left-sided tremor. People in Hitler's immediate environment, such as his secretaries and servants, confirmed the diagnosis with descriptions of the typical symptoms, which is backed up by interviews with military figures, reports in the literature, and evidence in film clips. Speer said that Hitler was:

shrivelling up like an old man. His limbs trembled; he walked stooped, with dragging footsteps. Even his voice became quavering and lost its old masterfulness ... his uniform, which in the past he had kept scrupulously neat, in this last period of life was stained by the food he had eaten with a shaking hand.

News films from 1943, despite being edited before they were shown to the public, showed unmistakable signs of Parkinsonism, including the stooped shuffling gait, left-sided tremor and blank, motionless face by the beginning of 1945. Two short clips in March 1945 that escaped censorship show the typical gait and posture, as well as the characteristic tremor at rest. By March 1945, when walking, Hitler needed constant support and had to rest every twenty metres.

Despite the censorship, the public were aware of the changes. Melitta Maschmann, a member of the League of German Girls, wrote in her diary: 'The newsreels showed an ageing man, who walked with a stoop and glanced anxiously about him. His voice sounded shrill with despair.'

Morell's diary has no comment on his tremor, gait or posture for the obvious reason that Morell did not recognise the presence of Parkinsonism until March 1945. To confuse the situation even further, his medication had an inadvertent impact on Hitler's symptoms. Dr Koester's Anti-gas Tablet, (up to sixteen a day), contained four milligrams of belladonna extract which could alleviate some symptoms of Parkinsonism. The amphetamine and caffeine injections could also have weak efficacy on some Parkinsonian symptoms but, at the same time, worsen the tremor.

While Hitler's tremor disappeared for a short period after the explosion in the July 1944 assassination attempt, it soon returned; he dragged his left leg as if it were lame, his head shook and there was a flickering and twitching of his eyes. The following month he told his staff that his death in the explosion would have relieved a 'severe nervous disease' — possibly the only intimation of the nature of his condition.

In February 1945 Professor Max de Crinis, the highest-ranking SS physician and Director of the Neurological University Hospital, Charite, Berlin, informed SS-General Schellenberg and Heinrich Himmler that Hitler had PD. De Crinis prepared an anti-parkinsonian mixture for Hitler, but Stumpfegger, a physician in Himmler's confidence, refused to deliver the prescription.

Neurologist Ellen Gibbels analysed eighty-three newsreel sequences and interviewed three people who had been in Hitler's entourage. What she described as 'a mild habitual hypoactivity of the left arm' was visible in 1939. She believed the disease began at the latest in 1941 with tremor on the left side. Left-sided slowing of movement then increased and became generalised. Gibbels came to the conclusion that the diagnosis of moderately severe PS was incontestable.

This line of speculation took an intriguing turn in 1986. Lieberman, a neurologist, stated that Hitler had PS from a relatively early age, an unusual development then and now, for which the likely cause was encephalitis lethargica (EL): There were three likely periods when Hitler could have contracted EL, the epidemic that swept the world from 1917 to 1925 (see the chapter on Constantin von Economo). Firstly, when he was eleven, his younger brother George (aged six) died of measles. One of the delayed consequences of measles is subacute sclerosing panencephalitis, which leads to protracted neurological and behavioural difficulties in adult life, in addition to early-onset Parkinson's disease.

Stationed on the Western Front between 1916 and 1918, Hitler would have been in contact with soldiers infected with EL. In October 1916, following a shrapnel wound to the left thigh, he was hospitalised for several weeks, transferred to recuperate at a military hospital in Berlin, followed by two months of guard duty in Munich where the EL epidemic was rampant.

Lieberman believes that Hitler developed EL at Pasewalk Hospital in November 1918, leading to the development of PS at a relatively young age. When the war ended the following month, Hitler remained in Munich.

Alternatively—and this is the least likely scenario—the encephalitis could have arisen at Vinnitsa, his Eastern Front headquarters, in 1942, where it was hot, humid and mosquito-ridden. Hitler complained of a constant headache. Morell's comments on his health at the time were picked up by historians, Alan Bullock referring to an episode of 'inflammation of the brain' from the entries in Morell's diaries which only indicate that he had symptoms consistent with a viral infection and headache, but recovered.

The paradox is that, of all the physicians who dealt with Hitler, only Morell would have had experience with EL from being a front-line doctor during World War I. Intriguingly, he once said that Hitler's problems could be summed up in one word: '*Kopfgrippe*', the alternative name for EL. However, he never wrote anything about this in his diaries, confirming that when it counted, Morell could not have made a diagnosis if it hit him over the head and wrote its name across his forehead.

Among its many features, EL can lead to character changes, sociopathic behaviour and a 'charismatic glow'. The most distinctive sign is oculogyric crises—a rolling upward movement of the eyes—which is not found in any other condition. During the Czech crisis in 1938, Édouard Daladier, the French Prime Minister, observed how Hitler's eyes suddenly developed 'a hard strained look' and turned upwards.

On meeting Hitler in 1939, the Swedish diplomat Essen Dahlerus commented that the German leader seemed to be in a trance. He described Hitler having an oculogyric crisis with facial spasms, palilalia (constantly repeating statements) and tics, which was supported by photographic evidence.

In 1942 Baldur von Schirach, a Nazi official, noted that during a conversation, Hitler's eyes would suddenly dart off to the side as if he were watching somebody else.

The most enduring demonstration of Hitler's PS can be seen in the changes in his signature on documents from an early point in his political career. Hitler's early handwriting has excessive rigidity, restrained and deteriorated motion, and lack of flow and rhythm. By the end of his life (for example, on his marriage certificate the day before he died), his cramped and sloping signature was almost unreadable, a typical example of micrographia.

The premorbid personality (premorbid means before the onset of the illness) of Parkinsonian patients includes obsessionality, craving for recognition, megalomania, limited interest in sex, inflexibility and pedantry. Hitler, a teetotaller, had no recreational activities, never smoked and only existed for the sake of his (terrible) work. He lacked any ability for self-criticism, never doubted his own abilities, and was 'a stranger to compassion and scruples'. His interest in women was very limited and hyposexuality (low or non-existent sex drive) can be assumed.

He did not finish school, seek any training (after his applications to art and architecture schools were rejected) and was content to lead a bohemian life. His surviving paintings and postcards lacked creativity, he only copied work by others in a stereotyped manner, producing a series of urban landscapes, highly schematic as if produced for an architectural draft, the few people depicted in them as stick-like presences devoid of emotion.

He was besotted by the music of Wagner and it played a major part in his megalomaniac ideology. Hitler's mystical obsessions ensured that the iconography of Nazism was derived from ancient Aryan roots, giving full support to the bizarre fantasies of acolytes such as Hess and Himmler.

The best evidence that Hitler had an episode of EL early in life is that he had bouts of uncontrollable rage and permanent restlessness while his intellectual functions remained unchanged. From an early stage, Hitler had difficulties establishing or maintaining personal relationships. He constantly accused others of treachery, while deceiving and betraying them for his personal advantage. He completely lacked sympathy with others and never showed any remorse.

Chronic insomnia, somnolence and reversed sleep–wake cycle are prominent features of EL—indeed, they were the characteristic features after the 1917 outbreak. After World War I, Hitler's sleep pattern changed drastically. He would spend most of the night with his party sidekicks, usually in restaurants and cafes, then sleeping till late in the morning. When asked, he said his insomnia had arisen when he was a despatch rider in 1916—just about the same time that EL first infected the soldiers. From 1935 he had almost total sleep inversion and would be up most of the night. Morell's sleeping tablets had only limited effect and he would then need a stimulant to overcome the drowsiness during the day. By the time of the war, the pattern was set of Hitler sitting up all night with his entourage who had to listen to him endlessly recounting anecdotes.

Typical features of PS include changes in appetite, polydipsia (excessive thirst), photophobia (sensitivity to light), sweating and sensitivity to noise. Hitler's staff observed that he constantly drank mineral water and tea, sweated profusely and required several baths a day. As a result, he would wear his hat brim low and at times use dark glasses indoors. A related symptom was hyperacusis (sensitivity to noise) and he would require people to speak in a low tone or whisper.

A number of signs point towards right laterality. First, his Parkinsonian symptoms were most pronounced, if not restricted, to the left side. The first visible symptom was a tremor in his left hand. As far back as 1932, his press agent noticed during a plane trip, when they were fearing a crash, how his left hand went into spasm, clenching and unclenching. Two years later, in Leni Riefenstahl's movie *Triumph of the Will*, it can be seen how he always held his left hand against his body to suppress its movement. As this persisted and worsened to the end of his life, his characteristic stance of holding it against his body with the other hand could not succeed in hiding the tremor, which extended to the left leg as well.

The perception of time, as opposed to space, is based on the left side of the brain. Hitler was notoriously unpunctual, understandable in a dictator, but more important, he could only function on a present-time basis. Consequently, Hitler insisted on immediate action in any combat situation when it was clearly evident that a delay to rebuild forces was far more appropriate. This may explain his absolute refusal to contemplate that the Nazi invasion of the Soviet Union could last until the arrival of the Russian winter, leaving his forces unprotected for the extreme weather—but this can be just as easily attributed to the belief in his invincibility after the smashing victories that preceded the invasion.

Another example of Hitler's inability to conceptualise issues in a verbal and logical manner was his obsession with running the war from maps, spending day after day in the war room, rather than gaining a comprehensive and accurate perception of events by viewing the scene of action or giving more credence to reports of observers. This is a caricature of how the right hemisphere deals with the concepts of language, symbolism and emotion.

That Hitler was irrational would only be expected of such a tyrant and was a key feature of his hold on power, impressing anyone who challenged him. What was unusual was the cult he made of this. Until the end of his life, Hitler would state his dislike of the rational, the intellectual and the learned response, instead pronouncing the superiority of his instinctive reaction. He refused to allow his officials to present a measured argument in which the facts would be carefully marshalled to make a case, insisting instead on a brief summary of no more than a page regardless of how important or complex the matter would be. This contrasted with his grasp of physical details, for example, the technical features of tanks and artillery, or the dispositions of front-line forces.

Hitler's notorious paroxysms of rage, described as 'seizures of violence' appear to have a neurological basis. His teachers and his friend Kubizek reported that the bouts of rage were present during his early youth. In 1934, Hermann Rauschnigg described how he stamped his feet, banged his fists, foamed at the mouth, his eyes fixed and his face distorted and purple. When the episode would suddenly subside, he would peer around the room to see if anyone was laughing at him.

In March 1945, when tank commander Heinz Guderian made it clear to Hitler that the war was lost, he described his reaction:

His face was marked with large red blotches. His left arm and whole left side of his body was trembling more violently than usual and he looked as if he was going to throw himself at the General ... [he] poured out invectives, accusations and loathing ...

To summarise, the factors favouring the case for PS due to EL are:

1 Onset of Parkinsonism below the age of fifty, in the era 1920–1950, was three times more likely to reflect post-encephalitic PS than PD.

2 Hitler, at thirty-four, had PS symptoms, albeit transient, by 1923. Historian Werner Maser claimed that Hitler had tremors in his left leg and arm with spasticity in the left hand after the Munich Putsch of 1923. This lasted until the end of 1924. After this, Hitler is observed in many photographs to hold his left hand with his right hand to suppress the tremor.

3 Oculogyric crises.

4 Palilalia. In 1940, Rauschnigg described how Hitler responded to enemy propaganda about Nazi atrocities in the captured territories: 'Yes, we are barbarians! We want to be barbarians! It is an honourable title.'

5 The report of a seizure in 1932—seizures are rare in Parkinson's disease

6 Personality features dominated by utter amorality, ruthlessness, exploitation and grandiosity while seemingly maintaining a coherent facade and high intellectual function.

To say that an infection causing EL induced Hitler to become both the greatest conqueror of Europe since Napoleon and the worst genocidal killer in history is speculation of the highest order, but speculation based on observable symptoms—which is more than other theories on Hitler which use only psychological speculation as evidence.

For the first thirty years of his life, Hitler was utterly undistinguished. He failed to gain entrance into the Vienna Academy of Fine Art or the Vienna School of Architecture, and never rose above the rank of corporal despite receiving rewards for gallantry. A man like this, it seemed, could never have transformed a defeated Germany. From the time he sent his troops into French-occupied Rhineland, he was able to outmanoeuvre his opponents by doing what no one expected him to do—the ultimate in brinkmanship. All his life, he was a supreme opportunist and gambler. This is one thing to do in a card game; it is entirely another when a nation's fate is the stake. His run of luck held until the invasion of Russia when the Soviet General Georgi Zhukov turned back his forces in the snows of Moscow. Had the Nazis succeeded in holding Russia, there is little doubt that the Slav *Untermenschen* would have been the next in line for extermination. From this point his luck deserted him and his strategic skills were shown up for what they were: the grandiose opportunism of an inept bungler.

In the last weeks of his life, the dictator of the Thousand-year Reich, a man who all his life could never stand to be contradicted, was left in control of a mere two Berlin street blocks, his denial only crumpling when Russian shells exploded above his bunker. This ending does not require the explanation of a psychiatric disorder, it is merely the collapse of colossal hubris in the face of overwhelming evidence to the contrary.

The Thousand-year Reich barely lasted twelve years, but the costs to the world were incalculable. It is estimated that fully fifty million people died, of whom at least twelve million were deliberately murdered in what can only be described as an industrial assembly line process of genocide. Knowing the cause was lost, Hitler continued his war against an enemy that could not fight back—the Jews—and took his own people down with him in the process. In so doing he does not deserve to be granted the exceptionalism of some sort of disability; rather, he should be seen as driven by an insatiable affinity with death that has never before been seen in human history, and hopefully never will be seen again. That, if nothing else, is as close to the definition of pure evil as we shall ever see.

CONCLUSION

This book starts with the events, both natural and induced, that led to Sam Kaplan's dissolution. If anatomy is destiny—and it surely is—then history is divinity. We have looked at the lives of a small and diverse group of individuals. What is admittedly no more than a microcosm has allowed us some insight into how their brains, in some cases pathologically altered, in others only functioning more definitively, produce some of the most endearing, important and, unavoidably, worst aspects of human nature.

Most of the individuals described were forces for good, in some cases amazingly so, who left the world a better place. The others did the opposite; Hitler will remain ever so the most evil human being who lived. His moral malignancy notwithstanding, Hitler too had a brain and it is hoped that the case put forward (and it is only a case, not a proven brief, however intriguing the premises), will be a small contribution to understanding perfidy, turpitude and depravity of cosmic proportions.

And, as the rabbi said to the actress, this is a group? The first two individuals have no known identity aside from the examples of their work that have survived to our era—but what class! Inscriptions and paintings by men with stones and powder that deserve to hang in the greatest galleries. Ezekiel, tossed into exile in the Fertile Crescent where settled society began, first raging, revoking, berating and baffling, then inspiring his disconsolate flock. The artists—Leonardo the-ever incomparable, Vincent van Gogh, his brushes and pen flailing like a manic combine harvester, Nijinsky the soaring balletic Icarus—driven ever further by their inner visions, never attaining the impossible goals they set themselves but leaving the world an immeasurably better place in which to live. The women, Frida the artistic documenter of the twisted, tormented tortured body, and Bertha Pappenheim, an icon for the misunderstood and misappropriated, who firmly turned her back on an experience that would have shackled most of us for the rest of our lives, instead becoming a lighthouse to victims, a light unto gentiles and a deeply resourceful intellect of whose work all too little survives. The criminals who all in their own ways show us that, *contra* Mrs Thatcher, there is always a society in which we have to function, most within it, some on the margins and others in its dungeons. And the oddities, Arthur Inman lying in a darkened room, peering over his notebook at a sweet-faced street girl he hoped to fondle. Jack Ruby ever wanting to be someone who counted but, fuelled by amphetamines and pushed past his usually shaky limits into taking the fatal misstep that left history in limbo. Where would the world be without them, instead populated by a collection of identical clones, all doing exactly what is expected of them? North Korea perhaps.

The utterings of those, from Karl Marx to the current crop of commentariat agnostics, who say that religion is no more than a medieval soporific, are ignoring the fact that spirituality is as crucial a factor in defining our nature as it was over 100,000 years ago in Africa when we first expanded beyond the physical constraints of a 1350-millilitre brain.

While the selection of the cases was based on no more than curiosity, coupled by the belief (or, at the time of starting, hope) that there was a clear illustration of how their brains functioned, the unintended symmetries emerged. Those artists described show how their natural talent, talent of extraordinary virtuosity, was powered by the surging voltage of the temporo-limbic system. While Trebitsch could never have been a Hitler, no matter how much he might have dreamed of it, if only Hitler had been a Trebitsch. If the astonishing organising skills and capacity to engage people of a Joe Silver had not been mutated by the psychopathy induced by social forces that made him marginal in a hostile world and the warping effect of progressive syphilis, how much could he have contributed to society?

From Blombos Cave on the divine South African coast to the sizzling cement plazas of Dallas, this voyage started a long way and a long time ago. Or so it seems; in fact, it is a mere blink of the eye in geologic time. At the start, we have a quotation of some uncertainty and pessimism. We can only end with a message from one of the great brain men of his day, Charles Sherrington who, as anyone who knows his work will tell you, was not prone to whimsy. But after a lifetime of working and studying our truly amazing, totally fabulous and simply incredible human brain, Sherrington could not restrain himself and leaves us to conclude with words that remind us that, when all is said and done, the science of the brain is nothing less than the art of life:

The brain is an enchanted loom where millions of flashing shuttles weave a dissolving pattern, always a meaningful pattern, though never an abiding one.

Robert M. Kaplan
Windhoek, Swakopmund, Cape Town, Austinmer
March–December 2010.

ACKNOWLEDGEMENTS

This book, as the introduction indicates, started a long time ago, but along the way some people have made contributions for which I will always be grateful:

The guiding spirit throughout this book has been Norman Geschwind, whose work remains for me the green light across the water.

Secondly, the late Lesley Kiloh, Emeritus Professor of Psychiatry at the School of Psychiatry, University of New South Wales, Sydney, who was not only brave enough to provide the opportunity for me to become a psychiatrist, but prepared to tolerate thousands of my seemingly pointless questions. A brain man who could hold his own among any of them.

My publisher, Sue Hines of Allen & Unwin, who was responsible for the genesis and accouchement of this book and bravely tolerated a thousand bad jokes, most of them about publishers. That she is prepared to take a chance on such a hapless scribbler remains a minor miracle of the age.

Fourthly, to all those who were involved in the production of this book by providing help, wisdom, tolerance and humour above and beyond the call of duty. They are many in number, an amazing fact in view of my avowed fecklessness, but I must mention by name Garry Walter, Editor of *Australasian Psychiatry* and, more importantly, endlessly encouraging of my wildest schemes; my inhouse editor, Siobhán Cantrill, for not boggling at some of the more tendentious paragraphs I inserted in the text; and, the librarians at Wollongong Hospital and the RACP Medical History Library, Sydney, without whom any such work would never be possible.

A number of people were kind enough to field questions or look at some text excerpts, tactfully giving advice when necessary: Professor Michael Besser; Professor Bernard Wasserstein;

Emeritus Professor David Lewis-Williams; Dr Sarah Wurz; Dr Keith Lethlean; Dr Milton Lewis; Professor Harold Merskey; Professor Charles van Onselen.

Finally, on a personal note, this book could not have been written without the help, encouragement and support of Marita Hodel Gutmundsen who was prepared to put up with the whining, self-pity and endless groaning of a despairing author for close to eight months during the work on the text. Not for nothing is she a candidate for Norway's finest, and I thank her from the bottom of my heart.

A closing note: While drawing on the work of legions of brain men, women and other writers, the opinions in this book are entirely my own. I am quite certain that some readers will not agree with my account of events or interpretation, in which case I can only agree to disagree and hope they enjoyed the other parts of the book. To the rest of my readers, I hope that the experience leads them to look at the brain in a new light; if it leads some to make further inquiries, then I can feel I have indeed been of some assistance.

FURTHER READING

It is impossible to write a book of this nature without accessing and searching several thousand sources, both articles and books. Were they to be individually cited, the list would extend for at least 25 pages and interfere substantially with the text flow for the reader. On that basis, I have provided a short list of articles and books on each topic for the interested reader who wishes to pursue the topic further.

Chapter 1: Daidalos

Bressloff, P.C., Cowan, J.D., Golubitsky, M. & Thomas, P.J. 2002, 'What geometric visual hallucinations tell us about the visual cortex', *Neural Computation*, 14:473–491.

Deacon & Deacon 1999, *Human Beginnings in South Africa: Uncovering the Secrets of the Stone Age*, David Phillip Publishers, Claremont, South Africa.

ffytche, D.H. 2002, 'Cortical bricks and mortar', *Journal of Neurolology, Neurosurgery and Psychiatry*, 73(5):472.

ffytche, D.H. 2004, 'Visual hallucination and illusion disorders: a clinical guide', *Advances in Clinical Neuroscience and Rehabilitation*, 4(2).

Henshilwood, C.S., Marean, C.W., Chase, P., Davidson, I., Gamble, C., Holliday, T.W., Klein, R.G., McBrearty, S. & Zilhão, J. 2003, 'The origin of modern human behaviour', *Current Anthropology*, 44:627–651.

Wadley, L. 2001, 'What is cultural modernity? A general view and a South African perspective from Rose Cottage Cave', *Cambridge Archaeological Journal*, 11(2):201–221.

Chapter 2: Heinrich Klüver

Cheyne, J.A. 2005, 'Sleep paralysis episode frequency and number, types, and structure of associated hallucinations', *Journal of Sleep Research*, 14 (3):319–324.

Davoli, C.D. 2007, 'Heinrich Klüver's "divine" plant', *Journal of the History of the Neurosciences*, 16: 318–319.

Griffiths, R.R., Richards, W.A., McCann, U. & Jesse, R. 2006, 'Psilocybin can occasion mystical-type experiences having substantial and sustained personal meaning and spiritual significance', *Psychopharmacology*, 187 (3):268–283.

Klüver, H. 1966, *Mescal and mechanisms of hallucinations*, Chicago: University of Chicago Press.

Nahm, F.K.D. 1997, 'Heinrich Klüver and the temporal lobe syndrome', *Journal of the History of the Neurosciences*, 6(2): 193-208.

Nahm, F. & Pribram, K. *Heinrich Klüver 1897–1979: A Biographical Memoir*, National Academies Press, Washington DC, 1998. See: http://www.nap.edu/readingroom.php?book=biomems&page=hkluver.html.

Chapter 3: Nqabayi

Bartocci, G. & Dein, S. 2005, 'Detachment: Gateway to the world of spirituality', *Transcult Psychiatry*, 42(4):545–569.

Cheyne, J.A. & Girard, T.A. 2004, 'Spatial characteristics of hallucinations associated with sleep paralysis', *Cognitive Neuropsychiatry*, 9(4):281–300.

Cheyne, J. Allan T. & Girard, T.A. 2009, 'The body unbound: Vestibular–motor hallucinations and out-of-body experiences', *Cortex*, 45: 201–215.

Hufford, D.J. 2005, 'Sleep paralysis as spiritual experience', *Transcult Psychiatry*, 42(1):11–45.

Lewis-Williams, J.D. 1986, 'Cognitive and optical illusions in San Rock art research', *Current Anthropology*, 27(2).
Lewis-Williams, D. 2002, *The Mind In The Cave: Consciousness And The Origins Of Art*, Thames & Hudson, London.

Chapter 4: Norman Geschwind

Geschwind, N. 1983, 'Interictal behavioral changes in epilepsy', *Epilepsia*, 24 (Suppl 1): S23–S30.
Geschwind, N. & Levitsky, W. 1968, 'Human brain: left-right asymmetries in temporal speech region', *Science*, 161(837):186–187.
Schachter, S. & Devinsky, O. 1997, *Behavioral Neurology and the Legacy of Norman Geschwind*, Lippincott Williams & Wilkins, Philadelphia PA.

Chapter 5: The Prophet Ezekiel

Callahan, T. 2005, 'Ezekiel's spaceships, *Skeptic*, 12(1): 70.
Devinsky, J., Schachter, S. 2009, 'Norman Geschwind's contribution to the understanding of behavioral changes in temporal lobe epilepsy: The February 1974 lecture', *Epilepsy & Behavior*, 15: 417–424.
Geschwind, N., 'Personality changes in temporal lobe epilepsy', *Epilepsy & Behavior*, 15: 425–433.
Masia, S.L. & Devinsky, O. 2000, 'Epilepsy and behavior: A brief history', *Epilepsy & Behavior*, 1: 27–36.
Roberts, J.K., Robertson, M.M. & Trimble, M.R. 1982, 'The lateralising significance of hypergraphia in temporal lobe epilepsy', *Journal of Neurology, Neurosurgery and Psychiatry* 45(2): 131–138.
Shetty, T. & Trimble, M. 1997, 'The Bear Fedio Inventory: Twenty years on', *Journal of Epilepsy*, 10(5): 254–262.

Simon, B. 2009, 'Ezekiel's geometric vision of the restored temple: From the rod of his wrath to the reed of His measuring, *Harvard Theological Review*, 102:4 411–38.

Trimble, M. & Freeman A., 2006, 'An investigation of religiosity and the Gastaut–Geschwind syndrome in patients with temporal lobe epilepsy', *Epilepsy & Behavior*, 9: 407–414.

Van Nuys, K. 1953, 'Evaluating the pathological in prophetic experience (in particularly Ezekiel)', *Journal of Bible and Religion*, 21(4): 244–251.

Waxman, S.G. & Geschwind, N. 2005, 'Classics in epilepsy and behavior: 1974 Hypergraphia in temporal lobe epilepsy'. *Epilepsy & Behavior*, 6: 282–291.

Chapter 6: Leonardo da Vinci

Eduardo, & Kickhöfel, H.P. 2009, '*Sine ars scientia nihil est*: Leonardo da Vinci and beyond', *Epilepsy & Behaviour*, 14(Suppl 1): 5–11.

Schott, G.D. 1979, 'Some neurological observations on Leonardo da Vinci's handwriting', *Journal of the Neurological Sciences*, 42 :321–329.

Schott, G.D & Wyke, M.W. 1981, 'Congenital mirror movements', *Journal of Neurology, Neurosurgery & Psychiatry*, 44: 586–599.

Schott, G.D 2007, 'Mirror writing: neurological reflections on an unusual phenomenon', *Journal of Neurology, Neurosurgery & Psychiatry*, 78: 5–13.

Chapter 7: Antoine Laurent Jessé Bayle

Brown, E.M. 1994, 'French psychiatry's reception of A.L.J. Bayle's discovery of general paresis of the insane', *Bulletin of the History of Medicine*, 68: 235–253.

Brown, E.M. 2000, 'Why Wagner-Jauregg won the Nobel Prize for discovering malariatherapy for general paresis of the insane', *History of Psychiatry*, 11: 371–382.

Claude Quetel, C. 1990, *History of Syphilis*, Oxford: Polity Press.

Chapter 8: Joseph Lis

Brittain, R. 1970, 'The sadistic murderer', *Medicine Science and the Law*, 10: 198–207.

Dubin, L. 2006, 'Introduction: Port Jews in the Atlantic world', *Jewish History*, 20(2): 117–127.

Kaplan, R.M. 2007, 'Searching the Silver trail: Charles van Onselen, Joe Silver and Jack the Ripper', *Australasian Psychiatry*, 15(3): 217–21.

Van Onselen, C. 2007, *The Fox and the Flies: The World of Joseph Silver, Racketeer and Psychopath*, Jonathan Cape, London.

Van Onselen C., 'Jewish police informers in the Atlantic world, 1880–1914', *The Historical Journal*, 50(1): 119–144.

Chapter 9: Jean-Baptiste-Édouard Gélineau

Austin, S.C., Stolley, P.D. & Lasky T. 1992, 'The history of malariotherapy for neurosyphilis', *JAMA*, 268: 516–519.

Bladin, P.F. 2000, 'Narcolepsy–Cataplexy and psychoanalytic theory of sleep and dreams', *Journal of the History of the Neurosciences*, 9(2): 203–217.

Cao, M. & Guilleminault, C. 2011, 'Hypocretin and its emerging role as a target for treatment of sleep disorders', *Current Neurological Neuroscience*, 11(2): 227–34.

Cheyne, J.A. & Girard, T.A. 2004, 'Spatial characteristics of hallucinations associated with sleep paralysis', *Cognitive Neuropsychiatry*, 9(4): 281–300.

Dauvilliers, Y., Arnulf, I. & Mignot, E. 2007, 'Narcolepsy with cataplexy', *Lancet*, 369(9560): 499–511.

Dement, W.C. 1993, 'The history of narcolepsy and other sleep disorders', *Journal of History of the Neurosciences*, 2: 121–134.

Passouant, P. 1982, 'Doctor Gelineau (1828–1906): Narcolepsy centennial', *Sleep*, 3(31): 241–246.

Chapter 10: Vincent Van Gogh

Arnold, W.N. 2004, 'The illness of Vincent van Gogh', *Journal of the History of the Neurosciences* 13(1): 22–43

Blumer, D. 2002, 'The illness of Vincent van Gogh', *The American Journal of Psychiatry*, April (4): 519–26.

Hughes, J.R. 2005, 'Review: A reappraisal of the possible seizures of Vincent van Gogh', *Epilepsy & Behavior*, 6: 504–510.

Van Gogh letters, see: http://vangoghletters.org/vg/

Voskuil, P.H.A. 1992, 'Vincent van Gogh's malady: a test case for the relationship between temporal lobe dysfunction and epilepsy?', *Journal of Historical Neuroscience*, 1: 155–162.

Chapter 11: Bertha Pappenheim

Borch-Jacobsen M. 1996, '*Remembering Anna O.: A Century of Mystification*, Routledge, New York.

Bristow, E.J. 1982, *Prostitution and Prejudice: The Jewish Fight against White Slavery*, 1870–1939, Schocken Books, New York.

Kaplan, R.M. 2004, 'O Anna: being Bertha Pappenheim—historiography and biography', 12(1): 62–68.

Merskey, H. 1992, 'Anna O. had a severe depressive illness', *British Journal of Psychiatry*, 161: 185–194.

Thornton, E.M. 1983, *Freud and Cocain, The Freudian Fallacy*, Paladin Books, London.

Chapter 12: Eugen Bleuler

Berlim, M.T., Mattevi, B.S., Belmonte-de-Abreu, P. & Crow, T.J. 2003, 'The etiology of schizophrenia and the origin of language: overview of a theory', *Comprehensive Psychiatry*, 44(1): 7–14.

Crow. TJ. 1997, 'Is schizophrenia the price that Homo sapiens pay for language?' *Schizophrenia Research*, 28: 127–141.

Crow, T.J. 2002, 'Handedness, language lateralisation and anatomical asymmetry: relevance of protocadherin XY to hominid speciation and the aetiology of psychosis', *British Journal of Psychiatry*, 181: 295–297.

Hanauske-Abel, H.M. 1996, 'Not a slippery slope or sudden subversion: German medicine and national socialism in 1933', *British Medical Journal*, 313: 1453–1463.

Kraam, A. 2002, 'The legacy of Kraepelin (essay review)', *History of Psychiatry*, 13: 475–480.

Zilboorg, 1957, 'Eugen Bleuler and present-day psychiatry', *American Journal of Psychiatry*, 114: 289–298.

Chapter 13: Vaslav Nijinsky

Acocella J. 1999, 'Secrets of Nijinsky', *New York Review of Books*.

Ansbacher, H.L, 1981, 'Discussion of Alfred Adler's Preface to The Diary of Vaslav Nijinsky', *Archives of General Psychiatry*, 38: 836–841.

Oswald, P. 1991, *Vaslav Nijinsky: A Leap Into Madness*, Robson Books.

Oswald, P. 1994, 'The God of the Dance: Treating Nijinsky's Manic Excitement and Catatonia', *Hospital & Community Psychiatry*, 45: 981–985.

Chaper 14: Hans Berger

Borck, C. 2001, 'Electricity as a medium of psychic life: electrotechnological adventures into psychodiagnosis in Weimar Germany', *Science in Context*, 14: 565–590.

Borck, C. 2005, 'Writing brains: tracing the psyche with the graphical method', *History of Psychology*, 8: 79–94.

Borck, C. 2005, 'Writing brains: Tracing the psyche with the graphical method', *History of Psychology*, 8(1): 79–94.

Borck, C. 2008, 'Recording the brain at work: the visible, the readable, and the invisible in electro-encephalography', *Journal of the History of Neurosciences*, 17: 367–379.

Gloor, P. 1994, 'Berger lecture. Is Berger's dream coming true?', *Electroencephalography and Clinical Neurophysiology*, 90: 253–266.

O'Leary, J.L. 1970, 'Review: Discoverer of the brain wave', *Science*, 168: 562–563.

Chapter 15: Frida Kahlo

Barnet-Sanchez, H. 1997, 'Frida Kahlo: Her Life and art revisited, *Latin American Research Review*, 32(3).

Budrys, V. 2006, 'Neurological deficits in the life and works of Frida Kahlo', *European Neurology*, 55: 4–10.

Herrera, H. 1990, *Frida: A Biography of Frida Kahlo*, Harper & Row.

Lester, D. 2010, 'The reasons for suicide: An analysis of the diary of Arthur Inman', *Death Studies*, 34: 54–70.

Lomas, D. & Howell, R. 1989, 'Medical imagery in the art of Frida Kahlo', *British Medical Journal*, 299: 1584–7.

Melzack, R. 1990, 'From the gate to the neuromatrix', *Pain*, 6 (Suppl): S121–126.

Merskey, H. 1980, 'Some features of the history of the idea of pain', *Pain* 9: 3–8.

Chapter 16: Woody Guthrie

Arévalo, J., Wojcieszek, J. & Conneally, P.M. 2001, 'Tracing Woody Guthrie and Huntington's disease', *Seminars in Neurology*, 21(2): 209–23.

Klein, J. 1980, *Woody Guthrie: A Life*, Random House, New York, New York.

Naarding, P., Joost, G. & Janzinga, E. 2003, 'The neuro-psychiatric manifestations of Huntington's disease', *Current Opinion in Psychiatry*, 16: 337–340.

Ringman, J.M. 2007, 'The Huntington Disease of Woody Guthrie: Another Man Done Gone', *Cognitive and Behavioral Neurology*, (4):238–43.

Chapter 17: Trebitsch Lincoln

Knightley, P. 1998, 'Reverse discrimination', *London Review of Books*, 10(10): 27.

Spence, R.B., 2009, 'The Mysteries of Trebitsch-Lincoln: Con-man, spy, "Counter-Initiate"?' *New Dawn* 116: See: http://www.newdawnmagazine.com/articles/the-mysteries-of-trebitsch-lincoln-con-man-spy-counter-initiate

Trevor-Roper, 1988, 'His brilliant career', *New York Review of Books*, 35(9).

Wasserstein, B. 1988, *The Secret Lives of Trebitsch Lincoln*, Yale University Press, New Haven, Connecticut.

Wasserstein, B. 1988, 'Chasing a chameleon: Trebitsch Lincoln', *History Today*, April, 38: 10–17.

Chapter 18: Arthur Inman

Harris, R. 1992, 'Posterity as exigence: Arthur Inman and his audience', *Rhetorical Society Quarterly*, 22(2): 51–65.

Hobson, F. 1987, 'The ordeal of Arthur Inman', *The Kenyon Review*, 9(1): 139–142.

Lester, D. 2010, 'The reasons for suicide: An analysis of the diary of Arthur Inman', *Death Studies*, 34: 54–70.

Chapter 19: Howard Hughes

Barlett, D.L. & Steele, J.B. 1979, *Empire: The Life, Legend and Madness of Howard Hughes*, Norton & Company, New York.

Cheyette, S.R. & Cummings, J.L. 1995, 'Encephalitis Lethargica: Lessons for contemporary neuropsychiatry', *The Journal of Neurosciences and Clinical Neuropsychiatry*, 7: 125–134.

Franklin, S.A., McNally, J.& Riemann, B.C 2009, 'Moral reasoning in obsessive-compulsive disorder', *Journal of Anxiety Disorders*, 23: 575–577.

Hollander, E. 2005, 'Obsessive-compulsive disorder and spectrum across the life span', *International Journal of Psychiatry in Clinical Practice*, 9(2): 79–86.

Hounie, A.G, Mercadante, M.T, Alvarenga, P.G, Sampaio, A. S et al. 2006, 'Obsessive-compulsive spectrum disorders and rheumatic fever', *Psychiatric Annals*, 36: 2.

Kant, R., Smith-Seemiller, I. & Duffy, J.D. 1996, 'Obsessive-compulsive disorder after closed head injury: review of literature and report of four cases', *Brain Injury*, Vol. 10(1): 55–63.

Kmsz, J.C., Koller, W.C., & Ziegler, K.D. 1987, 'Historical review: Abnormal movements associated with epidemic encephalitis lethargica', *Movement Disorders*, 2(3): 137–148.

Rajkumara, R.P., Janardhan Reddya, Y.C. &, Kandavel, T. 2008, 'Clinical profile of "schizo-obsessive" disorder: a comparative study', *Comprehensive Psychiatry*, 49: 262–268.

Rapoport, J.L. 1990, 'Obsessive compulsive disorder and basal ganglia dysfunction', *Psychological Medicine*, 20: 465–469.

Stein, D.J., Denys, D., Gloster, A.T., Hollander, E., Leckman, J.F. Rauch, S.L., Phillips, K.A. 2001, 'Obsessive-compulsive disorder: Diagnostic and treatment issues', *Psychiatric Clinics of North America*, 32(2009): 665–685.

Ward, C.D. 2003, 'Neuropsychiatric interpretations of postencephalitic movement disorders', *Movement Disorders*, 18(6): 623–630.

'The Keepers of the King'<http://www.time.com/time/magazine/article/0,9171,918528,00.htm> *Time Magazine*, Retrieved: 12 November 2010.

Chapter 20: Constantin von Economo

Altman, L.K., 'The doctor's world', *The New York Times*, 2 February 1982.

Fenelon, G. 2006, 'Hallucinations in Parkinson disease in the prelevodopa era', *Neurology*, 66: 93–98.

Lazaros C., Triarhou, 2007, 'Constantin von Economo (1876–1931)', *Journal of Neurology*, 2001(254): 550–551.

Lees, A.J. 2007, 'Unresolved issues relating to the shaking palsy on the celebration of James Parkinson's 250th birthday', *Movement Disorders*, 22 Suppl. 17.

Oppenheimer, D.R. 1980, 'Constantin von Economo: The man and the Scientist, by L. van Bogaert and J. Theodorides, *Journal of the Neurological Sciences*, 48: 45–58.

Pearce, J.M. 1996, 'Baron Constantin von Economo and encephalitis lethargica', *Journal of Neurology, Neurosurgery & Psychiatry*, 2001(60): 167.

Ransmayr, G., 2007, 'Constantin von Economo's contribution to the understanding of movement disorders', *Movement Disorders*, 22(4): 469–475.

Chapter 21: Jack Ruby

Bugliosi, V. 2007, *Reclaiming History: The Assassination of President John F. Kennedy*, WW Norton, New York, New York.

Friedman, L.M. 2001, 'An American tragedy: The trial of Jack Ruby' 1966, *Wisconsin Law Review*, 1188–1889.

Gutmann, L. 2007, 'Jack Ruby', *Neurology*, 69(9): 940–1.

Kaplan, J. & Waltz, J.R. 1978, 'The Trial of Jack Ruby', *Litigation*, 435(1): 43-55.

Langguth, J., 'Jack Ruby: Profile of Oswald's assassin', *The New York Times*, 2 February 1964.

Mayer, M., 'The trial of Jack Ruby', February 1966. See: http://www.commentarymagazine.com/article/the-trial-of-jack-ruby-by-john-kaplan-and-jon-r-waltz/

Posner, G. 1993, *Case Closed: Lee Harvey Oswald and the Assassination of JFK*, Random House, New York.

Waldron, M. 1966, 'Ruby's cancer is widespread; Drugs called his only chance', *The New York Times*, 14 December 1966.

Wehrwein, A.C., 'Chicagoans recall Jack Ruby as ticket scalper and chiseler', *The New York Times*, 25 November 1963.

Chapter 22: Adolf Hitler

Bugliosi, V. 2007, *Reclaiming History: The Assassination of President John F. Kennedy*. WW Norton, New York, NY.

Bullock, A. 1992, *Hitler and Stalin: Parallel Lives*, Knopf, New York.

Lieberman A., 1996, 'Adolf Hitler had post-encephalitic Parkinsonism', *Parkinsonism & Related Disorders*, (2): 95–103.

Lieberman, A. 1999, 'Adolf Hitler's cognitive disorder and how it affected his conduct of World War II', *Advances in Neurology*, 80: 459–66.

Maranhão-Filho, P., da Rocha e Silva, C.E. 2001, 'Hitler's hysterical blindness: Fact or fiction?' *Arquivos de Neuro-Psiquiatria*, 68(5): 826–830.

Redlich, F. 1998, '*Hitler: Diagnosis of a Destructive Prophet*', Oxford University Press, Oxford, UK.

Rosenbaum, R. 1998, *Explaining Hitler: the Search for the Origins of his Evil*, Macmillan, London.

Stolk P.J. 1968, 'Adolf Hitler: His life and his illness', *Psychiatria, Neurologia, Neurochirurgia*, 71(5): 381–98.